THE MUSIC INDUSTRY
DOESN'T HAVE TO KILL YOU

**Conversations with Remarkable
People from the Music Industry**

by John Clore
**Edited by: Michael Lasley, Mallory Redel
and Matt Ingle**

THE MUSIC INDUSTRY DOESN'T HAVE TO KILL YOU:

CONVERSATIONS WITH REMARKABLE PEOPLE FROM THE MUSIC INDUSTRY

By: John Clore
Edited by: Michael Lasley, Mallory Redel and Matt Ingle
Cover Design: Tyler Clark

All interviewees appear with expressed written permission.

Steady Cardinal Publishing
PO Box 121736
Nashville, TN 37212

For additional information, visit www.johnclore.com

ISBN-10: 061559848X
ISBN-13: 9780615598482

To Sarah, Harvey and Charlie,
my irreplaceable inspirations.

Contents

This Book Was Written While Listening to the Following:

The Hold Steady, The Black Keys, Counting Crows, Band of Horses, Kopecky Family Band, Mona, The Avett Brothers, Cold War Kids, Drew Holcomb and The Neighbors, The National, Arcade Fire, INXS, The Church, Pixies, Widespread Panic, Pearl Jam, Van Morrison, Mott The Hoople, The Who, Interpol, Foxy Shazam, Goldfinger, Foo Fighters, The White Stripes, Billy Joel, Elton John, Ben Folds, Metallica, Bon Jovi, Guns 'N' Roses, Hank Williams, Procol Harum, Kanye West, Jars of Clay, Rihanna, Lang Lang, Sonic Youth, Merle Haggard, Smokey Robinson & The Miracles, Arthur Conley, The Marshall Tucker Band, Keith Urban, The Temptations, Bill Withers, Johnny Cash, R.E.M., Megadeth, Jellyfish, Led Zeppelin, John Waite, Bryan Ferry, Andrew W.K., Hugo, Jay-Z, Smokey Robinson, Billy Currington, Toby Keith, Grizzly Bear, Aerosmith, Ray Price, Kent Blazy, Garth Brooks, U2, Bill Anderson, Mötley Crüe, Elvis Presley, Mahalia Jackson, Édith Piaf, Brenda Lee, The Rolling Stones, John Mark McMillan, Perry Como, Willie Nelson, Floyd Cramer, Bessie Smith, Louis Armstrong, Roy Clark, Ray Charles, Herman's Hermits, My Morning Jacket, Jesus Christ Superstar, Roxette, Eyes Around, The Apache Relay, Petra, Radiohead, Manchester Orchestra, Dolly Parton, Switchfoot, Quicksilver Messenger Service,

Kip Moore, Temper Trap, Explosions In The Sky, Burlap To Cashmere, Matt Maher, Charles Bradley, The Dirty Guv'nahs, NEEDTOBREATHE, Portugal. The Man, Incubus, The Head and the Heart, The Damn Quails, Barbara Mandrell, George Jones, Spacehog, Better Than Ezra, The Verve Pipe, P.M. Dawn, Blink 182, Faith No More, White Zombie, Fitz and The Tantrums, Eric Church, John Denver, Rod Stewart, Abandon, Death Cab for Cutie, Mat Kearney, Andrew Bell, Amos Lee, Bon Iver, Hillsong United, Gabe Dixon, Matthew Perryman Jones, Bruce Springsteen, Andrew Osenga, Marty Robbins, Marvin Gaye, Bobby Womack, Dan Deacon, Mayer Hawthorne, Tori Amos, Garbage, Asleep At The Wheel, David Ball, Randy Travis, The Highwaymen, Waylon Jennings, Broken Social Scene, Stone Temple Pilots, Rich Mullins, Phil Collins, The Frames, Flowers and Sea Creatures, Men At Work, The Bangles, Bonnie Tyler, When In Rome, Soundgarden, The Used, Rage Against The Machine, Phoenix, Lionel Richie, Britney Spears, Kenny Rogers, Paul McCartney, Wilco, Judy Garland, Tom Waits, LCD Soundsystem, The Killers, Red Hot Chili Peppers, The City Harmonic, Blondie, The Clash, Rosanne Cash, Amy Grant, Rez Band, Keith Green, Foster The People, MUTEMATH, Journey, Alan Parsons Project, Fisher Price Lullabies (while holding Charlie), George Harrison, Gomez, Bob Dylan, Cinderella, John Coltrane, Alison Krauss and Union Station, Ryan Adams, Michael Jackson, John Legend, The Police, Loretta Lynn, Conway Twitty, Patsy Cline, Righteous Brothers, The Platters, Fats Domino, Otis Redding, Todd Rundgren, Earl Scruggs, The Wallflowers, Beastie Boys, Green Day, Blues Traveler, The Jayhawks, Harvey Danger, Kid Rock, Dave Matthews Band, Stephen Stills, Coldplay, Dawes, Sly & The Family Stone, The Gaslight Anthem, Quiet Corral, Lana Del Rey, Roy Orbison, Lou Reed, Howlin' Wolf, John Lee Hooker, Ike & Tina Turner, Buddy Holly,

The Doors, Chuck Berry, The Impressions, Nirvana, Aretha Franklin, Sam Cooke, The Ronettes, The Lovin' Spooful, Sarah Jarosz, Kathleen Edwards, Soul Asylum, Ugly Kid Joe, Butthole Surfers, Meat Puppets, Cheap Trick, Blind Melon, New Order, Filter, Dog's Eye View, Alice In Chains, Tool, Brett Dennen, Young the Giant, When In Rome, Florence & The Machine, Orchestral Manoeuvres In the Dark, Craig Finn, The Darkness, Buck Owens, David Bowie, Tom Petty And The Heartbreakers, The Carpenters, Joe Walsh, White Heart, Newsboys, Neil Young, M83, Tiffany, Belinda Carlisle, Bonnie Tyler, Delta Spirit, Justin Timberlake, Cyndi Lauper.

Introduction

We all come from somewhere. We gain experience along the way: some good, some bad. We hurt. We long. We stay. We leave. We do our best to deal with what is inside. Some translate it to art. Sometimes, said art resonates with, and speaks for, the rest of us. Sometimes money is made. Often it is not.

Music has an extremely unique way of impacting each one of us; but the realities of the business that surround it are far from safe, comfortable or loving. Frankly, it can often be terrible and destructive.

But it does not have to kill you, or take your soul.

For me, nothing has more continuously impacted my heart and soul than music. From very early in my life, I met music with a fascination that only strengthens with time. From performances by my brother, sister and me for our parents in our living room circa 1988; to hearing Metallica's "Enter Sandman" in that Ford Probe in 1991; to seeing Billy Joel and Elton John together at Busch Stadium in 1994; to hearing The Hold Steady's Craig Finn sing, "from the Meat Loaf to the Billy Joel, certain songs they get so scratched into our souls," in 2009 – I simply cannot get enough of it.

I am fortunate to have spent my entire professional adult life working in the music industry – actually getting paid to work around the very thing I love so deeply.

During that time, I have had the privilege and opportunity to meet remarkable people, witness unforgettable performances, work as part of great albums, escort many great artists on the red carpet and, generally, see the behind-the-scenes of the music industry.

I have also encountered thieves and liars. I have seen sad and shady dealings. I have been disrespected, as I have disrespected. I have been lied to, as I have lied. I have been made to feel very unimportant, and I am certain I have made others feel as such. I have seen lives and families broken apart, and I have felt just enough of the latter to know without question that my dream is never worth more than those I love. And that is what this book is about.

The music industry does not have to kill you. Nor does it have to make you generally miserable.

This is not a self-help book. Nor is it a how-to guide. It is my first step in spending the rest of my life encouraging people in the music industry to think differently.

Contained herein are 23 interviews with some of the most remarkable people I know: people who have spent decades in the music industry; people who have recently joined; some who have found success; and those who are still searching for it. They are people who truly love everything about music. As you read their stories, learn from what they have done, what they have not done, and how they generally orient their life to the music industry. Consider how it all applies to you.

No one has all of the answers, and I cannot guarantee that you will not die – literally, emotionally, metaphorically – as a result of your time in the music industry.

You very well could.

Gene Bowen

"Last night I spent three hours with a group of a dozen kids in Road Recovery. We talked and we jammed and it was a great experience for me. Road Recovery is comprised of people with a hope of teaching kids that they can draw a map through this world that doesn't include a stop at the liquor store or the dope house. I saw myself in that room and I realized that to be 16 or 19 or 22... and clean... and totally uninhibited, was living proof of principles in action. What appears to be contrary to the laws of nature is HAPPENING in Road Recovery. If I hadn't seen it with my own eyes, I wouldn't have believed it. It's a true, hands-on program for young people, and it needs to be duplicated around the world. Do whatever you can to support them."

— Wayne Kramer, founding member
of the legendary MC5

The Rock and Roll lifestyle is often blown way out of proportion. Few are ultimately able to maintain the lifestyle that is expected to remain relevant in the music industry.

Gene Bowen has devoted his life to sharing that the music industry does not have to be a constant altered reality, where too many breaths are breathed knocking at death's door. He does this through his foundation, Road Recovery, which was founded in February 1998.

Bowen and co-founder, Jack Bookbinder (artist manager, type II diabetic) envisioned the day when youth, some considered outcasts and trash in society, would share a Broadway stage in New York City with some of Rock music's superstars. A decade later...with the help of countless dedicated entertainment industry professionals and support from the mental health field, Bowen and Bookbinder's dream became a reality onstage at the Nokia Theatre for Road Recovery kids, and the many international superstars that continue to support the organization's mission. Performers included Iggy Pop, Slash, Tom Morello, Perry Farrell, Denis Leary, Wayne Kramer, Jerry Cantrell, Jakob Dylan, Little Stevie Van Zandt, Juliette Lewis, Billy Bragg, Joseph Arthur, Ours, among many others.

Road Recovery's Mission Statement:

Road Recovery is dedicated to helping young people battle addiction and other adversities by harnessing the influence of entertainment industry professionals who have confronted similar crises and now wish to share their experience, knowledge, and resources.

With support from the mental health field, Road Recovery provides hands-on mentorship training, educational/ performance workshops, peer-support networking, and "all access" to real-life opportunities by collaborating with young people to create and present live-concert events.

Road Recovery empowers young people of all backgrounds to face their struggles and helps them develop comprehensive life skills, guided by professionals and supported by a community of like-minded peers.

Clore: Gene, please share how you got involved in the music business, and what life was like as a road manager.

My older siblings took me to concerts when I was in elementary school, and from the point the house lights went down and the band hit, I was hooked! I have absolutely no musical ability or talent, but experiencing live music gave me reason to be alive. My obsession for live concerts led me to explore how all the pieces came together for that amazing magic on stage to happen. I was soon following the trail, which led me to the stage door. I was in high school and very young looking. I was given the nickname, "The kid," and soon was asked to unload gear and hump road cases. By my senior year, I was eighteen and was offered my first tour upon graduation. My talents lay in logistics and soon I rose through the ranks from roadie to tour manager. I spent the next 15 years tour managing, and believe it or not, managed to get a BS degree from NYU [New York University] after completing seven years of part-time classes.

Clore: In general, what events, or series of events, led to you and Jack Bookbinder starting Road Recovery?

In 1992, my lifestyle caught up with me, and I got clean from drug and alcohol addiction. In 1994, my business partner Jack Bookbinder began managing Jeff Buckley, and I was asked to tour-manage Jeff's debut release tour, Grace, for two years. I was now two years sober and decided to break my anonymity in order to gain needed support from everyone involved (band, management, label, touring crew) as I headed out into the touring minefield. By letting everyone know my situation throughout the world, I not only gained needed support, but discovered that there were many people in the entertainment industry who sought a happy and healthy lifestyle based on the personal adversity they themselves had faced.

All of a sudden, I began to meet herds of amazing people in my industry; famous folks and workers among workers who were all striving towards the same goal, and willing to support each other achieve and maintain a happy and healthy life along the way. Jack was diagnosed with Diabetes Type II and we both realized how we could support each other based on our own personal experiences. The entertainment industry is such an attraction to young people, and we decided to harness that power and use it for good, helping young people find their way toward a healthy and amazing life. Road Recovery is unique in that we partner with the mental health field, as many of the young people involved with our organization are at-risk.

Clore: To the young person with lofty dreams of superstardom, what would you share with them?

Start with what drives you. Stick with what causes you to want to get up each morning. Follow that interest. Ask a million questions along the way and don't be afraid to let those folks you trust know when you're feeling scared or lost. Share what's going on inside you. Don't bottle any of your feelings up. Express yourself. Be open-minded and don't put all your eggs in one basket. If you want to be in the music business, explore all the many facets of the business – don't close yourself off to meeting, speaking or exploring something that seems of no interest to you. If you follow this honestly, you may not become a superwhatever, but chances are, you will find yourself doing something that makes you happy. Oh, and as Frank Zappa says, "Don't forget the next poor sucker on this one way train." Give back!

The Road

Life on the road is tough. Yes, often fun and exciting, but really, really difficult.

We often idolize our favorite band(s), wishing we could replicate their lifestyle; coveting a taste of that perceived fame and fortune; effortlessly striving to make some form of connection with them.

Oh, and we always expect them to be "on." No matter when or where.

Try to imagine for a second waking up in a brand new town with absolutely no idea how you got there – and doing this nearly every day, often for months on end. Imagine stepping away from your loved ones for extended periods of time. Imagine being at the mercy of the concert promoter's staff in the next town if you need to make a basic trip, like a run to the grocery store. Imagine dealing with asshole promoters that do not, and/or cannot, pay you what had previously been agreed upon. Imagine the exhaustion at the end of the show, of which every fiber of energy was just expended onstage. And now it is time to go meet and greet with a long line of your fans: fans that expect you to be 100% "on," treating them exactly as they have it built up in their minds for you to treat them.

Remember, they have come to see you, their idol, and idols do not get tired and cranky. No, idols live a perfect life, in perfect cars, with perfect possessions, and with no struggles.

That is the falsity believed by many.

Take fifteen minutes and listen to Jackson Browne's "The Load-Out" and "Stay," followed by Bob Seger's "Turn The Page." Few songs sum this topic up so well, describing the rigors and realities of what begins to happen as a result of day upon day of being in strange places with strange people. I assure you, the majority of artists on the road are not spending their time flying in a private jet, sleeping in air-conditioned tour busses, or showering on the fifty-second floor of the Palms in Vegas.

For maximum effect, and no offense whatsoever to Seger, but I think the only way to get the full, intense impact of the lyrics in "Turn The Page" is to listen to Metallica's powerful cover of the 1973 classic.

The road is essential. But the road is not always the glamorous, coveted wonderland it is built up to be.

Keep this in mind when considering your favorite act(s). Supporting them (in many ways) is vital to their successful longevity.

Your support counts.

Charlie Brusco

We got in this little small convertible car that he had and took off from Winterland. We went down and across the Oakland Bridge, and the next thing I know, we're at the Berkeley Community Center – or something like that – and we're going in because he's got Jackson Browne playing that night.

Charlie Brusco is a member of the Georgia Music Hall of Fame, an honor he counts among his highest. He has also managed, or still manages, a legendary assortment of musicians: Styx, Lynyrd Skynyrd, The Outlaws, Dickey Betts, Survivor, Bad Company and Peter Frampton. Charlie worked with the most legendary and infamous Rock and Roll concert promoter of all time, Bill Graham. He helped reunite The Police for a few shows in 1986. He has promoted concerts and/or tours for Bon Jovi, Sting, Fleetwood Mac, Ringo Starr and Janet Jackson.

Charlie has amazing stories, but he also poses strong challenges. Admire his greatness, learn from his stories, and use it all to make a better next step.

Clore: What are those momentous occasions that have stood out – and defined – your career?

If I sit and think about the big things that I consider big moments, the first one was when The Outlaws got to the point of being able to headline Madison Square Garden. There's just something that's attached to that place. It's funny, I had Styx playing The Beacon Theatre in New York this year [2010], and it's only a 2,800-seat hall, so it's not like Madison Square Garden or anything like that. John Scher, who has been a long-time friend of mine, and one of the major promoters in the New York market for at least the last 35 years or so, and I were talking on the phone about it. I was busting his chops about everything: "Let's do this. We want to make sure we sell out." We got into this conversation about how somehow, especially to people like myself, no matter how long it goes on, and no matter how much people act like the music business has shifted, there's something about New York, because when I started in the business, New York was the prime part of where all the business took place for all the touring and music/record business, everything. Everybody had satellite offices in L.A., but the main offices were in New York, and that's all somewhat shifted. Both Nashville and L.A. have become important, and New York sometimes is looked back on as not being the same thing it was before, but still, when you go in there to play a show, there's always a little bit more pressure – especially to a manager with history – to make sure New York is a big deal.

The first time The Outlaws played Madison Square Garden – and back in those days [early 1970s] you worked your way up to being able to play Madison Square Garden, some people playing Madison Square Garden now, they have a big record. I remember somebody saying the only other place Taylor Swift played in L.A. was [2,200-

seat] The Wiltern, and she went from there to [19,000-plus capacity] Staples Center.

In our day of building band's careers, you never made that kind of jump. Even Led Zeppelin played small halls before they got to the big halls, and they actually opened for people before they headlined. There was somewhat of a natural order in things back then. So, for The Outlaws to end up being the headlining act at Madison Square Garden – and on top of that we sold it out – we were selling out arenas everywhere else. We had built ourselves up in New York to getting to the point of being able to play Madison Square Garden. That was a real career moment for all of us. We had played New York as the opening act early in the band's career, before anyone knew who we were. We opened for The Jefferson Starship for a free show in Central Park. There were 100,000 people there, and it was just like looking out at a sea of people, but that didn't mean as much to us as selling out Madison Square Garden. I think it was 18,000 people – or something like that – there for us. We had actually played The Garden before on the Doobie Brothers tour, but going back to The Garden and selling it out? I mean – that was one real big thing.

Also, receiving a Heroes Award from NARAS a few years back, where my buddy Jon Bon Jovi flew in from New York to present me with the award, and Styx played a couple of songs for me. I was honored alongside Coretta Scott King, Usher and the B-52s. I really thought that was going to end up being the high point of anything for me. And then I was inducted into the Georgia Music Hall of Fame, which was on the same level.

As a result of the Heroes Award, I became involved managing Michael Bolton. And from that, Michael and I ended up at Coretta Scott King's funeral, on the side of the stage. We were there with Stevie Wonder, so the Heroes Award thing was really special because I met Stevie that night.

Same with Jimmy Carter, both of them, I felt kind of an aura about them when I met both of them. As much as I wasn't politically on the same page with him, when I met Reagan, there was a certain thing with Reagan. We met him with Styx. We ended up meeting him at a private meeting that one of the band members refused to go to. Everybody else figured, "Hey, we'll go and just meet him because he was a movie star. The hell with the rest of it. Forget the politics of it."

There were also the 9/11 benefits that we organized after 9/11. We organized them in like three weeks, and it was Styx and Journey and REO [Speedwagon] and Kansas and Lynyrd Skynyrd and we put together an all-star band, and John Waite and all of these other people – Eddie Money, Mark Farner – they all played. We did back-to-back; we did Atlanta on a Saturday night and Dallas on a Sunday. Just being able to pull that off and being able to take a check for over a half million dollars to the Port Authority people in New York, and handing them the check at ground zero. That whole experience was really special.

Another major thing for me, I got into the business of doing national tours and I had done 16 dates with Sting, on the Blue Turtle Tour, and I had done multiple cities all over the place for Bon Jovi. Another time, Doc [McGhee] was pissed off with Louis Messina, who was a promoter out in Texas. Louis was my partner, and Louis' company was putting up the money for my shows. So Louis was in what they called "Doc's penalty box," so Louis wasn't allowed to promote Bon Jovi or Mötley Crüe shows, so whenever they played a Texas show I ended up being involved. I got national. I ended up being a promoter, but the money was going back to Louis anyway, so it was just a way to tell him that he wasn't getting that because he was in Doc's doghouse.

Then I got into the business of trying to do national tours and we started buying. I got some partners that had very heavy money and they wanted to get into the business of doing national tours. We had done all of the dates on a Barry Manilow national theater tour. We had done one tour for Ringo, and we were involved in some other tours. We had done the Fleetwood Mac Reunion Tour. After The Eagles had done their tour, we went to Fleetwood Mac and made them an offer. Then one of the partners that had been involved in that tour left, and he went to form Live Nation Touring, with Live Nation. Actually, back then it was SFX Touring, and that developed into Live Nation Touring. He basically put it out in the street that the other three of us were no longer going to be doing national tours, that we were getting out of that business, and we *hadn't* decided that we were getting out of this business. We were like, "You snuck out of the office in the middle of the night to go work for SFX and made yourself a better deal and you're an asshole – but that doesn't mean that we're out of business."

I got a call from a guy that I had gotten into the business real early with as a tour accountant, and he was a tour accountant for Janet Jackson. We were in a conversation, talking about something, and he was telling me that he couldn't believe it. There were a bunch of promoters balking at Janet for her tour dates. I said to him, "Hey, what if we made an offer for the entire Janet Jackson tour?" Not knowing what it would involve. He said, "You and Roger Davies [who manages Janet] are similar kind of guys. Roger would probably get along with you really well. Let me see if Roger would be interested."

So he set up a meeting for me to meet with him and Roger in L.A., and my guys said that we could go up to $400,000 a show. I didn't know how many dates he was talking about. I walked out of the meeting and we had made a $16 million offer to Janet Jackson and they accepted. To this day, the Janet Jackson Velvet Rope Tour is the biggest and most successful tour that Janet Jackson has ever done. She was a pleasure to work with, and it was a great tour to do.

Clore: Do you care to talk a bit more about legendary concert promoter, Bill Graham? How he influenced you, anything specific that stands out?

Bill used to like to take in stray dogs and I was probably one of his stray dogs. There's a bunch of them out there. I was a young kid, didn't know what the hell I was doing. When I was in college I was the chairman for the school and I got involved with Belkin Concerts, which had a college concerts division, so I did stuff through college. When I got out of college, I moved to Tampa, Florida, because I figured I could just get some money from some people and become a promoter. I didn't really know the business.

The Belkins had always had a promoter office, as well as a management office, because Mike Belkin managed The James Gang, Joe Walsh, and other artists at that time. I always thought that promoters could both promote concerts and manage acts. I didn't really know that most promoters weren't involved in management at all, although Bill was. When I started out, I met The Outlaws the first night I went to Tampa, and then I started managing them. That was in '73. I got them a record deal with Clive

Davis in '74, made a record, and all the sudden we're out on the road and I start meeting all these different characters, all because I basically went on the road with the band. I was at most of the shows, just like I am today. I like to be around my artists when they're on the road.

I got to San Francisco and we [The Outlaws] were the opening act for Marshall Tucker and Charlie Daniels at Winterland. Bill Graham came in, he loved the band, and he was bigger than life.

I had been to New York a couple of times when I was in college and I had been to the Fillmore East. And here I was – the next thing I know, we're standing around backstage, and The Outlaws were done playing, and Bill was like, "Hey, what are you doing?"

"Nothing."

"Come on, take a ride with me."

I said, "Where are we going?"

"Don't worry, I've gotta be back before Marshall Tucker goes on," and The Outlaws had just come off stage. He had said hello to the band and everything like that, and he said, "Come on, we'll have a talk. I want to get to know you."

We got in this little small convertible car that he had and took off from Winterland. We went down and across the Oakland Bridge, and the next thing I know, we're at the Berkeley Community Center – or something like that – and we're going in because he's got Jackson Browne playing that night. So he was going to see Jackson, and as Jackson was just getting ready to go on stage, he was going to go back to Winterland to be back in time for

Marshall Tucker, and the whole time he wanted to know more about The Outlaws and what was going on.

I got back to my office, at that time either in Macon or Atlanta, and I was going through some stuff and I was like, "Oh, you know what? I wonder if Bill Graham would take my call." So I picked up the phone and thought of something I could call to ask him about, and it was really not important. I just wanted to see if we had any kind of a relationship at all. I called him up and two minutes later, "Oh Charlie, hold on one second, Bill will be right with you." He got on the phone, "Oh, how you doin', you back in Atlanta?" "Yeah." And as it went on, there's a million Bill Graham stories. There's some that can't be told, and there's some that I'll tell when I do a book, but Bill was the consummate fighter for what Bill believed was his way of doing the business. And Bill felt that he was responsible for a lot of things and he felt that he should get a little more than any other promoter because of that. So you always gave up and you always looked the other way on little things that Bill would add in that were coming out of your payment of the money. Like, he would have...I mean, the backstage at a Bill Graham show...I remember at a Lynyrd Skynyrd show we had a donkey backstage because he wanted it to look like a cowboy scene, and he had my picture, and Peter Rudge's picture, and somebody else's picture on the wall with a bulls-eye on it, and the guys could shoot arrows at our pictures on the wall. He thought that was really funny, and Rudge and I both had our pictures on the wall with bulls-eyes because we were the two managers. He did all of that stuff, but at the end of the night, out of the charges that would be paid back to the promoter for the night, there would be like a $5,000 charge for "backstage ambiance," and that was him charging you for bringing in the donkey that you didn't even ask for, and other promoters would do that stuff and they would never charge you for it. They'd do their little things, but nobody did it like Bill. I mean, Bill was as much of an artist as he was a promoter. He started out with a mime troupe and all that kind of stuff. I spent time with him at his house and he always treated me well, but when we got into arguments, all gloves would come off. And he was like that with 90 percent of the people he did business with because he could get away with it.

He was very instrumental in helping me, as he did the first five dates on the Lynyrd Skynyrd Tour in 1987 when I put the band back together for the first time. He did a bunch of the dates. The band left me at one point to go to Bill for management, then the band left Bill and came back to me for management. So there was this whole thing that went down between us on the management of Lynyrd Skynyrd for a few years.

He was really a special, one-a-kind kind of guy.

I was lucky enough in the years that I came up, and in the time that I came up, that – forget the business relationships – I had actual, real personal relationships with Bill Graham and Don Law and with Larry Magid, Jerry Mickelson and Arny Granat, Jack Boyle, Louis Messina – all of the guys that basically started the promoter's business. I started out as a manager that sold them acts, and when I became a promoter, I was taken into the promoter's club. I went to the international promoter's meetings where we had our secret meetings. I was in on all of that.

One day when Michael Cohl came to a meeting in Dallas – I think it was in Dallas – and we were all in this room, put the chairs around a big, square table so everybody could see each other. Bill was sitting next to me, and Michael Cohl came in, and this is the day after Michael Cohl announced that he had gotten The Rolling Stones

Tour. That was the beginning of Bill not being Bill in my eyes. He was never the same again. And I was sitting next to him when Michael Cohl walked into the room and he stood up, and he went into this tirade: "I will not be in the room with this motherfucker!" He called Michael Cohl everything, and to Michael's defense, Michael actually came in the room, sat down at the table and refused to leave – and finally, Bill left. And Bill stomped his one foot, up and down, when he was screaming and yelling, and my foot was underneath it and I couldn't get my foot away from him slamming it, and he actually didn't know that he was, he had to feel that he was hitting something but he was so in this tirade that he didn't notice.

To this day, I'll never forget him screaming and yelling at everybody, stomping on my foot the whole time he was yelling at Michael Cohl. If someone had a film from that, it would be like a scene from *The Godfather* or a scene from *Goodfellas*. It was an amazing thing to watch, but that's how passionate Bill was.

It is true, after that Stones thing – and there's been stuff that's been written about it – he was never Bill Graham again. He felt like how he did business, that that was all being questioned.

I just finished reading the Keith Richards book, who also is a guy that I know well and had the pleasure of actually promoting his first show ever as a solo artist in The X-Pensive Winos. He played that first show for me in Atlanta. He says in the book, about the transition from Bill Graham to Michael Cohl, and he even notes in his book that he had heard that after this thing that Bill, losing The Stones, was never the same. He says basically it was just something that The Stones had to do. That Michael Cohl made more sense to them. And he alludes to the fact that The Stones got tired of seeing backstage ambiance that was going to Bill; that he was always about taking a little bit more than anyone else.

As a promoter, for me, that's one of the things that got me really…like with Bon Jovi – Jon Bon Jovi – the reason he gave me so many dates on every tour, between him and Doc, was, when they looked at the bottom line, I never nickeled and dimed them, or I never tried to get extra money out of stuff that shouldn't be coming out, which a number of promoters just couldn't help themselves from doing. And Jon, when he would look at the bottom line, back in those days, everyone looked at what percentage of the gross they were making, and I was always two or three percentage points higher than anybody else. So it was like, "Hey, we make more money with Charlie."

So, sometimes on a couple of the Bon Jovi tours, I was doing 20 cities, and I started out only doing Atlanta, and just kept on getting asked if I wanted to do more cities. But Bill was one of those guys, and it's like the Ahmet Erteguns and the Clive Davises and, along with all of those promoters, those were all guys that we did business together, but we also hung out together. I picked up the phone and called any of them, and they picked up the phone right away. Ahmet – I did a bunch of stuff with. I had the pleasure of working with Tom Dowd, one of the great producers of all time. And with Glyn Johns, who did the early Eagles stuff, and did The Who stuff – and The Outlaws toured with The Who.

You know, there were all of those guys around, but somehow when you go back on it, I think there are still more special things about Bill than there are about most of the others. Bill did the music and promoting business 24 hours a day, seven days a week. He lived and breathed it. That's all it was.

The business wouldn't be the same without those guys.

Clore: It sounds like it truly was a community of people back then.

It really was, and I don't know if that will ever be recreated, because quite frankly, the rules were made up as everybody was going along. Originally, artists were given sometimes 50 or 60 percent of the net proceeds after the expenses. And back in the days of Sam & Dave and all of that stuff, promoters paid those people flats and didn't give them anything. They were lucky if they got paid. As it went, everybody kept moving the bar up in the artist's favor.

Then at one point, Peter Grant basically told everybody that if you got Led Zeppelin, you were paying Led Zeppelin 85% of the gross after expenses, and promoters were going to work for 15% and a lot of people balked at it and basically he [Grant] went to Concerts West and gave them the whole tour. All of a sudden everybody started saying, "Hey, some of these acts can pull off that kind of stuff. We better go along with what some of these deals are because we're making really good money." What happened was, once everybody heard that somebody was getting that kind of money, as soon as you knew you could sell out a building, you were like, "Hey, I want the Led Zeppelin deal. We're doing the same kind of business as them, I want to be paid like them." And now it's progressed to where it is today – where basically, the acts are asking for all the money up front.

Clore: What are your thoughts on where we are now, as we talk in 2010?

I think we're in big trouble. I think – and I've expounded on this with a bunch of people – my biggest worry for this business is, what's going to happen to the business when all the acts that currently can sell all the tickets, and are keeping the business going, are all retired – which is probably within the next 15 years. And the way that I figure that, is that from 1985 on, any artists that were spawned at their beginning from '85 on, there's almost no business. You've got Dave Matthews, Bon Jovi, and a couple of other acts that can still do major business, but 15 years from now, Jon will be 63. Alright, at 63, I don't know that he will go out and do the kinds of tours that he does. And what I'm saying is as going forward from that, Lady Gaga won't be able to sell out arenas two years from now. It'll be over. And because there's not a passion from people, in other words, people that we're still selling records to, and really, the music business has become the touring business, because even with an act like Bon Jovi, if Jon puts out a record and his net back from the record ends up being $5 million, of the Bon Jovi empire money, $5 million is from that portion of his business, his touring business is a $200-350 million business. You know, the record part, the new stuff is nothing compared to what the touring money is, and the merchandise money is, and that's what's driving the business. And that's what's also keeping amphitheaters open and keeping outdoor places open and those acts are going to.

I don't see the stuff that replaces when there's no more Styx, Journey, or Rolling Stones. When there's no more Paul McCartney; when all of those are gone. There's nothing. I don't see the stuff that comes up, in other words, even if there's four or five acts that are from '85 on, '85 to 2010, that can generate the business, there's not the other 40 or 50 or 60 of them that are out there right now that can do concerts every summer. And when that goes away, the people that are from our generation, they're still Pink Floyd fans. I was at the Roger Waters show a couple of weeks ago, and you know, you look around, and 70% of that crowd is probably 40 years or older, and 30% of it probably is younger people under 40, because that's about what it is with Styx now, and on these big shows, you do get a lot of younger people going to them because they've heard about these acts forever and they want to see them. And sometimes they only want to see them once. If you've seen The Stones, you probably aren't going to go back if you're 26 years old, or 17 years old, or you may become a fan and want to go back every time and see them, but you better have money to be able to see those kinds of acts.

My thing is, once all of that clears out, and I think we're within 15 years of that happening, because if The Stones tour again, they're going to tour one more tour, and that's going to be it. I mean they're going to be 70. I think Keith is 67. Charlie Watts is 71. So now you don't have the $200-300 million Rolling Stones Tour that happens every three years, or every four years lately. You start taking that out and all of the sudden, how do all of these people that are working in this business – in the live entertainment end – how do they make a living? How do you pay people to do stuff when that's not there?

The one business that seems to keep on going right now, and is actually, I think, building, is the Country music business. Because the Country music business feels like what the Rock business was in 1975 and '76 and into '80 and all that, because there's a good radio to support it, they play new stuff by new artists and established artists, so that end of it could keep on going, but there's only so many of those artists. And as the record stuff keeps on going little by little, it's going to be put in the hands of managers and people like that to be able to put records out for their artists on their own – which we're all coming up with those ways to do it – but I'm just saying, the business is, I can't see that the business can't do anything but shrink.

And I'll listen to anybody that thinks they've got an answer to that, but it's pretty tough to start manufacturing the acts that are going to go out there and do the business to sustain a Live Nation operation that's built on touring. And it takes hundreds of millions of dollars of gross to make that happen when there's not…you have to have artists and we're running out of them. There's no doubt about it.

Clore: To people who are in music business classes right now…

We came up with what worked for us, they better come up with what works for them, because we're not going to be around to do it for them.

Clore: If an act is trying to get started, or keep going, what are some of your philosophies about how they approach, how they sustain and survive…

My newest one is that they've got to be totally proactive in what they're doing for their business and their brand. When we were coming up in the business, you could have never mentioned to anybody that you were trying to make somebody become a "brand," because then you would have been labeled as being a corporate sellout, and now the business is all about, I mean you're great if you can figure out 15 ways to do a corporate sellout on your act. There's no stigma attached to that anymore, but I think we're in an age of the Internet, and these guys that are my age, that when the Internet stuff came out, people were burning records and everything like that, you know, the answer that Doug Morris and all those people that were supposed to be so smart and protecting their assets and all that, "Oh no, don't worry about that, that's just a phase. That Internet stuff will go away. That's not going to happen." And they didn't get proactive on it, and now it's beating the hell out of everybody. But, I don't think that that's the key thing that's the problem. I think the key problem is that people have lost interest, or music has become worth less than what is was before, because I've got a 25 year-old stepson, and he's had a band, he's played drums and all that stuff. But he's not as enthusiastic about the business, or music, as I was when I was his age, because half of what gets taken up with him, gets taken up in video and the Internet and all of that. They're getting hit from all different sides. I think acts and industry people have to be very proactive in going out there and establishing a relationship between themselves and the people that are out there that are their fans. They have got to do everything they can to keep those fans interested, because they're not going to be able to do it how we did it through radio airplay and all that. They're going to have to get them in a different way.

The preceding interview took place in December of 2010.

Older Artists Matter

One of the biggest mistakes we make is ignoring the elders around us. It is pretty ridiculous, really. The wisdom that exists and could be tapped into simply by talking with people that have "been there" is vast. I realize it is easier simply to not talk to people and avoid potentially awkward or failed conversations; but when you come across an elder willing to help you learn, it can be life-changing. Not everyone loves history. I have to remind myself of this often. But we all need help, no matter our interests.

In the Music Row neighborhood of Nashville, there is a Best Western Hotel on Division Street that contains a dive bar / music lounge lovingly referred to as the "Hall of Shame." Years ago I was there to hear some friends play a gig. As a 23-year old, I will never forget looking over into a dimly lit corner and seeing a seemingly alone woman with sad eyes, well along in years, sipping on a cocktail. That image deeply impacted my heart and soul. A couple of years prior, I arrived in Nashville with mostly naïve excitement about how great it was all going to be, nary giving thought to the glut of human souls that never realized their dream of stardom.

Whether this specific lady came to Nashville and did or did not find success, she represented the latter to me. In my mind, I stereotypically placed thoughts of failure on her. Not to be mean or intentionally judgmental, but because it was a learning moment for me, and continues to be. Theoretically, let's say she was in her late 60s in this moment, and she came to Nashville with a dream in her early 20s. That is 40+ years on the whole. Let us assume she had a couple of small breaks and she had some people encourage her and she genuinely, deeply thought she would be the next Loretta Lynn. As the days, months and years continued to pass, her self-confidence gradually decreased. All along the way, she had to make money somehow, always leaving herself available for when her break was going to happen. She would need to be ready to hit the road, get in the studio, be in the movies. Whatever.

The phone did not ring. Those that had supported early on were long gone because her potential value proved zero to them.

She stayed in Nashville. She held on to the dream. She developed a routine that positioned her where the industry people would be. She wanted to remain ready, no matter how many signs pointed to the dream's completion.

And there we sat, circa 2003. I did not talk to her. I would like to now, and I have seen her since, but in some ways, I am afraid to. I have built this story in my mind about what has happened to her. Truth is, it is a story I know as absolute fact from too many others. I have zero confirmation from the lady that it is her story, but I bet it is.

When I see her in my mind, the caption reads, "The Nashville Dream."

For all of the glitz and glam of the entertainment indus-try, there is a deep, dark underbelly of shattered hearts, dreams and lives, and the thing is, for even those who have been lucky enough to enjoy the spotlight, it fades. Often, really fast. The hot new thing comes along, and as the original star gets older – more often than not – they are completely forgotten. This is real life in the music industry, and these types of people can teach you more than you will ever learn in any class, book or article.

A personal pursuit of a dream should look long term. Consider how your actions are going to affect you, your closest personal relationships and your life on down the road. Do not hear me saying to not go for it. I guar-antee you I am as supportive about going for a life in the entertainment industry as anyone. Just do it within the confines of reality. If you are hitting closed doors at every turn, get a clue.

You will grow old, and that is okay. Please do not try to keep that from happening, you will only look worse. Grow old gracefully. Work hard to understand where you fit in, and how you can help those around you.

Just please do not ever look at older artists or music industry people as worthless. I assure you, they are our greatest asset.

Fred Buc

Part of my philosophy is that anybody, including you, develops their musical tastes around the ages of fifteen to eighteen years old. So, that means I will love Jethro Tull and Led Zeppelin until I'm ninety-five years old.

I was slowly introduced to Fred Buc over the course of a few years by listening to his fabulous Saturday morning show, *Retro Lighting,* on my favorite radio station, Lightning 100 Radio in Nashville – an independent, Triple A format station. On the show, Fred picks a year in "progressive radio history" and spends four hours playing nothing but music and sharing cultural events and information from that year. He has hosted the show nearly every Saturday morning since 1993. It is, and has been, a perfect way to learn more about music history.

Fred was born in Nashville and fell in love with everything about radio in his early teens. He attended Vanderbilt University, where he served as both program director and station manager of the campus radio station, WRVU, and earned a Bachelor's in Business Administration and Mathematics. Fred has been involved in radio for over

35 years, working in various capacities for WRVU, WKDA, WKDF, WYYB, WDBL and currently General Manager at WRLT/Nashville. Fred serves, or has served, on Leadership Music's Board of Directors, the Tennessee Association of Broadcasters' Board of Directors and the March of Dimes' AIR Awards Board of Governors.

I reached out to Fred as one intrigued with the complexity of pulling off a show like *Retro Lightning* for some seventeen years. He gladly agreed to get together in late 2010 for the following conversation at a coffee shop in West Nashville.

Watch for Fred's passion and how much time he puts in to everything. He embodies excellence in every sense of the word.

Clore: I'm fascinated with *Retro Lightning*, four hours every week since 1993. How do you do that?

My wife lets me. After all these years, she lets me.

We started the show in October of '93, at 8 am. And the then music director and I co-hosted it for about a year until he left town. Then I took it over. At one point, the general manager moved it to 6 to 8 am on Saturday, and I was waking up at 4:30 in the morning on Saturday. My wife couldn't figure out why I did this if I really didn't have to, you know, it's always been kind of fun for me. I've always had weekend air shifts. I've worked six days a week forever, and working Saturday morning even on regular radio when I was in Kansas City and in Charlotte, I was part of the weekend air staff, so I would get up and do 6 to 10 on Saturday morning without a blink. So it really wasn't a big deal for me.

This show stemmed from a show I started when I was a student at Vanderbilt [University, in Nashville]. I ran the radio station [WRVU] at Vanderbilt when I was in school and all through college, I had a weekend on-air job at WKDA, which is a Country station, and KDF, which at the time was a Rock station.

I graduated from Vanderbilt and came back as an alum to do a show called "Stuck in the '70s," and that would have been around '81 to '83. I had gone to school in the '70s. I had worked at the college station in the '70s. I was program director and music director there in the '70s. So that was music I grew up with, and then it had moved on into the '80s, well I did this special of just music from '70 through '79. And I didn't pick out a particular year, it was all over the place. So you would hear The Who from 1970 and then "Sniffin' The Tears" from '78 and then Elton John from '75. It was all over.

So, *Retro* picked up from where that left off, kinda of focusing on the same period, that would have been '93 at RLT when we did that. And it was structured like "Stuck in the '70s." It was old Rock songs from whenever during that period instead of focusing on one year. And it fit well with the station because the station's personality was depth and variety and obscurity. It didn't hurt to play that sixth or seventh deep track on the Jethro Tull album during the show, because it kinda fit the personality of *Lighting*, anyway. I can't tell exactly when, I think at some point the general manager had suggested that I focus on a particular year instead, so I started getting that together and that was quite a project, and you had mentioned that was an amazing feat, getting that together. Well, it was really easy when it was just anything because I could go to the album stack and pull out one of those and one of these and one of that – it wasn't hard at all. But, when I had to narrow it down, I had to know what year was what, I had to basically create a folder for each year, and that was a very time-consuming process. You've got to remember, too, this was like the early '90s, so there wasn't much done on the computer at all. So I pulled out a legal pad and did research through any *Rolling Stone Encyclopedia*, *Billboard*, Top 40, Joel Whitburn's book, just anything I could get my hands on, plus my own knowledge of knowing what albums came out what years that I grew up and just started building a song list for each year.

Clore: Do you still have those originals?

I still have my legal pad. For two or three years, I actually attempted to enter the songs on an Excel spreadsheet. I didn't get very far. Only a couple of my years are all on an Excel spreadsheet. But, you know, I can't even tell you how many hours worth of time and I can't remember if I, when it started, I must have had to just do it on the fly each week, you know, when we first started doing this. Okay, the first week – 1973 – so that whole week I was putting this stuff together, then I got to work on the next one, and the next one, and the next one... It was probably 10, 12, 20, 30 hours – I don't know how many – just putting these initial lists together. My point is, from that day – up until today even – I continue to build on those songs. Things I don't have, things I discover, the facts about the year, news happenings. I'm still adding to each of these files every day. I even did a bit of that today.

My show goes from 1967 to '83, and there's a reason for that. The reason I didn't go before '67 is the station didn't have a whole lot of material prior to that, enough where I could change it up frequently. The songs were a lot shorter. See, I hate doing '67 because all the songs are two and a half minutes long. We just didn't have enough material.

'83, on the other hand, was really the year I got out of full-time radio for a period of time. I was off the air as a full-time, six day a week personality. I continued to work weekends, but I tried another related profession or two.

I got out of it full-time at KDF in '84. So even though you continue to listen to the radio, you're not looking at trades full time; you're not playing music every day. My knowledge in that period waned, between '83 and when I came back to *Lightning* in '92. I wasn't up on the music, so we stopped it at '83.

Also, when I started the show, part of my philosophy is that anybody, including you, develops their musical tastes around the ages of 15 to 18 years old. So, that means I will love Jethro Tull and Led Zeppelin until I'm ninety-five years old. The Foo Fighters fans, [me, based on a story I shared with Fred prior to the interview] if they were 15 to 18 at that time, they're going to love them until they're ninety-five years old. So, the core group, the target of the radio station, was at an age where the music I presented on my show fell between people being 15 and 18 years old in the mid to late '70s. I was born in '57. I was eighteen in '75. In 1997, I was 40 years old. The target of the radio station may have been 35 to 44 years old, so somebody like me was in the core of that station. And that's the music I liked when I was 15 to 18. That's why the bulk of it falls between '73 and '80. Of course that's shifting up now, but at the time that's where it was. So when I jump around, I use a method where I'll take one from one end, late '60s, mid '70s, early '80s, back to '70s, back to early '70s, back to '60s, back to '70s, late '70s, early '80s. So, you get more in the '70s range than you do in the early part of the fringe, or the late part of the fringe. It's basically like a Bell Curve.

Will we expand it a year or two down the road?, I don't know, but we might. The original premise of the show was to get in that '67 to '83 range. And I'll notice that the people that listen, when they request, I'll always ask their age and their zip code. When I'm playing something from 1975, my year, people requesting it are 53 years old. When I do 1981, they're six years younger – they're 46, 47 years old. When I do 1967, they're 10 years older – they're 60, 61, 62 years old. So, it follows that path that I just described on when people form their musical tastes. It's fun, but it's also kind of been a science for me.

It's my relaxation of the week; to tell you the truth. Being general manager of the station, Monday through Friday, I have to worry about normal business things: I've got to worry about clients, I've got to worry about personnel, I've got to worry about advertisers and the problems they have, and making sure this is done on time and making sure sales are at this level and doing this and doing that. On Saturday morning, I can come in, nobody's there, I get to go in, as my wife says, "play radio." It's very relaxing. It's a lot of hard work. It's like doing a very intensive morning show, like Gerry House or somebody would do. I mean, I'm working my ass off, especially now with all the social media that I'm doing at the same time that I'm trying to do everything else. It's tough, but it's relaxing to do that. And to get to play the music I played when I was growing up and hearing people call, telling me what memories it brings back for them, and that's part of the show's mission, is to make people re-live. A song makes you think about some-thing, where you were at a certain time, or what you were doing when that song was playing on the radio on a regular basis. I get a lot of satisfaction out of making people happy like that.

Clore: Music evoking memories and deep meanings in people is very important to me. What is your favorite year in this era, and is it a music thing, a political thing?

I have different years that mean different things to me. I guess you could say '75 is one of my favorite years because in a period of five, six months, I graduated from high school, I celebrated my 18th birthday, and I went to college. So, that's what I remember. And I got to work at a college radio station immediately. Of course I was working at it when I was still in high school, but officially, as a Vanderbilt student, I came on, and boom, I was officially on the air. Which is part of the reason I chose Vanderbilt because I had already been on the air there, and it was kind of stupid because they didn't have a communications program there, and I could have gone to three or four other places, but I always knew I wanted to be in radio and I was already on the air there when I was still in high school and I figured that's whcrc I'll go, and I don't have to be a grad student or anything to get that opportunity, so that's where I ended up going.

So, '75 meant a lot to me there. '72 is a favorite year of mine because I was 15-16 years old at that time and really discovering music. I was listening to KDA-FM at that time, which was really underground, progressive FM station here [Nashville], and I was discovering all this music. I was in a band in high school like everybody is, so that was a big year of musical discovery for me. I often tell people I could do eight hours of '72 one morning and it wouldn't kill me. Even though I love the music, the late '60s – '70 even – I'm still kind of on the fringe there. I was a little too young to go to Woodstock, so I didn't do that. It was really '71 was the first year I was like really discovering music and started buying albums and things like that. So '71, '72, '73 I like because of the Southern Rock kicked in in '73, and that was real important to me and my friends at the time. '74 was my first day on the air at [W]RVU when I was still in high school. And through college radio, '77, that was a big disco year, but I was music director at the time, at the college station that year, and we did our best to find everything that wasn't disco. Consequently we were playing a lot of really deep, obscure tracks in '77 when nobody else was. I mean, it was all Top 40, Disco, Bee Gees-O-Rama. So, that year was important to me. After that, things kind of were slipped down for me, as far as my favorites.

Clore: Can you point to one year that was really the most important culturally in our Nation's history? A turning point – musically, politically?

Probably somewhere around '69 or '70, because you had Woodstock, you had all of these underground FM stations starting up in '69 and '70, like KDA-FM here started in '70. I don't know the exact year, but I'm sure stations like WNEW in New York were probably started about that time and, as well, KSAN, in San Francisco – stations like that were kind of popping up around that time. It was the birth of music as an art form – moreso than three minutes of hook, choruses and verses. That's what Top 40 radio was. I love it to death – I grew up with it, but that's what it was. A lot of The Beatles stuff, and all of the British Invasion stuff. I mean, it was hit, hit, hit. It was two and-a-half minutes of verse, chorus, verse, chorus, bridge, chorus – and that was it. But in '68, '69, really more so than '68, well, maybe '68 to a degree, all these bands started popping up and all of the songs, like I said, 1967, the song length was like two and a half minutes, you really had to fight hard to find something that was seven, eight minutes long. But in the next two to three years, The Grateful Dead and all these jam bands were extending all these compositions out six, eight, 10,

12 minutes, and it really turned Rock into an art form of expression, more than just a hooky hit. If I had to nail it down, that period is probably the most influential to really change what was going on during that period.

There are others that are probably less obtrusive. Disco in '77. New Wave a year or two after that. Then you had the techno pop of the early '80s, so there are other sections where music evolved into something else.

Clore: Are you a huge Beatles fan?

I'm not a huge Beatles fan.

Clore: I'm asking because every *Retro Lightning* show ends with a Beatles song.

The reason I did that is – they had a song in every year, or one of them did. That's why it's formatted that way. Not for any other reason, really. It's just so I can get some [Beatles] in every show and maybe, kind of police it a little bit. Every now and then, I will play two songs – I'll play something early in the eight or nine o'clock hour because I also finish up with The Beatles. But it's rare that I do that. And it will be a different one, or it will be – I guess '70 would be the only year that I could play a Paul McCartney song but also play a Beatles song. It allows me to get something in in every year. The only year we really have trouble with is '84, sometimes we've had to slip Julian Lennon in as our Beatles song.

They're important. They're great, and they changed the whole picture. But you know what? You can OD on them so easily. It's like there's so much else out there that I can't play them more than once. I only have four hours. I average about 10 or 11 songs an hour – and about 40-42 songs per show.

Clore: Where would we be without radio? It's almost impossible to consider that, but what do you think?

This is an opportunity for me to really toot radio's horn.

Clore: And I would love for you to.

It might sound a bit cliché, but until recently, radio was really the only way to expose material to the masses for a lot of years. It's really only been within the last eight or 10 that it hasn't – that it could be challenged that it hasn't. But how else would you know to buy that record? My friends still tell me what records, we still talk, they still tell me what records to buy, but where do they hear about it, originally? About the only place was, really, the radio. There was no *Grey's Anatomy* on TV to expose new material. You had to listen to it on the radio, then you would go to the concerts, or maybe, *maybe*, someone would drag you to a concert and you didn't know who in the hell it was, and then you bought their music afterwards. But it was really the only way to discover music. And in my opinion, it still is today. Not the only way, but it's still a major source in music discovery.

There are just so many other ways to get it now. Of course, radio's also good for other non-music reasons. The big arguments today when radio is challenged by others is, local, terrestrial radio – it's local. None of these other sources can tell you what's happening in [Nashville's] Centennial Park this weekend. Well, a lot of radio stations can't tell you what's happening in Centennial Park this weekend because they're syndicated. The FCC gave us this license to serve the community, that's why they gave out the licenses, to serve the community. And for that reason, you've got to support the community. It's also a good loudspeaker during disasters and emergencies.

As a local station, we're sitting proof that, with radio, you form relationships with the listeners. The listener's your friend. You wake up every morning and flip on that friend, because they're talking to you and you know them and you get to know their personality, day after day, you know what their personality is like and you feel like you know them. And you can't do that on an iPod. The whole element of surprise is important in radio as well, because you can put 20,000 songs on your iPod and shuffle them up, but guess what, they're still the 20,000 that you put on. And you know you put them on. Pandora's changing that a little bit with the element of "What is that? I've never heard that before. That's kinda cool." Then your new friend on local radio gets to tell you, or should tell you, hopefully will tell you, who it was, how it came about, or who sat in on sax on that particular song. Local radio can still do that. Not all of them take advantage of it, but music education is a big deal with us [WRLT]. For that reason, I think radio's always going to be important. No matter how many ways you can get your music, I think that's what really makes local radio stand out from everything else. I think there's always going to be a need for that.

Clore: I feel that, in a lot of ways, radio is the backbone of the music industry, not the record industry.

If you think about it, you know, music discovery via radio has been going on for 80 years. My parents and grandparents were discovering music on the radio in the '30s and '40s. So to that, it was the original backbone of music discovery of the music industry. Like I said, it fueled people's knowledge to go out and buy, whether it was sheet music in the early days, acetate in the early days, or whatever it was. That's where they usually heard the music first.

Clore: Why do you do *Retro Lightning*? Outside of just your love for it, is there an underlying music education element that you really want to help people? People like me.

I don't want to sound selfish, but I kind of do it for me. And hey, if the byproduct is educating other people, then great. I really get off on finding rare stuff. I am not a record collector.

Clore: That is very interesting. I would assume you would be.

No, I'm not. I mean, I am, but I'm not. In fact, all the years I've been in radio, it's really funny – I used to bring promo copies of things home, then I'd go through my albums three years later and the shrink wrap was never opened on them. And I'm going, "Why did I bring this home?" You know what I did? I took them back to the station. I have about 2,000 albums. I could have about 20,000. But I only have 2,000. And now I've probably got maybe 1,000 CDs. Most of that is newer material, recent stuff.

I'm a collector for the *Retro Lightning* purpose.

Here's what I did today – I have a half a dozen of my *Retro* listeners that love turning me on to stuff, and they send me things that I end up playing sometimes. It's all licensed material – we pay all of our ASCAP and BMI fees – I'm not worried about all of that, but I'm just saying that – and I've actually bought a number of songs on iTunes for the sole purpose of playing them on *Retro*. I've probably spent $200 of my own money on like 200 songs that, hey, I just can't find this one anywhere.

Clore: Does Fred Buc own an iPod?

Fred Buc does not. Fred Buc wants one.

Clore: Back to the element of surprise, I call the iPod the "music graveyard." Not all of it, but most of the stuff you put on your iPod – my generation, younger especially – you're probably never even going to listen to it again, let alone hope it pops up in a random shuffle. That is a very sad thing to me about the switch to so much that you have no idea it is there any longer.

Yeah, and that's again where I bring up the element of surprise with radio that you wouldn't get in that iPod graveyard. My kids say, "I have 10,000 songs." Well, that's nice – how many will you listen to? Or when's the last time you heard that one?

Clore: Advice to young people? Or anyone trying to get in the business?

Here's my advice: get your foot in the door. Whether it's radio or music industry, through internships...the way I got into it was I begged on my hands and knees. I got lucky when I went to WKDA at the top of the Stahlman building in 1975 – 18-year old kid – my first year of college, and, you know, "I'll do anything, I'll do anything." The receptionist, who's now one of the heads of the Tennessee Association of Broadcasters, she was the receptionist at KDA at that time. She said, "Don't tell anybody, but I think we just lost a part-time person on our AM station, they might be in a bind." I said, "Okay." The long story short was I, when all my friends, on Friday and Saturday night were going to fraternity parties and having a ball, I was going to work at midnight. And I was sitting there from midnight to six am, the graveyard shift, playing Country music which I had never even heard of before, until four a.m., and then I'd put on these big church tapes, thirty minute church programs, on a big reel of tape, every thirty minutes, and I'd snooze for twenty, then I'd get up and get the next one ready, until six in the morning.

I wanted to be in radio so bad, so that's what I did. In my day, that was your foot in the door, was begging for a graveyard shift and changing church tapes at 4:30 in the morning. Today, it's internships, and it's usually through the promotions department, in radio. Sometimes, every now and then, I'll get someone who's interested either in audio engineering, which would go in to our production area, or very rarely, I get someone who's interested in sales or marketing, but nine out of 10 end up in promotions, and they get to go out to the events and hang up our banners and set up the table and the giveaways and all the swag on the table. We didn't have those when I was going to school, and now you can earn credit for it.

I've hired several interns. They already know your system. They've already been inside your door. If you're going to naturally expand in a department, that's the first person I look at. It's a great advantage for somebody.

If you don't get hired, you still get to put it on your resume and go on to the next place.

<u>Clore's Summary</u>:

- Go with what you love. Work hard to determine what your "thing" is, like radio is for Fred. Put heart and soul into making it happen. It is not going to come easy, but with a natural interest and passion for something, you are well on your way to spending your life doing that.

- Radio matters. It is far from being a "new" technology, but it is still a very important element of the music industry. Learn and know about radio.

Quotes not to miss:

- "As a local station, we're sitting proof that, with radio, you form relationships with the listeners. The listener's your friend. You wake up every morning and flip on that friend, because they're talking to you and you know them and you get to know their personality, day after day, you know what their personality is like and you feel like you know them. And you can't do that on an iPod."

- "If you think about it, you know, music discovery via radio has been going on for 80 years. My parents and grandparents were discovering music on the radio in the '30s and '40s. So to that, it was the original backbone of music discovery of the music industry."

Remaining a Fan

I am a *huge* fan of music. Rarely do I lose the passion I have felt for it since I was very young.

Life has afforded me the amazing opportunity to pay my bills by spending my days marketing music. I am very grateful for this. Very.

My challenge is remaining in-tune with this original love despite the cynicism that surrounds me. I am not claiming to not be cynical, but I do claim to fight it.

I moved to Nashville in 2001 to finish my (music) business degree at Belmont University. I came from a small town in Illinois where, relatively speaking, I knew a decent amount about music. At Belmont that no longer mattered as the place was full of people like me, plenty of them far superior to me in both talent and knowledge.

Either way, we all thought we had it figured out. We would graduate as executives at big music companies.

Hardly.

During this time in my life I became an asshole about music. I hate that this happened, but I am now aware of it.

I continue to learn how much I do not know about this industry I love.

Thomas Cain

I promise you're going to have a series of issues in your life, but you just deal with that one, and with whatever else comes up, you deal with that, until life is no more.

I f I can be half of the man Thomas Cain is when I grow up, I will be doing well.

I had the tremendous privilege of meeting Thomas at a NARAS [National Academy of Recording Arts and Sciences] educational event at a high school in Muscle Shoals, Alabama, where we both spoke. He was immediately welcoming and sincere with me, and in every interaction with him since that first day he has been nothing but the exact same: a consistent, genuine and well-mannered man.

When I think of Thomas, I think of calm, humble and self-confident excellence. In every way, he is someone to look up to and learn from.

A native of Athens, Alabama, Thomas Cain is passionate about playing piano, organ and trumpet. He attended college in Nashville at Tennessee State University, where he earned a Bachelor in Music Education. He is Senior Director, Writer/Publisher Relations at BMI Nashville, a fantastic company he has been a part of for nearly 30 years.

Cain's songs have been recorded by artists such as Ronnie Milsap, Trace Adkins, Kenny Rogers, Albertina Walker and Diamond Rio. He has opened for artists such as Ray Charles, Dave Brubeck, Johnny Mathis and Bill Withers. His jingles have been used by McDonald's, Rubbermaid and Oscar Mayer, among others. Thomas' original compositions have been used as television background features on The Weather Channel. In 2009, he was honored in Washington, D.C., at the Kennedy Center for the Performing Arts as part of the "105 Voices of History Celebration," and is a member of the Alabama Music Hall of Fame.

In early 2011, I spent time with Thomas in his office at BMI Nashville, where we had the following conversation.

Clore: Around the mid-'70s is when you officially became part of the music industry. Can you talk about that time in your life, and some of the events that took place?

I kind of always wanted to be – you know, when I was in college in the late 1960s and early 1970s, I always wanted to be a songwriter. I didn't really know much about it – we just played music at TSU [Tennessee State University] and played in bands. I actually had kind of dabbled on Music Row in the late '60s and in the early '70s. I met a guy named Arthur Alexander, met some cats named Rob Galbraith and then I discovered Combine Music Corporation – which is now part of EMI Music Corporation. I had been coming over on my lunch hour writing songs with Dennis Linde, who wrote "Burning Love" and "Goodbye Earl" – such great, hit songs.

Bob Beckham, who was the president and co-owner of Combine Music Corp., they kind of just let me come and be a part of that organization, and when I gave up – I was teaching young kids in the Metro Parks System – and I quit in '76 and I came to the music business, I took a job there as a staff writer. It was my only publisher, until I started my own business with them, a co-publishing deal.

Clore: And now BMI, and you've been here how many years?

This is my twenty-seventh year, and it's been really good. This is a really great company. A lot of great activity always going on. A lot of mind-bending things as far as new concepts in technology and how we adapt our new business models. So many other things that are going on that just kind of keeps you moving, revitalized, and of course I keep my creative side going, too. I blend that with the business world, just kind of helping songwriters listen to songs – helping them with the structure of the songs, because that's what I am, a songwriter.

Clore: I want to compliment you on the example you are – to spend 27 years at a company. I know there are a lot of factors that go into that, but, at the core of it is you, and that is a tremendous example for myself and many others.

Well, thanks so much. Back in 1980 when I started my publishing company with Combine – the lady who was the president of BMI – she actually ran this office [BMI Nashville] and set this office up. Her name is Frances Preston; a well thought of, very astute businesswoman.

Back in the day she loaned me seed money to start my business up. I remember $13,000 was what she gave me back in 1980. It was what they were giving back then – advances to songwriters and publishers and so forth. She gave me the money and we had number one records. John Scott Sherrill was a songwriter that wrote for my company called Sweet Baby Music, at the time. When the partnership was dissolved, I actually started a new company called Candy Cane Music. EMI took their portion of the copyrights, and I took my portion of the copyrights, but she [Preston] was the one who was really a mentor for me.

[*Note: Frances Preston opened the BMI office in Nashville in 1958. She eventually became President of all of BMI and served in that position from 1986 until 2004.*]

I was told we had to wear suits and ties, and I told her I had the suits. [laughter]

Clore: I was actually at, and I'm sure you were, at the Dale Franklin Awards ceremony for Frances in 2007. I was thoroughly informed of her impact that night.

Amazing human being. I certainly want to give a certain amount of homage to Bob Beckham, as well. He reached out to me, a black person…when it was kind of unfashionable that you saw black people on Music Row, or writing songs. He reached out to people like Arthur Alexander, myself and other writers that have come along the way. He gave me a key to the building. Way back in 1976 I had free range of that building. We'd go in and it'd be three o'clock in the morning. You'd hear people over there writing songs, playing piano. It was always activity, and that's how Music Row was back in the day, and I suppose it's still that way now. But man, you talk about a buzz that used to be on this Row – it was unreal, unbelievable. Just energy for days. People were sharing and working with one another.

Clore: What was TSU like when you were studying there?

TSU was a melting pot – an eclectic mixture of all kinds of musicians. They came from everywhere. They came from Michigan. They came from small towns in Alabama. They came from the West, the East, the North, the South. They came from everywhere. And the big draw was, TSU, back in the day, had a phenomenal music department, and I guess they still do, but that was a time when, certainly in the mid to late '60s, even further back, and I used to hear stories about it, but there were so many profound music teachers on that campus. I mean, these were people who really, really cared about you. I mean they cared about you. So much so that they'd do anything for you. I mean literally. Mr. Frank T. Greer, who's long gone. Mr. Danny Owens. Dr. Lewis. All of these people – certainly one of my dearest friends is Dr. T.J. Anderson, who is a noted American classical composer, who lives over in the Carolinas – Raleigh-Durham area.

The competition was fierce. It was so fierce that we had so many components. You know, you could be a piano major, you could be a trumpet major, you could be a woodwind major, you could get a degree in music theory or that kind of thing, music education. Most of the people that came out of that program were people who were being prepared to be school teachers, or high school band directors, or music teachers within a public school system. But we worked, ah man, I tell ya, they gave us a kind of discipline that I don't see a lot of today. They gave us a kind of pride, man, a kind of passion for what you do that – they made you want to do something. They made you want to practice your horn, and consequently, it was that way.

You'd go to the music building, I'd be in the music build-ing sometimes at 3 o'clock in the morning, especially on "T" days…you could go there anytime of night.

I remember these great musicians that were so good. There were other musicians – Mr. Danny Owens kind of hand-picked you to be in his band – but there were musi-cians that'd come up there every day and they'd be out in the hallway, just waiting for you to mess up, if you messed up. The same thing with concert band. Mr. Greer with the concert band, if he heard somebody make a mistake, he'd go down the row and make every musician play a passage. He'd just point and tell you to play something, and you may not have been the one who made the mis-take, but people were so nervous when he came down, because he was a no non-sense band director. He didn't joke with you. He let you know that he was in charge. He was the grown-up, and basically you were the child, and as a result of that, he'd go right down the row, and the person who may not have made the mistake, he would make you pack your horn, and you'd have to get out of the band for a minute. And the way that you got back in – you would have to go to his office and audition pri-vately for him. He would take a Klose method book for the woodwind instruments and he would take his baton – I can see him right now, just turning a page – "Okay, play that right there." Turn a page, "Play that right there." He was just a great guy, a great, great man.

All of these guys – there were women, too – but just great people, and I got so much out of their love for the stu-dents. So it helped mold my life, from a business point of view, from a work-ethic point of view. I used to do the same thing around the same time every day – on Monday, Wednesday, Friday – I had the same thing. I did that for the whole time I was in school. Then on Tuesday, Thurs-day, I had the same thing, and we'd go to band practice at six o'clock in the afternoon. They meant that we started at six, not like 6:01, 6:05, 6:10. If you got there at that time you were running laps or doing push-ups. They meant serious business. If it was six o'clock, you better get there a quarter til six and be ready to go at six o'clock.

But it was just wonderful.

Clore: I hear you saying "excellence."

Excellence.

Clore: That's a word that I feel is not thought of enough these days, certainly not taught and instilled in universities enough. Also, you were on the road there for a while at one point, right?

This is the other thing that we did. In marching band we had just all these great players and went out of the marching and concert band, there were musicians that played in pick-up bands or they played in somebody's band around town, and I played in The Tyrone Smith Band, with Tyrone, "Super-T" they call him now, but The Tyrone Smith Revue is what we did – and there was the same kind of discipline in that band. We all had music stands in front of us, like you see Duke Ellington had those music stands, we all had music stands with charts on them, with lights on them. We had people who traveled with us, our sound company, and we played joints, but Tyrone, I must say, he was a public school teacher, and he always kept a fantastic band. The guys in the band were writing music and charts and arrangements, and we'd play some of the songs that were popular on the radio, we'd write jazz pieces, and we traveled all over the place.

I remember one of my favorite trips was one summer when we traveled to Montreal, and we were playing behind Rufus Thomas, who did a song called "Walking the Dog." And we played behind this guy at that same show – a guy named Arthur Conley – "Do you like good music? Yeah, yeah. That sweet soul music." But we'd have all those horns and trumpets, there'd be about three trumpets, and they'd be blasting away. Sometimes we had a trombone, tenor saxophone, alto saxophone, two guitars, bass and drums. It was just fantastic.

I remember one of the worst gigs I think I ever played. We went from Nashville to Memphis and we had to drive to play a gig, from Memphis to Johnson City, Tennessee. That was the longest gig I've ever been on in my life. We drove across the state of TN, and that is long, but we did it. We got there and we did it, but we were worn out. We played the gig, rocked the house and came on back home.

Saturday night in Memphis, Sunday night in Johnson City.

Clore: What years were you on the road?

This was probably 1968-69-70, something like that. Maybe in to '71. It may have been a little bit later, at least four or five years.

Clore: Four or five years on the road. I know there are tremendous stories.

It was great. It was great. We were young in those days. We could withstand anything. The only thing that wore us out was the trip from Memphis to Johnson City, but we were young. We could withstand anything. There was nothing. We didn't even think about being tired, and it was always a real good bunch of guys. We always got along – we had our difficulties, relational difficulties – but, by in large, ya know? Everybody was on everybody, too, man. I mean, you mess up and they were all over you.

If you was slacking, man, they'd be all over you, and that was it, but I loved it.

I carry those same principles into my life right now. There are some things, as you get older, you get a little tired [laughter]. But by in large, it's like everyday, I get up every morning – I was out at six o'clock – I hit the floor between 6 and 6:30, and I'm out. I walk three or four miles in a day. I was out doing it this morning in the rain, but it keeps me feeling great. I feel so good all the time, man. I'm going to leave here, I'm going to the Y and I'm going to pump some iron, but I feel good, I really feel great all of the time. It's very rare that I really feel bad – I just don't feel bad. I feel good all of the time. I really do.

And you have mental stresses, I mean, the business will bring a lot of mental stresses, but by in large, once I hit that gym or something like that, it's gone. I'm out there laughing with my friends, my buddies and talking and running in to good friends – we're talking business. Last night I was talking to my friend and we were talking about real estate – it's so wonderful.

Clore: Staying active, working out – what else do you do at this point, after a few decades in the music industry – how do you maintain what you're describing?

Well, I think that one of the key things – I like reading a lot, and I love to write, and I love to play the piano, I love to travel. I just came back from Texas this weekend. I went to this big Gospel music event that we had, that BMI put on – called The Trailblazers Awards – we went to that. I left that at three o'clock in the afternoon and I was on a plane heading to Austin, TX – and I got down there and taught three classes, and then got back on a plane on that Sunday and came right back to Nashville.

I like to work around the house, too. I like to have projects in my home that I like to work on. My wife and I have little things that we work on. It's simple stuff. I really don't have any real crazy, crazy things. I'm inspired to write books. I'm writing my first fiction book, and once I finish that, I'm going to write some more books. I have a lot of ideas – I'm going to write about my journey on Music Row, which I think would be, may be fascinating – because, you know, nobody of color has done this – has stayed over here on Music Row. From the day I came here, this is pretty much all I've ever done, is music. I've seen 'em come, I've seen 'em go, and it's been a wonderful thing.

But I think that perhaps, more than anything, being in love with God and Jesus, that's the most fascinating thing I know. It's more fascinating than anything else I do, and I kind of look at my other things in life – my music and all of these other things as my recreation – but my real application is prayer, prayer. Praying for other people, helping somebody, being a servant, and I really enjoy that part of life – being a servant. There are so many people that are hurting, so many young people that are having issues and problems. So many songwriters that are trying to make it through this maze of the music business. To be able to counsel with them and be able to talk about it – after you listen to them – you can say, "I think this is maybe what you should or could do." That's pretty much it, man – simple stuff. Get in my car and go to the country. Go to country towns and see what's going on out there. I've been doing that around Tennessee – go to little country towns – places I've heard of but have never been.

I really have enjoyed my life. I've traveled so much throughout this country, and this is a fantastic country. I've traveled it up and down, and certainly a lot of the traveling has been because of what I do here at BMI. It kind of sparks new adventurism; you want to go and be adventurous.

Clore: There's a calm and a peace about you, that to anyone that will someday read this book, I want to communicate that to them. As I sit here with you, you alluded to one of the books you want to write about your history on Music Row. You mentioned a person of color being able to stick around for all of these years. When I think through that history, and to see and hear the way you view all of it, embrace all of it – it's remarkable to me. Are there moments along the way when you didn't really feel this way?

Well, you know, man, it's like – this is what I did. I always prayed before I went into a situation. I still do that. When I go into meetings, not all of the time, but when I can think sometimes in the evenings, at home, when I know I've got some meeting coming up, I just ask God to be my guidance, to help me to not be mean, or say anything mean-spirited towards anybody, or towards a situation. And also, things that you may encounter. I try to separate.

I know one thing that drove me here, and that was music. It wasn't somebody's personality. Bob Beckham, certainly, out of the goodness of his heart. But he liked my music, he loved the way I could sing and play the piano, and thought I had a little bit of talent. So, he embraced that. He didn't embrace the fact that I was black or whatever – I don't think he really cared. He didn't even give two cents about that. The only thing he cared about is, he said, "You've got talent. Come on in here and go on over there and write with Dennis Linde." He didn't care to get off into all of these left field kind of things.

One of the things I did is I separated the personalities from the music, and whatever personality a person's personality is I don't want their personality to affect what I'm about, or my daily travel. Sometimes you have to bite your tongue, and keep on going on. Forget about it, because by in large, what I think about life and troubles is that it's going to be over within a minute. Everything's going to be over with. If you're having some issues, they're going to be over within a minute. You're going to go on to something else – something else will come up. I promise you're going to have a series of issues in your life, but you just deal with that one, and with whatever else comes up, you deal with that, until life is no more. Until life is no more. And I believe in heaven – I think that's a beautiful thing, and that's what I strive for, is to have that inward peace.

Clore: With all the hats that you wear: writer, producer, BMI representative, author – from a business standpoint, which one of those makes you feel the most alive, or is it all of them?

All of them. All of them, because it's all one when you think about it. They're all connected to one another, it's just like the parts of the body. You need your arms to keep your balance, your eyes to see. All of this stuff is the same thing. To write is somehow connected to the business part. To make a record is connected. To write a song, it's all connected to that business part. It's all interchangeable to me. If one part of it messes up, you're going to have an issue. If you don't write a good lyric, or if you've got some wacked-out chord changes in there – dissonant or whatever it might be – it's not going to be good. If you don't connect the song with good business practices, then you're really going to have issues when it comes to finances. I really see it all the time. People that don't pay attention to the details, and that's the most important. If I can say anything that causes falter is when you don't pay attention to the details. It'll stumble you up every time.

Clore: From an advice standpoint, what are some specific things people such as myself should pay attention to? Maybe organizations to be a part of, how to best spend my time in the music industry – what are some of those things that you feel are most important?

I certainly think that reading is at the top of the list, and reading the right things. There are some books on the music industry, which you can go to an organization like NSAI and they can be a mentor for you in a lot of ways. It's a music membership organization that puts on songwriter critiques, they put on Tin Pan South, where you can come see how other people write songs. There are showcases and so forth you can attend.

And the other thing, for example, when I got into the music business, none of this technology was available. You can go online and get an answer to mostly any question you want. And I think the other thing is find out for yourself what you should do. Ask questions – then join a PRO, like BMI, because there is a world of information to be garnered here that is free.

I think that if a person is trying to become active in the industry, you're going to have to invest in yourself. You're going to have to buy some books (Donald Passman). Applying yourself. I certainly think that in the music business, two things that must go hand in hand – and that is a good mind and a strong body. I think if you work your body from a physical standpoint – keeping yourself strong – I really think it does help you to stay up and motivated and moving around and full of energy, and it takes energy to be in this business. It really does.

Don't hang out with the wrong people.

And a lot of times you're going to find a good person to work with.

Find a good mentor.

Just live.

Don't do anything that would cause you to falter. People get drunk, and drive. People drink alcohol and take drugs and they get caught and busted. You wind up losing what God has given you, and if you feel like you've got to do that, certainly be moderate. Just don't be crazy with it.

I mean, I don't tell people about their personal life, you know, that's what they want to do. But as far as the practices of the music industry, that's pretty much what I do. Get up early and get at it. When other people are sleeping, the guys that are working are going to be the guys that will have the edge.

Clore: Profesionally speaking, what has been your highlight?

I suppose being able to get my songs cut by Kenny Rogers, to get songs recorded by Diamond Rio, to get songs recorded by Ronnie Milsap. Getting my music on The Weather Channel, to be able to play and open shows for people like Ray Charles and Donnie Hathaway, and people like George Benson and Bill Withers and Ramsey Lewis – to get to know these people when you do these shows with them, back in the day. These are things I really have kind of archived within my subconscious mind so when people mention it it comes to the forefront and I like to talk about those things.

I did a show for PBS with Johnny Mathis where my friends and I, we were the background singers and the dancers. We had to go through days and days and days of rehearsing and learning all the parts. We were on the stage and we were whispering to each other, "This is the next move," so that we would be perfect. This was at the Opry House – it was packed out. [whispering – "Okay, next you move to the right, crossover"] it was so wild, man, but we made it through the night.

The year before last [2008] I was in New York City at the Russian Tea Room. BMI had put on this thing they called "The Masters Series," where they honor all of these incredible jazz musicians, and in that room was The National Endowment for the Arts – they're the ones who put this on – but it was George Benson, Dave Brubeck, it was Billy Taylor, it was all of these incredible, great musicians and we were all in this room. And I had to get up and speak – Wynton Marsalis was there. Then wc wcnt down to the Rose Theater in Lincoln Center to hear these great performers. Then after that, I got a chance to play the grand piano in this big atrium where everybody came out, like a reception for all of these people, and it was just so wonderful to be able to have those kinds of moments in your life. It was just like heaven. But I still love writing songs. I love writing Gospel songs. I love writing jazz pieces. I love Country songs.

To do all of that, it's heaven, man. I can't describe it any more than that. It's just heaven.

Clore's summary:

- Practice, practice, practice, and then practice some more. That is the point Thomas is making when he is discussing the teaching style of Mr. Greer at Tennessee State University.

- Be excellent. Thomas talks about how much preparation goes in to his live performances, and pretty much everything he does in life. You have to be ready.

- Read. Know what's going on. Don't ever stop paying attention. One thing is certain – you do not know everything.

- Live a balanced life. Do things that do not involve your work-life. Spend time with family and friends, with no agenda whatsoever. Relax. Pay attention to the important things going on around you. They will be gone before you know it.

- Difficulties will come, and go. Don't let them freak you out. Be ready as best you can, deal with them, and move on. They aren't going to stop.

Quotes not to miss:

- "Don't do anything that would cause you to falter."

- "Get up early and get at it. When other people are sleeping, the guys that are working are going to be the guys that will have the edge."

- "I think if you work your body from a physical standpoint – keeping yourself strong – I really think it does help you to stay up and motivated and moving around and full of energy, and it takes energy to be in this business – it really does."

Networking

Connecting with people can be difficult, and often takes months of repeated and quality interaction. Without it, life is hard. Well, life is hard anyway, but at least when you have a network of people around you, there is something to fall back on.

I attended Belmont University in Nashville, where I graduated with honors from the Music Business Program with a Bachelor of Business Administration degree. Before I even arrived on campus in the fall of 2001, I had heard all about the importance of networking through Belmont's marketing literature. On campus, I heard about it even more. I rebelled at first because I felt it was being over-emphasized, and believed I could survive without it, but as a transfer student, I started realizing I was behind in the relationship department. It was time to immediately step up my networking efforts.

A college campus is a fascinating place. You are surrounded mostly by like-minded people striving for a quality life. You are physically together almost constantly. Everyone has arrived from their prior domain, the one they grew up in, the one they had likely mastered. Talent, drive, obligation and/or scholarship bring everyone together and it is time to get along and enter adulthood together.

During my time at Belmont, which followed my attendance at two prior colleges, I was simultaneously fascinated and challenged to be surrounded by people that loved music as much as I did. People that could, and would, sit around and talk about every single aspect of music and its industry for hours on end. New friends that shared a passion for live performance, recorded product, music's history and its future.

People just like me.

Networking with these new friends was natural, but we all knew we were in a competition from the first day on campus, and transfers like myself were a couple of years behind in the race.

I began thinking in my mind that I wanted it more than the person sitting next to me in class. I would often literally think that to myself as I sat in class and self-motivated. Fortunately for me, it came naturally and I knew it was true. Granted, I could have upped my on-campus involvement a bit, but I knew that through my studies, the relationships I was building and the places I was physically positioning myself, I was in a fight that I was not going to lose.

We all have some sort of innate ability and talent: God-given gifts. I firmly believe that it is not difficult for each one of us to determine what those things are. For me, it is a deep love of music and everything about it. I also have a passion for being a part of excellent work as it relates to all facets of the music industry. So I knew this life in music is all I really wanted. Although I tried my hardest to derail myself with a safe and boring (to me) job as a pharmacist, thank goodness for those crazy organic chemistry equations that confirmed what I already knew but was afraid I could not make a living doing.

Enter Belmont, after their unsolicited catalog somehow made it to my parent's house. Dad called to tell me about a Music Business program they offered. I knew it was for me. A year later, I was on campus.

As my time at Belmont progressed, I had to get serious about finding an internship. My first internship was with an amazing organization called Compassion International, where I worked under the supervision of a great man who would quickly become a dear friend. His name is Mark Hollingsworth, and he is interviewed in this book.

My second internship came about accidentally. During Fall 2002, I went to interview Pam Lewis at her PLA Media office on Music Row for a paper I was writing in my Artist Management class, where Tandy Rice was the professor – also someone interviewed in this book. The person answering the door was a classmate of mine at the time, Heather Lewandoski. I had no clue Heather was interning there, but it turned out to be one of the most important occurrences of my career.

Heather was soon leaving Nashville for Los Angeles to attend Belmont University West for a semester, and Pam needed to fill an intern role. Simply by showing up to do this class project interview, I was selected as the guy to take Heather's spot. In January of 2003, I began interning at PLA Media. In April of the same year, I was hired full-time as a publicist at the same office. This was my official entry into the music industry.

About a year later, I started hearing a whole lot about an organization called SOLID [Society of Leaders In Development], a networking, education and community service non-profit organization comprised of music industry people. Once again, I found myself feeling above the need for help on the networking front, so I initially resisted joining SOLID. I sure did not want to fill out that application and have to prove my worth. I was already *in* the music industry. Was that not enough?

My better judgment won out and I filled out the application. I can genuinely tell you that SOLID has connected me with some of the most amazing, like-minded people in the music industry, and provided me priceless opportunities. Namely, being a part of putting together a panel with my friends Justin Levenson, Chip Petree, and many others in 2005, comprised of Alan Parsons (who is interviewed in this book), Eddie Kramer and Tony Brown called "Making Masterpieces: The Stories Behind Some of Music's Greatest Albums." I will never forget that October night as long as I live. Between those three legends, they have been instrumental in some of music's greatest albums, including: Pink Floyd's *Dark Side of the Moon*, Jimi Hendrix's *Electric Ladyland* and Steve Earle's *Guitar Town*.

Networking is essential. You truly do not know when it is going to help you, catch up with you, be watching you, call you or be in a position to hire you. Be strategic in all you do. Think ahead. Consider your actions, your words, your tone and generally how you treat each and every single person around you.

Kris Kristofferson was a janitor at Nashville's Columbia Studios in the 1960s. He is now in the Country Music Hall of Fame and is the author of a tremendously special catalog of songs, including one of the greatest songs ever written, "Me & Bobby McGee."

You truly never know what is next. As you meet new people, treat them with respect. Give them the time of day. Follow up. Keep your word. Show up. Know your role, but respect others in theirs, no matter how much disparity there may be between you and them.

As your network expands, always keep in mind where you came from. Do not lose sight of where you are going, but do not ever forget your foundation.

I sure would not have wanted to be a jerk to the janitor at Nashville's Columbia Studios in the 1960s.

Peter Cooper

I wonder what life would have been like for some of my musical heroes if they had been expected to blog and tweet and update about every day of their lives. Would Townes Van Zandt have been updating his Facebook page with, "Heroin again this morning, LOL!"?

Peter Cooper is not only a great musician, he is also a great music writer for a major daily newspaper, Nashville's *The Tennessean*. It is impossible to say he excels at one over the other; Kris Kristofferson is a fan of his music, while the late Johnny Cash was a fan of his newspaper writing. In other words, Peter can count the guy that wrote "Sunday Mornin' Comin' Down" and "Me and Bobby McGee," along with one of the most influential artists in the history of recorded music, as two of his fans. Suffice it to say, Peter Cooper is a GRAMMY-nominated stud.

Cooper's albums have been praised by *The Washington Post*, *The New York Times*, *No Depression* and *The Philadelphia Inquirer*, among others. He is a senior lecturer in Country music at Vanderbilt University's Blair School of Music.

Peter has worked in the studio as a performer, producer or session musician with Patty Griffin, Emmylou Harris, Tom T. Hall, Bobby Bare, Nanci Griffith, Todd Snider, Kenny Chesney, Ricky Skaggs, Jim Lauderdale and many more.

From Kris Kristofferson – "Peter Cooper looks at the world with an artist's eye and a human heart and soul. His songs are the work of an original, creative imagination, alive with humor and heartbreak and irony and intelligence, with true beauty in the details. Deep stuff. And they get better every time you listen."

Brad Barnes, of Barnes Storming, sums Cooper up best. "Aside from being a quick wit and a kick-ass writer of newspaper stories, Peter Cooper is a great singer-songwriter."

You will be hard-pressed to find an individual anywhere that has had this much access to "famous people" and general music industry experience, yet remains so in love with the original point – the music.

Clore: One of the things I love most about you is your genuine and obvious love for music first. How does this shape how you view the world, and how you spend your time?

Anytime I think I'm getting burned out on music, I go home and listen to music. It's like hair of the dog. Sick of what you're hearing on the radio? Put some Tom T. Hall vinyl on the turntable. Works every time. As for my worldview...well, I wouldn't want to blame music for that. Except that when I'm thinking about people and situations, lyrics from favorite songs come to my head. If someone's having a going-away party, I think about John Gorka singing, "People love you when they know you're leaving soon." If it's a New Year's Eve party, I think of Townes Van Zandt singing, "Bid the years goodbye / You cannot still them." I spend most of my time either writing about music, reading about music, playing music or traveling somewhere to play music. Oh, and watching baseball. But I usually watch baseball with a guitar in my hands.

Clore: Your music has not only been approved, but endorsed, by the guy that wrote "Sunday Mornin' Comin' Down," "For the Good Times" and "Me and Bobby McGee." How does it feel to know Kris Kristofferson is a Peter Cooper fan?

As someone who writes music criticism, I'm very aware of the subjective nature of music-listening. And I have a general philosophy regarding music-making, which is that you should do some internal excavation – in other words, write something that either makes you feel a lot better for having revealed it, or that makes you feel a lot worse for having revealed it – and then people can take it however they want. And so I shouldn't be worrying about what anyone will think of a song I'm writing when I'm writing it. That said...well, Kristofferson is not "anyone." He's Kristofferson. First concert I ever saw was Kristofferson. I was five-years-old. His songs have been of enormous impact to me, and if he'd heard my songs and said, "This is crap," then I probably would have taken him at his word and felt bad and diminished. So his kind words have been bolstering and encouraging things for me. There's also an added kick-in-the-butt there: If I'm writing a song now, I know that Kristofferson might hear it. That'll kind of put your feet to the fire.

Clore: What are your thoughts about the music industry as it awkwardly transitions into the Digital Age?

As a musician, there are elements of that transition that are disheartening. There are a lot of empty buildings where record companies used to be, and that means there's a lot of nothing where recording and touring budgets used to be. It would be great to live in an era like the early 1970s, when singer-songwriters could hope to get $100,000 or so for a recording budget, and could then get funding from a label to take a band on the road. Those things happen with great rarity these days.

On the other hand, it's now much less expensive to record, and the Internet provides instant distribution. So those are huge positives. As a music fan and journalist, there are great benefits and great problems. Yesterday, I downloaded a Bob Carpenter album called *Silent Passage*, from iTunes. An out-of-print album from 1975, and I'd never heard it before. Well, it's a killer album. So, there's something wonderful that the Digital Age brought right into my home. The biggest problem for me is that the industry is now so fragmented and distracted. Trying to get a music consumer's undivided attention is like trying to have a conversation with a lunch date who won't stop checking her iPhone and texting her friends. When people listen on a computer, they've got little windows popping up, and they're having e-conversations and they're listening through cruddy speakers. Buying an album used to be followed by an evening that involves putting the album on a turntable and sitting there and listening to it. That's practically gone now, as is the relation between one song on an album and the song that follows. So many people download only singles now, and the crotchety old guy in me wants flow, pacing and tempo to play a greater role in the listening process. Listening to singles, or on shuffle mode, is like going to a comedy show where one comedian after the next comes onstage, tells a joke and walks offstage. Really discombobulated, to me at least.

Clore: What musician has impacted you most, and how has this shaped you?

On a personal level, Todd Snider asked me to open shows for him, which allowed me to get in front of large rooms for the first time, and which handed me a portion of his audience, and which allowed me to watch a true modern master at work. Big impact there. But it's impossible for me to narrow things to one musician. Lloyd Green is my favorite musician. He played steel guitar with The Byrds, Paul McCartney, Don Williams, Charley Pride, Nanci Griffith and so many more, and his playing is as emotionally intelligent as it is technically complex. I've never had to go in and record my songs without Lloyd on them, and witnessing the way he comprehends a piece of music and then elevates it has been a profound thing for me. Now, in terms of songwriters I rip off most regularly... er, I mean songwriters of great influence to me... my short list includes: Snider, Kristofferson, Tom T. Hall, John Prine and Eric Taylor. And in terms of my vision for how to make coherent albums and how to put the proper people together in a room to play music, Emmylou Harris is the most impactful for me.

Clore: You write about music for a major newspaper, perform your own music live and work in the recording studio with some of your personal heroes. Is there anything you would do differently?

I'm not one of those "no regrets" guys. Every day, I've got dozens of 'em! But as for what I do everyday for a living and for fun, I'm thrilled with the way it's all gone. Every now and then, I'll catch myself wishing that I was writing a song rather than writing another newspaper story. But a big part of what I do for the newspaper is sit down with songwriters and talk about songwriting. I mean, I get paid to do that. And those conversations with Kris, Tom T., Emmylou, Guy Clark, Loretta Lynn, Johnny Cash, Neil Young, Nanci Griffith, Keith Richards, Patty Griffin and so many more are absolutely priceless, and they can't hurt your songwriting, either. It's not like anybody ever said, "Yeah, I was doing pretty good with the songwriting until Guy Clark told me a bunch of dumb, ill-considered stuff that screwed it all up."

Clore: What has been your proudest moment to date?

Isn't pride one of those deadly sins? Is this a trick question? Let's go with "the moment for which I'm most grateful," 'cause nobody ever preached against gratefulness, right? I'm going to say that moment was probably when my phone rang in Spartanburg, SC back in 2000, and the person on the other end of the line told me I could come to Nashville and write about music for a living. Back then, I traveled to Nashville a lot, and I knew it's where I wanted to be, but I was either too responsible or too afraid to come here on a bus with $45 in my pocket. So here was a chance to get paid for being around music and musicians. Here was my backstage pass to the Grand Ole Opry, and my invitation to sit in Earl Scruggs' living room while he picked the banjo. I've seen a lot of lottery tickets, and never seen one with that kind of payout.

Clore: What is your songwriting process? What do you do to "get better," and how do you go about coming up with new ideas?

My process differs every time I write a song. It can start with a lyric, a melody, a guitar pattern or any other little bolt of inspiration. I try not to worry about getting better, because I don't think songwriting is a sport, at all. I can't compare, say, Neil Young and John Prine. I love 'em both. They both reveal truths to me. I tend to stick with a song if it either makes me feel better for having written it and for revealing what it reveals, or scared for having written it and revealing what it reveals. Then I take it on the road and see how other people react. I also have a few people – Todd Snider, Don Schlitz and Eric Brace are among them – who I'll bounce songs off in hopes of getting advice, criticism or affirmation. As for coming up with new ideas, that isn't much of a problem. I just participate in life, mull it over and write some of it down. I have a song called "Elmer The Dancer" about a guy in a Milwaukee polka bar that wasn't so much written as reported. Turns out writing songs and writing newspaper articles can be pretty similar. The rhyming is all that's different, and there are dictionaries for that.

Clore: How do you handle the business side of Peter Cooper, the musician, considering your day job at the newspaper and your professor role at Vanderbilt?

I have terrible business sense and am very bad at working angles, securing guarantees and getting tax credits. If you're talking about separating each job, though, then I have come to think that they don't always need to be separate. It's all music to me. I'm either playing it, writing it, writing about it or teaching it, and those are all just different angles on the same thing. I notice that when I'm watching a football game on TV, one of the commentators usually played the game. I'm not saying that all music journalists would be better at the journalism thing if they actually played, but I do think that personal experience as a musician has made me – not speaking for anyone else here – more capable as a journalist. As for teaching at Vanderbilt, all I'm doing there is sharing my love for Country music and my stories about Country music. That's an easy gig, and a fun one.

Clore: You mentioned interviewing Johnny Cash. What were your experiences like with him? When? Where?

The first time I met Johnny Cash, it was probably a year or so after I moved to town (I came here [Nashville] in 2000). The interview was in Nashville, at an office. I'd never done this before and haven't done it since, but I actually said something like, "Hey, before we start, I just want to say 'Thank you,' because your music has helped to shape me and so many others, for the better. I'm a fan." He was gracious and said thanks, and then he said, "I'm a fan of yours, too, Peter. I read you everyday in *The Tennessean*. We've had a subscription for many years." And then he mentioned a story that I'd just written and said kind things about that. At first, I probably blushed. And then I thought, "Wait, the stuff I write on deadline...Johnny Cash reads that? I've got to be more careful, and I've got to be better." Later, I found out Tom T. Hall was reading it, too. It was a lesson, and I took that lesson to mean that in Nashville there is no time when you should write ill-considered words. I certainly have written ill-considered words since then, but it wasn't for lack of consideration! After that, I spoke with Cash on the phone several times, and I spent a wonderful weekend in 2002 up at the Carter Fold in Virginia, hanging around June Carter Cash, Carlene Carter and other wonderful folks. June kind of adopted me for the weekend, and I was happy to be adopted. I don't claim to have been friends with Johnny Cash, but I think we may have understood one another, and a mutual friend of ours – the great bass player Dave Roe – once presented me with a CD that Cash signed to me.

Clore: As we get further away from an era where people purposefully focused on listening to music, often together, what are your recommendations about how to keep that spirit alive? Visit used record stores? Own a turntable? Get better friends?

I do believe owning a turntable is a good thing, both because it requires a more intense attention and because there's a lot of great music available on vinyl that isn't on CD or on iTunes. Mostly, though, I think it might be nice if people would listen to music – on vinyl or CD, through computer speakers or earbuds or in live venues – without doing something else at the same time. Cut off the deal on your computer where it pops up and tells you that you have a new email. Turn off the cell phone that buzzes when someone calls or texts or emails. Listen to music like it was a friend of yours and you were having lunch together and it was telling you something important. You wouldn't check a text message in thc middle of something like that. And it's my belief that it often IS telling you something important.

Clore: What are your thoughts about the separation between artist and fan, a la, Pink Floyd's *The Wall*, especially now that fans have more of a direct voice to the artist via social media?

My thoughts on this are confused and conflicting. I enjoy meeting people who listen to my music, and my songs have made wonderful friends for me. I am happy to hear from people who hear my music, and we often have things in common. On the other hand, I wonder what life would have been like for some of my musical heroes if they had been expected to blog and tweet and update about every day of their lives. Would Townes Van Zandt have been updating his Facebook page with, "Heroin again this morning, LOL!"? Can you imagine

Guy Clark telling his audience to please sign his mailing list or to follow his Twitter feed? For the most part, though, I think that artists hearing directly from listeners is a good thing. There's an Uncle Tupelo song I like about how every star on the back of the bus is just waiting for his cover to be blown. Social media means that there are fewer stars and that there's very little cover. And the music industry has dictated that there are fewer and fewer busses. I ride around in vans, and if I'm not driving I'm happy to pull out my iPhone and answer questions from listeners who are happy to ask. The magic isn't in the mystery, it's in the sharing.

Clore: What has been the single biggest moment in the history of Rock and Roll? Also, what has been the single biggest moment in the history of Country Music? Or, as I feel, should it all just be grouped in to one singular question? And if you can't land on just one, how about one per decade since the 1950s?

Elvis' recording of "That's All Right, Mama," with Scotty Moore and Bill Black, is the biggest moment in Rock history. Read Peter Guralnick's *Last Train To Memphis* book for further information. Basically, the guys in the room had no idea what had happened, but in three minutes they changed the culture of an entire world. After that, people sang differently, played differently, talked to their parents differently, wore different clothes, etc. It all changed right there, on a hot day in Memphis. It changed Country music, too: People like Webb Pierce and Ernest Tubb, who were at the top of the Country world, suddenly found themselves struggling to find an audience. But I guess I would separate the Rock and Country moments, because the Bristol Sessions in 1927 – where the Carter Family and Jimmie Rodgers were discovered – ranks as the top moment in Country history, in terms of influencing all that came after. I mean, Elvis wouldn't have thought to do what he did without Jimmie Rodgers.

Clore: I often experience this feeling where I think, "That's why I love music!," or "That's why I came to Nashville!" Specifically, and in addition to sitting in Earl Scruggs' living room while he picked the banjo, what are some of those moments for you?

I have those moments every day. A good one was when I sat down recently with Tom T. Hall to tell him about a project I wanted to produce, where different artists would come in to his home studio and record new versions of his children's album, *Songs of Fox Hollow*. He wanted to know what artists I had in mind, and I had a long list of them, including Buddy Miller, Patty Griffin, Bobby Bare and Duane Eddy. Tom T. went through each artist – none of whom except Bare I had any idea that he was particularly aware of – and told me all about them. And when it came to Duane Eddy, the first instrumental hero of Rock 'n' Roll, Tom T. said, and I quote, "Duane Eddy... Oh, boy!" Tom T. gave his blessing, and Duane came and showed up at the studio, and they met, for the first time. Duane was a huge Tom T. fan as well, and he was asking Tom T. about "Homecoming," "Old Dogs, Children and Watermelon Wine" and other songs. And Tom T. just kept smiling. Here were two people with seemingly disparate musical histories – one a twangy Rock 'n' Roller, one a storytelling Country singer – and yet they were bound by songs, by joy and by geography. They live just down the road from one another. Sometimes I hear people griping about Nashville, and usually those people are from Texas, and usually they're talking about so-and-so "Going Nashville." Look, there's plenty of laughable music coming from this and every other town. But what does "Going Nashville" mean? Does it mean going John

Prine? Going Emmylou Harris? Going Tom T. Hall? Guy Clark? Todd Snider? If so, I'm ready to go. Sign me up.

Clore: The Beatles or The Rolling Stones?

Both, and I mean that. Both. They are both necessary, and wondrous, and righteous and visceral and brilliant. I read Keith Richards' autobiography, and he writes about his joy in getting a visit from Paul McCartney. This isn't sports. The Colts play against the Patriots, but The Beatles don't play against The Stones. All together, now.

Clore's Summary:

- Don't lose your original love. Stay focused on the music. Don't let the business and the people and the heartache get you down. It will. Don't let it.

- Write honestly. Let people in, and they will decide what to do with it. If you never put it out there, you will never know if anyone is interested. I can tell you that is how I felt about my own writing just a few years ago, and still do sometimes.

- Know history. Know who matters and who has paved the way, especially in your area of interest.

- You do not need to compartmentalize segments of your life. It all works together. One thing flows in to the other. It may take years to see why and how, but it does.

- You can always be better.

Quotes not to miss:

- "Anytime I think I'm getting burned out on music, I go home and listen to music."

- "It's not like anybody ever said, 'Yeah, I was doing pretty good with the songwriting until Guy Clark told me a bunch of dumb, ill-considered stuff that screwed it all up'."

- "Turns out writing songs and writing newspaper articles can be pretty similar. The rhyming is all that's different, and there are dictionaries for that."

- "It's all music to me. I'm either playing it, writing it, writing about it or teaching it, and those are all just different angles on the same thing."

- "Wait, the stuff I write on deadline…Johnny Cash reads that? I've got to be more careful, and I've got to be better."

The preceding interview took place in November of 2010.

Talk To Your Bandmates

Hang out with your band, on purpose. Talk with them. Talk with them about all of the business stuff that you think is never going to affect you – or tear you apart. Get to the bottom of the issue(s). Don't let it fester. Put things on paper.

If you think being in a band is all about writing, recording and playing songs live, you are wrong (*most* of this also applies to individual artists; not talking to your band about business stuff, but pretty much everything else).

Check your motivations. You first, then ask your mates: "Fame? Fortune? Love of the music?"

It *will* get hard. You may be one of the FEW that hit it quickly, but even those few will encounter hard times.

Most encounter more hard times than good. Most never make it to start with.

Getting signed is not the answer. Nor is getting a booking agent or a manager. Getting your music in film/TV is not the answer. Getting on late night TV is not the answer. Getting on a certain tour is not the answer.

All of these things matter in their own unique and right-time manner, but they will not save you. Many stars must align before "making it" will ever take place. Chances are, it will not be you.

That is not discouragement; that is reality.

You must work, work, work and then work some more. You must practice until you no longer can. You must hone your art in each and every way you know how.

If you are not doing all of these things, someone out there is. And they will have what could have been yours.

Liberty DeVitto

I can remember standing on stage at Madison Square Garden, thinking, "This is it?"

Liberty DeVitto is a legendary Rock and Roll drummer. One of the most visibly passionate. One that truly loves the music. Simply, one of the best.

He spent three decades of his life playing drums (in-studio and on-stage) for Billy Joel. He has also performed with the likes of Elton John, The Carpenters, Meat Loaf and many, many others.

Clore: I know The Beatles had a huge impact on you. What other artists have had a significant impact on you?

The Rascals, Cream, Hendrix and Traffic…a long list. I like any music that is played with passion…Classical, Jazz, Rock, Soul, anything! My belief is, "It's not what you play, but how you play it." There are a lot of musicians that can "Play the part," but there is no emotion in it. That sucks to me.

Clore: What part of the music world gets you going? The studio, the live concert atmosphere, etc.?

They are two different animals. When you record in the studio it is like an out-of-body experience. The drummer concentrates on what he and the other musicians are playing and is totally engrossed in the emotion and spirit of the song. The drummer becomes the listener, and listens to how the drummer's part transcends through the speakers and how his part fits with the rest of the group. He becomes the judge. Live, there is the exchange with the audience. You play a song, the audience reacts in a positive way. You play the next song better. It's a give-give situation.

Clore: From a professional standpoint, what is your proudest moment?

First, let me say there has never been anything greater in my life than having children. Period. Hands down the best! I think musically it's when a young person says to me "I practiced to your records," or, "I saw you play and I said, 'That's what I want to do.' You are my Ringo."

Clore: Do you have a daily mantra you live by?

I try to treat people how I would like to be treated. I try to look at everyone as someone's son or daughter.

Clore: Can you share a little about the downside of the business and what happens to a person after years of actually living the dream like you've been able to?

The dream is always bigger than the reality. I can remember standing on stage at Madison Square Garden thinking, "This is it?" It was nothing like I imagined when I used to think how Ringo felt in The Beatles playing Shea. When I was on stage at The Garden, it was nothing like I imagined. Don't get me wrong – it was a cool feeling – but there were club gigs that were as exciting or more satisfying.

Clore: What keeps you motivated and interested after all of these years?

Girls!

<u>Clore's Summary</u>:

- Liberty has seen and experienced most of what the music industry has to offer, and yet he remembers standing on stage at Madison Square Garden, thinking, "This is it?"

- What you think you are looking for is often not what you hoped it would be. Keep this in mind as you press on toward your dreams. Be very mindful of what you sacrifice along the way.

The preceding interview took place in November of 2008.

Merle Kilgore Saw Right Through Me

I'm a Rock and Roll guy. I was not raised on Country music, and prior to Nashville, I wasn't around it much. Then I decided to attend college at Belmont University, in Nashville.

Like many of my classmates, I had a stupid, arrogant, anti-Country music attitude because I thought the music was dumb, or insert whatever stereotypical prejudices you can think of relating to the South, Country music fans, whatever.

Side note: Nashville is far more than just Country music, but that's not the point here.

In early 2003, I was sitting at my desk as a more than slightly arrogant intern at a PR firm called PLA Media, which is on Sixteenth Avenue right in the heart of Nashville's Music Row, an area founded upon the successes of Country music. I answered the phone and had no earthly idea who the guy on the other end was. Merle Kilgore was calling to talk to my boss at the time, Pam Lewis.

Merle, being about as quick-witted as they come, picked up on the fact that I did not know who he was, and he decided to confirm it. We had a brief, super-awkward conversation where he filled me in on his credentials.

As long as I live, I will never forget the feeling I had after that conversation. In that moment, I decided that even though I didn't (and still don't) love Country music, I am going to respect the hell out of it. I am going to learn about it and quit making fun of an important genre of music, both in Nashville and beyond.

By the way, Merle Kilgore, who co-wrote "Ring of Fire" with June Carter Cash, was the long-time manager of Hank Williams Jr., and was named honorary state senator for Tennessee in 1987. In 1998, Van Morrison recorded a version of the Kilgore-written "More and More" with a guy named Bob Dylan.

Mr. Kilgore passed away two years later, in 2005. I was fortunate to attend his funeral at the Ryman Auditorium, where Kid Rock sang, "I Saw The Light," a song written by Hank Williams Sr.

John Ettinger

You really start to think – yeah, that whole chase of the music business, and I don't mean to judge it, but it's kind of silly in the long run.

John Ettinger is a guy to emulate. He has been wildly successful in the music industry, and he is happily married with two beautiful children, making him a great example of accomplishing great things while keeping a family intact. The latter is a worthwhile and necessary challenge that seems to elude far too many in the name of industry advancement.

For as long as I have been around Nashville and its music industry, Ettinger has clearly been one of those guys that you need to know. A graduate of Cornell University, he started his career in management for The Kentucky HeadHunters before spending 14 years in radio promotion at Mercury Records, then Disney's Carolwood and Lyric Street Records, where he also worked in promotion. John has played absolutely integral roles in the careers of Sugarland, Shania Twain, Billy Currington and Toby Keith, among many others. Not a bad list for a resume.

And he actually did important, hard work for these artists – he didn't just sit back and make a couple of phone calls while everyone else did all of the work.

Give careful consideration to John's stories and his approach. He is one of the good ones.

Clore: Was there a moment you knew you would be around all of this stuff?

No.

Clore: Then how did you get in to it?

I graduated from Cornell in early 1990, and moved to New York City later that year. I was looking for work – thinking I'd be a sportscaster – but found it in the music business.

In Ithaca [New York, location of Cornell], I was working at a newspaper and a radio station. I was writing a column and I was the morning guy, sports guy and play-by-play for a couple of sports. So I thought I'd be a sportscaster. There were some budget cuts at the radio station. So then I took a job at the big newspaper, *The Ithaca Journal*, and it's like I have the career gig, because this is the big paper in my hometown. But very quickly there was just something in me that said, "No, you're not going to live in your small hometown your whole life." When you get your college degree, you think you can go conquer anything. So I moved to New York City thinking I would be a sportscaster. I thought I had a gig at WFAN in New York, and it didn't work out. The guy just never called me back.

I went to New York City and I lived with my sister. She's sort of in the business – she's a broadcaster.

I was looking for work. I took a part-time job working for a radio network there with Bruce Williams, who was a big talk radio, advice guy. I did his show out of New York.

Then I got a call from my buddy who was at the Country station in New York City. We were in college radio together. He said, "Hey, you're looking for work. The Kentucky HeadHunters – have you heard of them?" And I said, "Yeah. I just saw them on the CMA Awards." I think you'd call me a passive Country fan. I had a few albums – Rodney Crowell's *Diamonds and Dirt* – terrific album. I had Randy Travis' two first albums. I had George Strait's last album, and I had everything Willie Nelson ever did – because I thought he was really cool.

I took this job with The Kentucky HeadHunters. They were blowing up at the time. They had just won Album of the Year at the CMAs [*Pickin' on Nashville*, 1990 CMA Album of the Year], and [Vocal] Group of the Year [1990 CMA Awards], which was a big deal back then. They beat Alabama for top vocal group, so it's like, "Wow!"

So I took that job, which lead to them moving me to Nashville. I'm a young 23-year old, looking around Nashville saying, "Wow, this is a cool scene." The HeadHunters were blowing up, and I was their assistant manager. I became label relations, promotion relations, I was on the road for nine months, I toured with them all of 1991 and in to 1992. That was awesome, to be young, and I didn't have very much to do out there. I wasn't hauling speakers around or anything. I was just learning.

Clore: Were you doing any road management?

Sort of. I had one of the busses. You know, the band split up not long after I moved on to another job. I think they split up in '93.

As I joined them on the road they had split busses. Two who are brothers went on one bus, two who are brothers went on the other, and the cousin went with the guys he is cousins with. There are five guys in the band. So I rode with the two brothers and the cousin. I had to make sure the bus got there on time. I would to talk to the bus driver so he wouldn't fall asleep – that was my road managing. But the real road manager was on the other bus. It was great. It was pretty awesome. The road manager was a great guy, so I learned a ton from him.

We didn't have Internet. We didn't have cell phones. Think about that. We talked to each other on CBs. Often the busses got split up. You had to choose your destination before you left. It was a different ballgame.

Clore: It's like we're talking about a hundred years ago, and we're talking twenty, less than twenty years ago.

I try to remember, and it's hard to remember, when I would sit in my office in Chicago with no email, no Facebook, no text messaging. People talk about the old days, but how did we communicate with radio?

Clore: It was phone or go see them, basically, right?

Yeah. We didn't have the luxury of getting and giving info technologically, so we had to talk it out in every way. Programmers didn't click in each day to see the charts, or videos, or any of it. These days I train my staff to write the perfect e-mail, get the perfect answer, and get out. Be quick! You know, you don't have time, sometimes. And radio, certainly, doesn't have time to talk on the phone like they used to.

Clore: In the midst of all of that, though, what is still the number one way to connect with radio people?

Face to face, certainly.

Clore: Isn't that amazing? And discounted by so many.

Well, I know. I do think that part of this professional promotion is still a young person's job, because of that need for travel. As you age you can't help but think: "Alright, I'm going to be fifty soon, and to be great at this I'm going to need to be on the road one hundred days a year." The bottom line remains that you need somebody who will get on a plane and spend a week seeing radio. There's still important radio being made in Peoria, Illinois and Tuscon, Arizona and Spokane, Washington and Syracuse, New York – whatever. It's still where music is being heard by real people.

I'm big on that. I like the fact that I'm in Country music and the listeners are salt of the earth Americans. They don't care what Lindsay Lohan is wearing. Country listeners care about if the kids are being raised properly, and that's cool to me.

Clore: You mentioned being a bit of a passive Country fan.

Well, I knew I was rabid for Hank Sr. and Willie Nelson. I knew those two. But like plenty else in my life, I know a little about a lot of things, and so Country was interesting to me, but I didn't carry it on my sleeve. I remember discovering the *Willie Nelson Live* album, which was in my dad's collection. Still one of my all-time favorites. My dad liked Country, but my dad didn't pay attention to it, he just liked it. We sit here in the music industry and pay attention to it to the point where we try to figure it out, and then you go talk to somebody who isn't out there trying to figure it out, and they just like what they like.

It makes you crazy sometimes, because you think you've just found the next greatest thing – "Sugarland made this awesome new song, dad!" – and you play it for him and he's like, "Ah, that's alright, but I really like that 'Baby Girl'."

"But, dad, this one's another generation better than 'Baby Girl'." They don't know. They know what they love.

But yeah, I suppose I was passive. My entire generation of dudes were cranking Aerosmith, Elvis Costello, AC/DC, Skynyrd, Journey, The Police, and REO Speedwagon. The usual suspects.

My first big Country show was Randy Travis in New Jersey, when he was big, at an amphitheater. I was on a college party weekend with some friends and we saw that Randy Travis was playing near the beach where we were staying. Four of us were in to Randy, and another three of us were like, "Ewww, no – Country music." I'm glad I was on the side that was in to Country, because Randy put on an awesome show.

Clore: You know how you have those moments, where you're at a show, or whatever, "This is why I'm in Nashville," or "This is why I'm in the music industry." Can you think of some of those over your career?

Seeing Sugarland in a tiny club in Seattle was one, and seeing Shania in Lake Placid during rehearsals for her first tour are two exact examples of that idea. Both were big "Wow" moments for me.

A couple other stories:

About a year after my move to Nashville, I got an offer from the Halsey Company, run by legendary music guys Jim Halsey, and his son Sherman. Jim had managed Roy

Clark and The Oak Ridge Boys to stardom, along with working with, and booking, other Country superstars. Sherman had managed Dwight Yoakam to stardom and was making ground-breaking videos with him and others. Sherman was the first to make cool videos in Country, and I helped him on that side as well.

One afternoon, Jim asked me to attend what we thought was a standard meeting at RCA Records with the Oak Ridge Boys. We went into the office of the label president, and a few minutes later he let's us all know that they were dropping The Oaks from the label. Shocked. Stunned. All four Oaks and Jim Halsey were just stunned.

I remember calling my mother later that evening and saying, "Mom, you won't believe this, but I was sitting next to the deep-voice guy from the Oak Ridge Boys as they were dropped from the label." A moment I'll never forget.

I went to Farm Aid in Dallas in '92 with The Kentucky HeadHunters. I was so fired up that I might meet Willie Nelson. I was going to make sure. What I did was stand near the HeadHunters for that entire Saturday, and of course here comes Willie to thank them for being on Farm Aid. Shaking his hand was pretty cool to me.

The day before that I was sitting at the lobby bar of the hotel in Dallas as everyone arrived for Farm Aid. They kept it pretty simple, so all of the musicians stayed at one hotel. Kind of like you'd see in that movie, "Almost Famous."

Clore: My favorite movie.

There you go. It was like that hotel [The "Riot House," in Los Angeles. Now known as Andaz West Hollywood]. We got there at like three o'clock and we just started drinking beer in the bar. Me and this guy from Sherman

Halsey's crew that made videos. So he and I sat down, he was a real quiet guy, and I'm a real talkative guy. People started sitting around us because we had the best seats in the lobby, and we had a waitress that would come out of the hotel bar. It was just a Holiday Inn, or whatever. Anyway, I spend probably four hours on that couch, watching the entirety of cool American Country and Rock music walk by. And about three hours into it, the guy next to me, who I didn't know – I had just met him – he said, "Do you know who the guy sitting next to me is?," because we'd been sitting in this intimate conversation. I go, "No, what are you talking about?"

"Well, that's Toy Caldwell, the lead guitarist of The Marshall Tucker Band, and the guy that wrote, 'Can't You See'." That was really cool. He died within a few months of me meeting him. [Caldwell passed away on February 25, 1993].

Clore: You mentioned a Chicago office. I don't think I know that part of your history.

Not too many years ago, all of the big labels, and many of the medium and small labels, had branch offices where regional sales or promotion staff would work from. I was lucky enough to be placed in the Chicago branch office at Mercury Records in '94, and I stayed up there for my first seven years with the label.

I should add that in the early '90s, in Nashville, every young hotshot wanted a label gig, mainly because it paid very well. Some chose to stick with a particular artist out of a personal passion. They'd work as young managers or in management, and I have some friends who became millionaires sticking with Kenny Chesney or Rascal Flatts. I needed to pay off college and the very best way to grow financially was to get to a bigger label. It was terrific training and there was much excitement in that world, especially at Mercury, which was changing under the leadership of Luke Lewis.

Each label inside the Mercury/Polygram family had a representative for the Midwest, either in the discipline of promotion, or in the discipline of sales who worked out of the Chicago branch. In some cases they would put marketing people. New York or L.A. based labels would spread out radio promotion into all the other genres of Rock, Urban, Top 40, which actually was separated from Urban and Hot AC then. These labels had a lot of money, and they would put a different person into each genre.

Inside my building in Chicago was a mish-mash, a zoo, of promotion and sales people. It was pretty cool, because your boss isn't there. There is a head of the branch, who's not your boss, so he's just sort of a great character who runs the branch. The place was dominated by the sales force, who had the task of getting all Polygram records into stores like Target, Wal-Mart, Best Buy, and the smaller stores across the Midwest.

I had a chance to learn from so many different characters during my years in Chicago. One of my mentors was an A&M Pop / Top 40 promotion VP named Ross Grierson – holy crap, he was a caricature of the high-flying, hard-nosed promotion type. One of the first times I walked into his office, he was just getting off a call with a major Pop radio programmer. He hangs up the phone and says, "Well, that one cost $1,500."

I had heard of payola, and it's not like he gave cash to the programmer, but he took $1,500 and he did something nice for the radio station, and he got his record added – Del Amitri, or whatever.

So in that branch I got to meet all different sides. There was a guy named Frank Chaplin, who was a promotion guy for Mercury Urban. What a great guy. Just had been around forever. He had broken The O'Jays, or he had broken The Jackson Five. So I learned from those guys. They were really cool people. There was also a branch in Dallas; Washington, DC; a small branch in Detroit; L.A. and on Long Island.

Clore: In theory, that still exists today, correct? It's just that it's usually someone in their house?

Regionals now primarily work from home, exactly. When I was promoted to VP of Mercury, we hired a girl to go to Chicago. It was funny, I loved working in the branch and she hated it – primarily due to the commute. But then while she was there, the branch shut down. So she went from having that commute, which she hated, to working out of her house.

There are still a couple of branches left, but not many.

Clore: You have been a part of multiple superstars' careers: Toby Keith, Sugarland, Shania Twain, etc. There are highs and lows that come with that, and I know you've experienced that more than most have. From your perspective, what are your thoughts regarding the human behavior side of dealing with the ups and downs in the midst of the successes and failures, and sometimes the successes that never return?

Good question. Pursuing success in music is just such a subjective thing. All the artist stories go down different paths.

Shania, Sugarland, Toby Keith, even Rascal Flatts – who I worked with later in their career – all have different paths and different stories to tell.

Bon Jovi was another great, different story. If you ask Jon, or Richie Sambora, we played a very important part in their career. We got them their first GRAMMY, which was really big for Bon Jovi.

Clore: What?

Think about that. They were so psyched about that, because Jon was already such a superstar, arguably one of the biggest stars in Rock/Pop history. But I'll say this about the great commercial music artists – part of what plays into this for them is that when you achieve any level of success, there's usually somebody who is more successful, and these stars want to reach for that.

Bon Jovi came to Nashville with a song Jon thought could be a big record in Country. At first we thought they were just poking around and having fun in the format, but I soon learned that Jon was dead serious about having a number one record in Country. The song was "Who Says You Can't Go Home," sung with Jennifer Nettles of Sugarland. Oh my, she was terrific on that record.

My Mercury staff pushed and pushed, and there were real times we thought we wouldn't even get to Top 20. When we got the number one, the GRAMMY, Jon was over the top in his appreciation.

I think about Shania, and how focused she was. She went through the process of becoming a superstar and handled it really pretty well. I think she was very aware that she was becoming a superstar, and some people either aren't aware of that, and that non-awareness can be fun, but that non-awareness normally is debilitating. Shania was always aware. She never actually got surprised by it, but I think that's part of being married to Mutt Lange and knowing that he's made quite a few superstars in his life, and it was just a part of the crowd she was among. She had Springsteen's road crew with her during her first tour, and they were extremely professional.

I think when you are part of a small team that breaks an artist, you're doing something that you have to give your heart to, and you want to maintain a connection with the artist that is personal. It's funny, you listed three names: Toby Keith, Shania Twain and Sugarland – I maintain that friendship with all three of those. Some more conversationally than others.

I've chosen to go on a path now where I participate in different ways with artists. I'm managing and running my own promotion shop. I did this consciously, because I have to tell you that for me, breaking another artist at a big label would not be as satisfying as smaller successes from being truly there and inside the artist's world.

After breaking Toby Keith, Shania Twain, Sugarland, and Billy Currington – and then getting married, and living a life, and getting older – I sort of developed a very calm and focused perspective on what I want to do with my life.

There's this whole cool factor in the music business. People always ask, "Oh yeah, who have you worked with?" And then you throw a Shania-bomb out there and everybody goes, "Well, okay, what did you do with her?" And most people then automatically think you didn't do much [laughter]. Most people think, "He probably sat there." But to feel at ease and look people in the eye, and go, "Well, I took Shania and Sugarland to radio. I took them to Kansas City and Minneapolis and I ate in a Denny's with her in Omaha."

I took a year off after leaving Mercury. I took a year and wrote a book. Not about the music business, but about a subject I'd been studying and building on for some time. More of a philosophy book.

That year was when my wife and I got a terrific chance to stop and think, "What are we really doing in life?" I don't mean to pick on anybody caught up in the business being their life, but is any company really the big family we sometimes believe it is?

At the end of the day, the satisfaction was definitely there for breaking Sugarland, Shania, and my relationships with those artists was, and is, great, consistently. And I know sometimes they go bad in the music industry, but they haven't for me.

Clore: Leaving Mercury must have brought changes in your personal life.

I think that's one of those things people don't consider until it's gone. It was pretty wild, and wonderful for the strength of my marriage and family.

The year off was just perfect, but being away from the big company life – the social scene – was tough at times. It started hard, my wife and I both knew it was becoming an amazing thing to have that year. We knew it as we were living it. Stress just flowed out of my being and we grew closer as a couple. You really start to think – yeah, that whole chase of the music business, and I don't mean to judge it, but it's kind of silly in the long run.

Clore: What you just said could be the title of this book.

It's like in most any corporation. You're caught inside a trickle-down, political scene, inside of any organization.

It could be Exxon, The Democratic Party, a church. When it exists in the music business, it is a particularly stronger group of rogues and scoundrels, who maybe aren't informed by any greater purpose, you know? There's no hand guiding them. The music business has the same problem most businesses can get. Anytime you're chasing the dollar, it can get weird, inhuman.

Clore: So, becoming a dad changed how you view all of this, I'm assuming?

Oh, yeah. This revolution of being able to work from home, because of technology, hit me at exactly the right time. Exactly. I do tend to see things in a positive light, but I think I'm right on this. I will go back to my house after this interview, and my daughter has the day off from preschool, and I will get ten interactions with her today that would have been out of the question a year ago when I was working for Disney. What is each of those interactions worth? I think they're worth over $100,000 a year, to tell you the truth.

And I'm really glad I've come to that notion.

Clore: That is a great example. For people like me, anyone younger than you, probably people older than you, too. Thank you for that.

Well, we're all competitive. We're all trying to think we've got something figured out. And usually that comes from a financial angle. For me, I didn't have a lot of money when I came out of college. I didn't have a lot of money when I was in college. I put myself through college. So I've got the financial chip on my shoulder like a lot of people around the country. We all think ours is unique, and stronger. But the bottom line is, the best thing you can do is knock the chip off yourself, and get rid of it, and just live more authentically, and the money will come, I think.

Clore: Greatest career accomplishment?

Straight up, it's Sugarland for me. As I became more experienced at all aspects of record promotion, my theories and my opinions became stronger. I wanted more control.

Basically there were some changes inside Universal that abdicated control of the promotion department to me. In '03, '04, '05, on through '07 – I was really running the show, which was cool, and then I get handed Sugarland. I actually asked for them, because there was a question of whether they would be on MCA or Mercury Records, and MCA, as I put it, blinked. They just weren't sure what was up with Sugarland, thinking they were not quite Country, not quite down the middle enough. I won't say who felt this way, but they said, "Mercury can have them. They aren't for us." I literally raised my hand in a meeting and confidently said, "We'll take Sugarland." I wasn't all certain they'd make it, I thought, "You know, that would be a cool act to work with."

So we got them and I worked the hardest I'd ever worked to make the right moves for an artist. I was everywhere with them and our team had to do everything beautifully to get them broken.

Clore: Which basically is running it.

Yeah, and there were a lot of decisions being made very quickly. Album launch will be in Houston and Chicago for the second album. We'll do Seattle, Detroit, put a station show into Phoenix. Advertising will feature nothing but positive thoughts – for the band and toward radio. We'll say "Thank You" a ton! We'll go to L.A. and do our media there, then we'll go to New York. It was really a lot of fast decisions being made and hits happening. Hard work and smart decisions.

Clore: That's fantastic. And knowing a bit about your background, I wouldn't necessarily have landed on that particular act.

I know, but Sugarland really was an unlikely thing with country radio, and it's the weird ones that bring satisfaction. I once told an artist manager that doing overall radio promotion is like playing a video game. Breaking Sugarland, you had to play this game at the highest levels, using all your weapons to fly around and shoot the bad guys. I joke that with some pure Country artists – dudes in hats – you kind of just have to stand there and roll a ball into a hole from a foot away. Not with Sugarland.

The other satisfying footnote I'd mention is the song "Good Directions" from artist Billy Currington. That one was unlikely and a couple of us had to put our butts on the line for that one.

Our senior Mercury executives didn't want to release "Good Directions." The head of A&R and I, we basically put ourselves on a limb and said, "Let's release it," and then I was directed to not spend more than $30,000. Well, major labels can spend over $300,000 behind just one single – especially Top 10 singles. We actually spent just about $42,000 on that one. I still remember the number. It was a three-week #1 and I ended up probably getting too much credit for it. The team did a great job.

Clore: How does that crowd response feel when you see it?

It is awesome. After I left Universal, I hadn't seen Billy in a year, and I saw him in Chicago at a concert. He's playing in this club and the crowd's going crazy. I said to the Mercury rep, who used to work with me, "Has he played 'Good Directions' yet?"

She said, "No, it's coming up. We'll go watch him."

So we go watch from these stairs to the side of the stage, and I can't really hear him because we're behind the PA. I know he's singing the song, I just can't hear the words. The crowd is going nuts. Nuts. And in the middle of it I see him look at me and give me a thumbs up – which was really cool.

A bit later, one of the members of the band I had that was warming up, came up to me in the VIP area after the show, and he says, "Did you hear what Currington sang?" I said, "No, what did he sing?" He says, "Right at the end, he sang, 'Thank God for good directions, John Ettinger, and turnip greens'," which is the last line of the song.

I got chills. It was truly a "full-circle" moment for me, my career, and my time at Universal. Later that night I called my wife Jill and said I'm at peace in so many ways, just because Currington sang my name in Chicago. Funny.

Clore: Can you explain the day-to-day life of a radio promoter, and just how grueling that can be?

It's almost compartmentalized. There are two sides to promotion and I'll start with the positive side. You have an expense account. You have a list of radio stations, and you are expected to call them, and schmooze them, and it is a lot of fun. You are the guy, when they came to town, you're having fun. You're out for dinner, drinking beers, bringing your music around and playing it for people. You are the cool guy. Now, that's fun and those interactions can be a lot of fun, because I'm a people person. The other side is rather different and much tougher.

The other side is the station tracking and the charts. In promotion you wake up every day and get a readout on how you're doing. In our more informational world, you see the daily updates of what your songs are doing on the chart. And, if your song is even just minus three for the week, you are simply angst-ridden. You end up developing stress muscles that are stronger than any profession I've been in. You're basically holding on to a lot of stress – a lot of implied stress – that makes you think you're great at your job or you stink at your job based on how a single is doing on the charts. It's crazy. You don't even have to be yelled at by your boss, or you don't have to be threatened for your job. You just feel it.

So, I often say, promotion people have a real high tolerance for stress, because the charts are not predictable. Well, they are predictable for George Strait and Mariah Carey, but they're not predictable for B and C and new acts. So that's the normal life, you know? You can have fun all week, but if on Friday you don't have 1 or 2 adds on each of your records, and you're not positive on the charts, you are just angst-ridden. It is hilarious. I don't recommend it.

I've had really personable people either interview with me to get a job, or actually get the job and that one element of the angst of having to get the charts taken care of, or the tracking sheet taken care of, it crushes them.

It's not fair and it's a very tough game.

Clore: Due to the consistent interaction with certain people, have you developed some good friends at radio stations across the country?

Oh yeah. Here's an example. When my wife and I got married, we consciously said, "It's not going to be a music industry wedding." We certainly invited most everyone at our current company, which at that time was Universal, but we weren't going to make business decisions with our wedding. But soon we realized that I have some very, very good friends at radio stations across the country. Like, I think we only really ended up inviting six maybe, but it was so hard to pare down.

You know, these relationships can be pretty fake sometimes. Promotions people make friends with radio people because it's so important to the job. If you have a playlist, then you really get your butt kissed pretty strong by professionals at the art of making friends. Radio gets their butt kissed so much. We as professional promotion people can tell who's affected by it, and who's not.

Nonetheless, you do end up making close friends and I can say I have terrific friends in Kansas City, Milwaukee, Seattle, Indianapolis, Hartford, everywhere. I'm still very close with some guys not even in radio anywhere.

Clore: Achieving a number one – how hard is that? And what are your memories of your first number one?

You know, it's funny, I don't denote my first number one. My assistant, of a few years ago, counted, and I have 34. I think my first one was either Toby Keith's "Wish I Didn't Know Now," or something from Sammy Kershaw or Kathy Mattea. I honestly don't remember which one it is.

There were a couple of epic number ones. Terri Clark getting her first one was big, because her first two were number twos. Sugarland's first number one was a song on their second album. They didn't have a number one on their first album. They had two number twos. But their second album had a song called, "Want To." That was big.

Getting a number one is a moving target. It changes. The way you got a number one in 1995, the way you got a number one in 2005, the way you get a number one in 2011 – they are all very different. It's just the way the charts are compiled, and the types of radio stations that make up the charts, but it's pretty hard. Right now it's a game of universal acceptance of your song, and in Country you have to have every station. In other genres you don't, but in Country you pretty much have to. You can actually get a number one with one or two not there, but it's very difficult.

And then there's the syndication game that's being played, because any time you create a game, smart people will get good at playing it. There's no purity. You can argue that when Tim McGraw has his biggest hit he didn't need any syndication, and you know that's true. But for a developing artist, or an artist that isn't universally an icon, you have to put it in syndication.

You have to line up your timing. Some radio stations may have a song burned and they want to get rid of it, and they were your best friend when you first put the song out, and now they've been playing it 35 weeks and they want to get rid of it, and you're somehow angry at them?!?

We used to have a station in Madison, Wisconsin that would always add stuff he liked for you right at the beginning. He didn't add everything, but he added what he liked. Then you get 25 weeks in and he'd start saying, "Listen, I've got about a week or two left, and I've got to move this record in to my recurrent rotation." Then everybody would get mad at him, and this is what I didn't like about corporate stuff. So I'm sitting near the top of the chart, but not yet at the top, and the label head decides they're mad at Madison. And you're like, "Let me explain to you, Mr. label head, why you shouldn't be angry with Madison. They're the ones that actually started this record." Minneapolis was very similar.

For a brand new artist, the reason it's so difficult to get a number one is because the inclination of radio and listeners is not to believe in the artist until they know much more about the artist. That happened for Sugarland. That happened for Shania Twain. I could tell you stories about the beginning of Shania's career, people telling us, "The music's just stupid, and it will never be anything." I can tell you the story of me arguing with a programmer in St. Louis for a year, or the guy in Green Bay who said the *Come On Over* album was going to kill her career, and as we sit here, it's the number one selling studio album in Country music history. Funny how people get it wrong.

Clore: My goodness. I don't think people realize how short the window of opportunity is for an artist to be successful at radio.

You don't realize how many big songs over the years never got to number one, some never even close. It's a theme for me now. I talk to Emerson Drive about it a lot. It's a theme about making interesting music that the fans care about, versus making nice music that we think radio will play. I mean, it's a theme for all artists, in all genres, from Michael Jackson to Radiohead to Bruce Springsteen, who's never had a number one he recorded. Think about that. We all like to site these live touring artists that have made a ton of money, and touched a lot of fans, but in Country, radio is still the starmaking medium.

When I went through the wonderful program of Leadership Music [a music industry nonprofit 501(c)(3) educational organization established in 1989], 80% of that crowd was not major label – not mass-market music people. They were all making a living, and all happy. If you interviewed everybody in my class, you'd have a whole other book. The guy who wrote, "She's Like The Wind," was in my class. The publicist for Kris Kristofferson was in my class. A producer out of England was in my class. He was John Waite's producer, and produced "Missing You." There are so many stories! They can go on forever. And if he told the story about John Waite and The Babys, I could listen for two days, because I love that band, and I know nothing about them. I just know that I have that greatest hits CD and it's awesome.

[laughter]

You know what I mean? We all want to be part of a bigger story, and that is something that's definitely inside me. Being a promotion person isn't wholly satisfying to me anymore, and certainly playing the corporate game to maintain a certain salary level, in the position of a promotions person, isn't wholly satisfying. I'm not saying it's a stupid profession or that people shouldn't do it, but I'm seeking variety. When I leave this interview, I'll go have a talk with the head of CMT Canada. I'll have a talk to our road manager [for Emerson Drive]. I have to do some calendar work. I have to approve some advertising images for Quarterback Records. I have to write a slogan for that advertising. It's really a cool, varied thing, and the music business supports that. All of these cool little things. It's awesome.

Clore: Are you good on time?

You know, it depends on what this [Blackberry] says...

Let's see, I've got a Brian...

[At this point, John shows me his Blackberry, which has a text message from Universal Music A&R guy, Brian Wright, that reads: "Mutt Lange says hello."]

How cool is that? There's a music business moment. You get a note like that, right? Mutt Lange wanted to say hi.

Clore: That is very cool, man. – What do you look for in new artists?

I talk a lot with new artists now, a lot. It's basically about authenticity. However you find it. However you do it. Some artists are confused about what's authentic to them. I get why they're confused. I get it. They see Taylor Swift and they want to be like that, because they have a story to tell, too, but it may not be authentic for them to write the songs that tell that story. And for Taylor, it is authentic for her to write those songs. And she got through all of her vocal troubles, because of the authenticity of Taylor, it doesn't matter how well she sings. So, that's a big thing, and I'm very focused on it. At Mercury we ran around saying, "The authenticity of Billy Currington is that he's primal and he gets the girl." To be blunt.

We started to joke about it, but it became part of how we thought. We'll have a hit with Currington, as long as he gets the girl during the song.

The authenticity of Shania actually is flashy, and big, and produced – that's authentic for her. She looks like that. It works with her voice. Dancing, whatever. She looks like a star – let her go be fabulous.

There are a lot of people struggling to figure it out: "Why am I a great singer, but I'm not as big as Tim McGraw, who's not a great singer?" "Why am I a great singer, and I'm not as big as Taylor Swift, who's not a great singer?"

I don't argue with the realities of authenticity. You can spend your whole life in the music business sort of wasting negative energy arguing about why.

The other thing you look for is drive. It's not an easy game. I have a lot of songwriter friends, some of whom want to be artists. Sarah Buxton being a great example. She's a great songwriter and an amazing singer, and tried it as an artist, and somehow the audience didn't respond. Part of it is that she didn't really research with Country listeners, because her voice, I think, is a little raspy. I've got a whole theory on that. But part of it is her DNA wasn't perfect to be an artist. I hear she's giving up now and I wish she wouldn't. She's just amazing. This is why many bands break up – the stresses of being thrown out there. You've gotta have drive to keep doing that.

<u>Clore's Summary</u>:

- Do not bother with the corporate hassle/chase.

- Find your identity in something that will remain.

- Determine what you are authentic about.

- Without drive, forget it.

The preceding interview took place in February of 2011.

How Are You Treating Your Fans?

The concept of fan involvement/appreciation/recognition is not a new thing, but some artists and industry types really struggle with connecting the dots. Yes, some mystery is always important – as the artist must be set apart – but I believe too many overthink and overvalue that aspect, and elitism is often the result.

People want to feel as if they are part of something. There are a number of ways to accomplish this without sacrificing all privacy.

I fully realize – and actually somewhat understand – that it was more readily accepted and easier to remain insulated in the pre-social media age, but that is no longer reality. And I am glad it is not. I love knowing what Adam Duritz is doing between concerts and who he is pulling for during the NCAA tournament. Or that Blake Hawksworth (former St. Louis Cardinals pitcher) is asking his Twitter followers what running back he should draft for his fantasy football team.

If you have any control, influence or say into an act's career direction, consider what you personally want from your favorite band/team/whatever. Are you helping guide your artist in that direction? Are you fighting for what you know the fans want?

If you claim to not be that much of a fan of anything, or are too "cool" to admit it, and simultaneously help steer an act's decisions, I strongly encourage you to reconsider your role. Maybe it is time for you to go home.

Maybe you are the act. What are you doing to facilitate genuine fan involvement? Are you paying attention to them? When was the last time you shared a thought or what you were doing, and did you actually share something that helped your followers know something new of you – not a marketing message? Do you stay after your show to meet every last person waiting to meet you? When was the last time you checked in to let people know of a restaurant you visited (just after you left)?

People who interact with you online should be treated the same way as those waiting in your autograph/merchandise line.

Use new technology to your advantage. Do not let it freak you out.

John Feldmann

My dad definitely did the best he could, but he definitely told me, "You will never make it in the music business."

John Feldmann is a Rock star. He leads a successful band he started in 1993 named Goldfinger. Feldmann is also a tremendous songwriter, producer, mentor and A&R guy. He has worked behind-the-scenes, either writing with, signing, or producing amazing artists, including: Foxy Shazam, The Used, Story of the Year, After Midnight Project, The Veronicas, Panic at the Disco, Good Charlotte and City Sleeps, among many others. In 1996, Goldfinger played 385 shows, a Guinness world record.

Feldmann's house has been raided by the FBI, a fact that solidifies his Rock star status. He is one of those guys who lives out the Rock and Roll stereotype. Learn from his approach, his attitude, his tenacity, and his undying energy.

The following interview took place Monday, March 14, 2011.

Clore: I want to talk about some of your heroes. People that have influenced you to not only become who you are today, but when Goldfinger first got started, and before that.

Star Wars is definitely my first influence as far as scoring. Really noticing a score in a movie when I was in third or fourth grade, buying the *Star Wars* soundtrack and really getting moved by music. I used to watch *Monty Python* a ton as a young kid. I was so influenced by "I'm a Lumberjack and I'm Okay" and the "Holy Grail" and the humor, which to me there has to be some kind of sense of humor in music. Those are probably my two biggest influences as a kid. [The Who's] *Quadrophenia* certainly changed my life. Seeing that movie, and bringing fashion into it. I really remember, now that I look back on it, I think the visual is a precursor to the music, because way before I heard "London Calling," I saw Paul Simonon smashing his bass on the cover of the record, and I said, "Oh man, that looks cool." I saw the dudes in the tight, skinny suits behind Deborah Harry on *Parallel Lines*, and really being influenced by the fashion and the look before I even heard a note. I said, "I want to look like that." All of these things that are not musically related influenced me probably more than anything musical. When I realized it was music that I wanted to do as my creative, artistic outlet, that became almost secondary, if that makes sense.

Clore: Absolutely. How about The Beatles' *Revolver*? I know that's a specific album for you.

Yeah, I study The Beatles. I actually just met Ringo Starr last week, which was pretty fucking cool, man. I definitely study The Beatles. George Martin's my favorite producer, because he's a classic producer in every sense of the word. He helps with arrangements of songs, arrangements of vocals and he actually orchestrates his own. He really was the fifth Beatle by writing musical parts to enhance Lennon and McCartney's compositions. Without him, it would have been a completely different band. *Let It Be* is my least favorite Beatles record, and that was the one Beatles record not produced by George Martin.

Clore: Do you have a preference for the recording studio, being on stage, or is it a balance?

For me it has to be a balance. I get pretty stir-crazy if I get locked in the studio for too long a period of time, and I can't really, just physically, as a 43-year old man, it's much harder for me to do what I do onstage – like jumping off the balcony and that whole thing. It's just much harder to do the older I get. I've definitely physically damaged myself. I tore my ACL, herniated a disc in my neck – I've really hurt myself. And I still, everyday, I wake up and I know, "Hey, I hurt myself onstage." So I can't do the 385 shows like we did in 1996 any longer. We'll probably tour two or three months this year, and that's it. But I feel like this day in age, things happen so fast, and styles and people change. People just don't hold on to anything as much as they used to. Like when I was growing up, it was like, I liked The Police their entire career, from *Outlandos d'Amour*, all the way to *Synchronicity*. Granted, maybe that was only a four or five, six year period, but that just doesn't really happen. Obviously, bands like Coldplay or Muse or Radiohead are going to be standouts, but I want to be in touch with what kids are listening to, and when I go out to play shows, people that love music, and that are still in touch with bands, and scenes, still come out to shows, and I get to talk to real life people instead of just the Internet, which is the scene. I mean – the Internet is the scene. There's no more Seattle or Austin or San

Diego or whatever that may have been scenes in the past. The Internet is the scene.

Clore: Your point about the physical damage to your body is intriguing. I saw Goldfinger at The Pageant in St. Louis a few years back, so I've experienced it first-hand. I've seen what you do. As you mentor younger bands, do you talk about being careful physically?

Aww, no. These days I consider myself a wuss. I'm like, "This is all you've done?" The goal is, by 30, in a wheelchair. I mean, that's the goal for bands I work with. You've only got a certain window. I guess you can start at 18 or 19, if you really are living hard, or if you've really had a rough parenting experience. If you've been beaten up and abused as a kid, and all of that stuff. I mean, you could probably have enough life experience to start writing songs as a teenager, and be really ready to tour at 18. So you've got a window of like 18 to 27 to really, that nine-year period, of really getting it going and making it happen. And during that window, it's got to be full-on. There's no shoe-gazing. You've got to go all the way.

Look, I say that sort of jokingly, but this band Foxy Shazam that I signed and produced, the singer's [Eric Sean Nally] the craziest front man I've ever seen, but he doesn't eat any sugar, he's very, very slim – he's on like a crazy actor's diet. He has no body fat, he runs, he's super trained, and he doesn't drink or smoke. Nothing. He stretches and really takes care of himself. When he puts on a show, you look at him and you go, "Man, this guy could die doing that, what I'm watching him do." But he does take care of himself, so there is hope that you really can have it all.

I really view it like training, and granted, look, there are people who are talented enough, like Christina Aguilera's voice. Even Adele's voice, you just hear it, and you go, "This is something that's been given like a gift, that these people have that no one else has. They're on a different level when it comes to what their talent is, and that's enough." But someone like me, who's not gifted with a Freddie Mercury-style voice, I feel like it's gotta be the whole package. And most people in Rock and Roll, I don't know, I guess the guy from Muse and Thom Yorke have that similar type of vibrato, classy sort of thing going on. But Dave Grohl isn't Freddie Mercury either, and he puts on a phenomenal show. Same with Billie Joe Armstrong – their voices are fine, but it's not like you go see them because they sing like Michael Bublé. You go see them because it's the whole package. They write amazing songs, and they have a great live show. For me, it's always going to be about, you know, to make up for my lack of Freddie Mercury-ness, I've got to write better songs and hookier pop songs. And we've got to really think about fire and jumping off the PA and what kind of modern song can we make fun of, and "Twinkie in the Ass," and whatever it is that we want to do to make it a fun, funny show. That's what we do.

Clore: By the way, "FTN" and "Prank Calls," at the end of *Open Your Eyes* – those tracks still make me laugh to this day, no matter how many times I hear them.

Like I said, man, *Monty Python* was huge for me. I love comedy and I listen to *Raw Dog* on Sirius pretty much every time I drive. I just love it. I mean, stand-up, that's the real shit, man. You're in the moment, and if you fuckin' start floundering, it's over. Live, you can fuck up and mess up a song and break a string, have a couple of minutes of dead space – but you cannot do that shit in stand-up. That shit's rad.

Clore: You're a good dude: as an artist and a successful band guy. Most people become harder to get to, or make themselves very unapproachable. You're not that. I'm curious how you've maintained that sort of personality, especially with this whole open door policy on accepting demos from bands?

Thanks, man. It's definitely not a planned-out thing on my end, it's just kind of who I am. I think when you come from nothing, and I had a middle class upbringing – it's not like I came from nothing – but there was certainly no silver spoon, and there was no support. My dad definitely did the best he could, but he definitely told me, "You will never make it in the music business."

As a teenager, as hard as it was to swallow, and no matter how much I rebelled against it and how much I knew he was wrong, having kids of my own now, I understand that he was just trying to protect me to get an easier career to kind of fall back on when I had my own kids so I wouldn't have to be so competitive. I know his intentions were good, so ultimately I did this all myself. I sold shoes for years and years and years, and worked retail for years and years, and it's like, "I know what the other side is, I know what my options are, so how could I not allow some other kid to have the same experience that I have." There are probably 50 bands a day that MySpace me, and now that there's Twitter and Facebook, there are all of these avenues. I feel like it's my duty. And the greater feeling I have, of playing live, signing bands, producing records, mixing records, writing songs – all of the shit that I do – the thing that gives me the most satisfaction, is finding young talent, and developing them, and getting them record deals, and seeing if we can get their dreams to come true, and allow them to play music for a living, and get them on the road, and all of that kind of stuff. To me, it's what I do. It's not something that I think of.

If I say that I can't talk to anyone after a Goldfinger show, or if I say you have to send the demos to the label first and then all of the interns go through them, then I'm missing opportunities for what makes me feel good, which is obviously being a service to younger bands. And hopefully we all win in the end. We all win if the band gets big. You know, we all win from that financially and emotionally.

Clore: To a 15-year old kid in the middle of the country, who's at home practicing his guitar – what do you say to a guy like that? Who has Rock and Roll dreams, and like you were, he's being told he won't make it?

If you truly have that gift, you don't need to have that conversation, so it is sort of a catch-22, because ultimately it's harder than it's ever been. Three and a half million bands on MySpace. With *Rock Band* and *Guitar Hero*, everyone thinks they can do this. When I was a kid, Pete Townsend was cracking his kneecaps sliding across the stage. I mean, he was larger than life. There's no way I could do that. I just look up to these people, going, "They're really touched by something I don't have."

And kids these days – everyone thinks they can do this. And ultimately, now, *Garage Band* – I just got it on the iPad – anyone can really write a song, and kind of put it together. But, you know, there's no easy answer to that question, because ultimately, I really believe that if anyone has a dream, and that is all they think about, and then the negative thoughts come in, their dad says they can't do it, all that shit, and they push it aside, and they say, "They're wrong," and they have a real purpose, that this is the real purpose, and they make a decision that, "This is it," I really do think anyone can do whatever they want in life. I just believe that we are what we think, and what happens to most people, after the fifth rejection letter or whatever, or bands fail, people just give up and quit.

Like every single person I went to high school with, that we were playing in bands together, maybe a dozen of us, we all said, "Hey, we're going to do this for a living, we're definitely musicians, we're going to go for it."

But, everyone got a back-up plan. They said we're going to go to college just to have a back-up plan in case it doesn't happen, and I never had a back-up plan. There was only one goal and that was for me to play music, and do this for a living. Out of every single guy, they're all doing their back-up plans, because it gets hard, you know? After a couple of years of really struggling, and living in your car, and having to sell shoes and living with five guys in a studio apartment, and all of that stuff that I went through, most people just don't have the drive and the perseverance to make it work, and that 15-year old kid in his bedroom – it's impossible to tell what's going to happen. And 99% of the people are going to go the safe route – and I totally understand. The parents are going to pay for college. They get the back-up plan – whatever that may be – and that's what they end up doing for a living. It's typically what happens.

Clore: What has been your Goldfinger, or professional highlight?

Watching The Used get off the plane for the first time in L.A. when I flew them out here [Los Angeles] to do their first demo, and them having never left Orem, Utah, this little trailer community outside Salt Lake City. They had never left that city their whole life, and they're like 17-18 year old kids.

To watch them come off the plane, and be like, "Whoa, we're in L.A., and this is really happening." And they had played one show in front of family before, and to watch that happen, that was probably the highlight. To really watch their dreams come true, and have them trust me, just me, I mean it was really just me, there was no one else. I found this little demo cassette that they had given me at a Goldfinger show, and that was just me. I really just said, "This is the band that's going to fucking change shit," and I really had a vision, and to watch it all happen, to watch these kids, like really humble, they were really humble and were like, "I can't believe that this is happening." That was the highlight of my producing career.

Goldfinger, it's sort of a harder thing. I guess the biggest moment is still, like I was working on The Promenade [in Los Angeles] at this place called Na Na selling shoes, and I remember I had slipped a demo tape in this guy's shoebox that I knew was an A&R guy, who knew me from an old band I was in, and he signed us a week later.

I was able to quit that job, but I gave my two weeks notice, so I quit on good terms like I think any stand-up guy should do. We had recorded a song while I was still working there, and there's a station here [Los Angeles] called KROQ, that's sort of the defining radio station for all alternative stations. Most alternative stations kind of follow their format, and whatever they play, everyone else sort of copies. They added "Here In Your Bedroom" while I was still finishing up my job at the shoe store. They started playing it like 36 times a week, which is a tremendous amount of airplay. Like every two or three hours they played that song. I would be driving in my $100 Dodge Colt that was falling apart, with windows that didn't work, and all of my Bad Religion and NOFX stickers on the back. Hearing it on the radio was like – I mean, of all of the great things – like playing in front of 100,000 people, and playing with Max Weinberg from Bruce Springsteen's band, and meeting all of my heroes down the road, and doing all of that shit – but that was really the defining moment for me. Hearing myself on a station that really influenced me in L.A. was definitely huge.

Clore's Summary:

- Focus. Stop long enough to learn. Go deeper than listening to one song, or reading one sentence of an article. Learn about a band, an album, an individual, and continue to learn about what you love.

- Feldmann says the goal is in a wheelchair by 30. The point is to give it your all. Do not let up, because someone out there wants it too. Do not lose your soul in the process, and always keep a balance, but you better give it your all at every turn.

- Do not forget those that helped you, but mostly, help those after you.

- There is a very good chance you will sacrifice something, maybe a lot, to be successful in the entertainment business.

Quote not to miss:

- "I was able to quit that job, but I gave my two weeks notice, so I quit on good terms like I think any stand-up guy should do."

My Lunch with Jim Foglesong

There used to be a Longhorn Steakhouse on Lyle Avenue in Nashville. I met Jim Foglesong there for lunch one day in 2004. I knew it was a big deal at the time, but the value I place on that lunch only increases with time. People like me are not supposed to have lunch with people like him. I grew up in a small town in Southeastern Illinois. I did not come to Nashville with the right last name. I was not tagging along with someone else on their way to lunch with Jim Foglesong. It was a very special moment in time for me.

My life changed that day. He told me that someone is always watching, and to be excellent. Ever since, I have thought about those two things on a nearly daily basis.

At the end of our time together I attempted to pay our bill, but he took the check holder and told me when I became head of a record label someday, then I could buy his lunch.

I have had lunch with Mr. Foglesong a number of times since that day, but when we met specifically to discuss this book, he let me know he and his wife had just celebrated their 60th wedding anniversary. I can assume, that maybe outside of his children, that anniversary is Jim Foglesong's proudest accomplishment.

As you will see in the following chapter, he is a special man.

Jim Foglesong

Being a member of the Country Music Hall of Fame as an executive is unbelievable. I still have trouble realizing that this took place.

In any industry, there are important figures, and there are those who transcend. Some appear, make a brief impact, and then are gone. Some continue to impact, over, and over, and over again.

Jim Foglesong has been part of the music industry since the early 1950s; essentially for the past 60 years. He started approximately 13 years before The Beatles played on Ed Sullivan (1964); 18 years before the original Woodstock (1969); 30 years before Michael Jackson released *Thriller* (1982); 40 years before Nirvana's "Smells Like Teen Spirit" broke through (1991); 50 years before *The Concert for New York City*, which followed the events of September 11, 2001; and 60 years before Spotify launched in the United States.

A few of Foglesong's accomplishments: Veteran, World War II; Bachelor of Music, Eastman School of Music, Rochester, New York – Class of 1950; as a professional singer, worked with Ray Charles Singers, Arturo Toscanini and the NBC Symphony, Robert Shaw, among others; as a background (studio) singer, appeared on records with Neil Sedaka, Mahalia Jackson, Connie Francis, Rosemary Clooney, among others; produced records for Robert Goulet, Julie Andrews, Bobby Vinton, Joe Williams, among others; joined Columbia Records in NYC, September 1951; produced records for RCA Records in NYC between 1964-1970; named President of Dot Records in 1953 where he worked with Roy Clark, Donna Fargo, Hank Thompson, among others; through his career as a label executive (Dot, MCA, Capitol), signed Barbara Mandrell, the Oak Ridge Boys, Freddy Fender, Don Williams, John Conlee, George Strait, Reba McEntire, Terri Gibbs, Lee Greenwood, Garth Brooks, Sawyer Brown, Tanya Tucker, among others; inducted into the Country Music Hall of Fame in 2004 (non-performer category), along with Kris Kristofferson; awarded honorary Doctor of Music degree by the University of Charleston (WV) in 2007; former Director of Trevecca Nazarene University's Music Business program; and is an adjunct professor at Vanderbilt University's Blair School of Music.

In 2009, Trevecca honored Dr. Foglesong with the award, "Distinguished Professor," an honor that, including Foglesong, has only been conferred three times in the university's 110-year history. In his remarks about Foglesong's impact upon Trevecca, Trevecca President Dan Boone said, "At age 70, when he could have retired and enjoyed life, Jim Foglesong chose to return to college to become a really cool university professor. He crafted a music business program that would serve well the music business industry by producing graduates with the same humility, honesty, and character that he has. He clones himself! In a world of arrogance, he has produced students who have his simple grace and dignity."

Clore: Can you talk about what you were doing just before your Epic Records days, along with how you landed at Epic?

I went to work at Columbia Records in 1951 as a Musical Assistant in the Engineering Department. As I neared the end of my first year, my wife and I (both singers) signed up to tour with a show, Fred Waring's *Festival of Song*. It was a six-month tour that ran from September 1952, through March 1953 (approximate dates). When I turned in my notice at Columbia, that I would be leaving, they encouraged me to take the tour but we would call it a "Leave of Absence." It was a great compliment. They liked me enough that they wanted me to come back if I wanted to. The "tour year" was what I was doing prior to becoming a member of the Epic staff.

Shortly, when I returned to work at Columbia, the Personnel Manager told me that they would like me to become part of a new label they were starting. (In fact, they hadn't named the label yet). My job would be in the Artists and Repertoire [department]. Because of my diverse musical background and tastes, my main job was to listen to product from around the world: Pop, Classical, Folk, Cabaret, etc., and recommend what we should release in the United States.

Clore: What were your highlights during those early Epic years in Manhattan?

The pop A&R man, Marvin Holtzman, asked me to assist him on some projects. He did not have a budget to raise my salary, but, as remuneration for this "extra" work, he would call me to sing backup on some of his recording sessions. All of this led to my producing a concept album – a minstrel show – that became the biggest seller on Epic and was in *Billboard*'s Top Ten album chart for six or seven weeks. This led to my becoming a full time A&R man for Epic. In other words, a producer.

Clore: Person you should have signed?

Barbra Streisand, Kenny Rogers, Ronnie Milsap, to name a few that I had opportunities to sign.

Clore: How does it feel to be a member of the Country Music Hall of Fame, as an executive?

Being a member of the Country Music Hall of Fame as an executive is unbelievable. I still have trouble realizing that this took place. Being inducted along with Kris Kristofferson, the same night, was the icing on the cake. I feel that Kris brought a whole new dimension to songwriting and deserved becoming a member of the Hall of Fame.

Clore: As former Director of Trevecca Nazarene University's Music Business School and an adjunct professor at Vanderbilt University's Blair School of Music, what is the number one thing you try to instill in your students?

My number one thing with the students is to take advantage of as many opportunities as you can within the music business while you are in school and in Nashville. The importance of establishing relationships (contacts) cannot be over-emphasized. You meet people who introduce you to more people, etc., etc. The other parts of this challenge are (1) give every job a 100% effort; (2) do your schoolwork, again, with a 100% effort; and (3) be a sponge. Listen and soak it up. Volunteer. People are watching whether you realize it or not. Do not have an "attitude."

Clore: How do you stay on top of an ever-changing industry?

Realize that things are changing constantly, then do your best to stay on top of the changes. Study, observe and try to make the changes work for you.

The world needs music. It is a privilege and a responsibility to work in the music industry. We make people smile and relax all over the world.

The preceding interview took place in July of 2009.

Kid Rock Is Good For Music

Yes. Kid Rock is good for music. The guy represents an important aspect of the musical spectrum. I would argue that he is one of the very few true Rock and Roll stars that have come on the scene since the 1990s.

Rock represents what we wish we could be, and were, doing.

Many seem embarrassed and/or offended by Kid Rock and communicate their disdain via snarky comments, like "red neck," "can't sing," "womanizer," "white trash," et al., but really and truly, I believe they are jealous. Come on, the dude commands a room like few ever have, or will. He is a stud.

Maybe his personal style is not quite up to your standard(s), but I say he represents a strong portion of America: a never-ending, whirling, twirling, amalgamation of cultures, backgrounds, musical styles, likes, dislikes, values, standards and sometimes the lack of every single one of the aforementioned.

Robert James Ritchie, a.k.a. Kid Rock, has had plenty of success simply being himself: a white dude, born in the

North, sometimes performs with Lynyrd Skynyrd, was married to Pam Anderson, owns a "General Lee" Dodge Charger, opened a tour for Ice Cube, frequently hangs out with Hank Williams, Jr., has worked with Eminem, owns "American Badass Beer," and has sold millions of albums.

Whether we want to deal with it or not, we are mixed together, constantly. How do you think we got nearly every genre of music we have today?

Maybe if you are a self-proclaimed "musical purist," you can call him a musical whore. But I assure you he's having more fun than you.

Pinky Gonzales

One of the key elements that makes a career worthwhile is the giving back. Not because you need to donate your time to charity, but because I think one of the most effective ways to learn is to teach.

Pinky Gonzales is one of those guys you feel lucky to know. He is loved and highly respected by countless people. Pinky's combined intelligence, charisma and passion puts him on a level that few will achieve, regardless of effort. By the time you think you have a good idea, he has come up with four, and the first one is headed into production.

When I reached out to Pinky for a meeting, I assumed he would have no idea who I was, but it turns out the guy already knew who I was and had heard my name a number of times. Learning that was a compliment.

Pinky has a number of remarkable accomplishments to his name, but one of the coolest is selling Echomusic to Ticketmaster for $25 million in 2007, as one of five partners in the Echomusic business. During his Echomusic days, Pinky worked with, and for, acts such as: Robert

Plant, Janet Jackson, Kanye West, Rascal Flatts, Bon Jovi and many others – on hundreds of marketing, brand development and community growth initiatives.

Gonzales was named Belmont University's Adjunct Professor of the Year in 2010. The *Nashville Business Journal* honored him in the publication's "Leaders Under 40" article in 2009. As chief proprietor of Pinky Gonzales Unlimited, LLC, Pinky's clients have included: Bubble Up Ltd., Richards & Southern Inc., Carazel Inc., Cuestion Spirits Company and auraMIST Inc.

Simply put: Pinky Gonzales is an entrepreneur. Not in the way that Joe Blow down the hall calls himself an entrepreneur, but never actually accomplishes anything. Pinky defines the word, and has the resume to back it up.

Hang on his every word. He has plenty to share, and fortunately he has the golden heart of a teacher, and is happy to impart his wisdom on those smart enough to listen.

Early in 2011, at a coffee shop in Nashville's Hillsboro Village, I had the honor of buying Pinky a cup of coffee and having the following conversation with him.

Clore: I'm looking for your summary of the evolution of the music industry. From your time specifically, but if you want to go back even further, that's certainly fine.

Well, there's my perception of it, and then there's my experience with it. I'll answer on both levels.

The way I see the history of the music industry working, is that for starters, humans are creative creatures, and I think that's important to remember forever because there's so much "sky is falling" paranoia about the industry going away, or copyright lobbying – it's all about,

"Well, if you don't protect the creative work, people stop doing it." To which I say, not only is it untrue, you can go look at cave drawings to this day and see how humans expressed themselves. There's songs, there's folklore and there's always been creative expression, and that, to me, is the core of what we have turned into a business, which is a nice way to make a living, or a way to make a living, or a great way to make a living, but we are not incentivizing the creative works themselves. Anybody who's driven for the money should be in TV commercials or something, and out of the music business anyway.

So, with that premise, that foundation, we create with or without an industry. The way I see it having evolved is, scarcity is the only way to make a profit on something, so you got in to the live performance stuff – operas and musicals and plays and all of that kind of stuff – things you could sell a ticket to, but we didn't have the means to record, and then you fast forward a million years in time, and somewhere between the '30s and the '50s, this thing really caught on as a viable, reproducible, sellable medium and by the time The Beatles hit, you had the perfect storm of revolutionary sound, social upheaval worldwide, and an incredible thirst for what this all meant. And music is, in my opinion, the most direct form of communicating emotion there ever has been. It is pure emotion. Happy lyrics to a sad melody is a sad song, and vice versa. So you had all of those forces colliding at one time, and all of a sudden you went from being an industry based on live performance and ticketing to being an industry based on recorded works, which were far easier to make once and sell again and again and again, so you had scale and the profits were outrageous and a corporate culture took over, which didn't take long, because if you say "There's money up there in the hills," you get a gold rush. So, that's how it all happened. And the players that were in the right place at the right time cleaned up.

I love the story of Richard Branson, because he started Virgin Records by selling CDs out of his dorm room, and that's what a record label was to begin with.

So, enter Pinky Gonzales in the late '90s. By then, we'd gone through the Grunge revolution, prior to that, of course, the hair bands and Pop and all of that stuff, so there was a well-established method to how things were done. I feel very fortunate that I started my career in San Francisco, because we were close enough to L.A., where, if you were serious about going down to showcase, it was just a long drive, but we were far enough away that it wasn't an industry town. So the ethos was, "If you're going to make it as a serious mainstream Rock band," and I was a Rock guy, "You have to build a following, play and sell out live shows and you need to be able to do that regionally before some executive in almighty Los Angeles is going to take you seriously."

And so I always thought it was hard. I've always known it was hard. I've always thought it was as much about sweat equity and hard work as it was about great songs, but one without the other doesn't support us. So, great songs with no hard work is a failing formula, just like anything else. And I had a band, they were extraordinary performers, great, interesting dynamic live show – but there were too many people in the band – there were seven of them. They could never agree which direction things should go strategically. You couldn't get everybody to travel very far for a show and so it just fell apart, even though to this day they're one of the greatest bands I've worked with in terms of entertainment, it was unmanageable because they didn't have one piece of business focus, and they needed that balance.

1999, Napster hits. I'll never forget the day I heard about it. I was just starting a new job down in L.A. I had moved from San Francisco to L.A. for work, and my job was to physically set up our office. That's the first thing I did for this company. I bought computers and desks and insurance and got credit cards – physically set the company up, under the guidance of my boss, and there was a phone guy from PacBell who was installing our phone system, and I had just seen this whole thing on Napster, and I was like, "Hey dude, name an artist, any artist."

"I don't know, uh, Madonna."

Enter Madonna – and her whole catalog shows up.

I said, "Pick a song."

"Like A Virgin."

We clicked on it and it's playing right there, and the look on his face was exactly how I was feeling, which was like, "Can you believe this?" Like, everything you want, right here, you can pull down an entire album – we all know how that story plays out – so that's what signals the changing of the guard, the old from the new. You're no longer protected. There's no longer such a thing as scarcity and that's obviously going to affect the bottom line. What was interesting for me is I still had no money, so for me it was a great way to collect music that I wasn't in a position to buy anyway, and because I was never the corporate fat cat with the leer jet and a $400,000 salary, it never hit my bottom line. It didn't change my lifestyle because I was starting at the bottom in the first place, and that's something I've tried to keep with me my entire career. I've never had to take a step down because I never got beyond myself in terms of what I was making, or however you want to say it.

Clore: Which affected how you received Napster?

Yeah! For sure. And I've always felt like you have to earn your money. I'm fortunate that what I have in my brain now is of certain value, where it used to just be what I could physically do with my hands was all that people would hire. You look at job listings and it's crazy that we – you know, you want to be a coal miner – any idea how physically intense that job is? How many hours and how much danger, yet how little they make?

Clore: Oh yeah, I grew up around it.

There you go. So I feel fortunate that what is in my brain is worth something and that there are fewer of us than there are just strong people, but it's a strange paradox – not to get off course.

So that's where I see the current state of affairs. You had the floor drop out. You had digital sales continue to rise until this last year. Physical sales have dropped. Digital sales have risen, but they plateaued this year. Part of that is we have even more competition out there with applications on our mobile device, as well as movies and video games and all these other things that can be factors. So I don't see things getting substantially better in digital music anytime in the near future. Maybe a long-term trend, but not overnight are we going to replace everything that we lost. And that's just where it is.

So, that's all well and good except you also had over-building in the live performance space. You've got Ticketmaster and Live Nation that have now consolidated. The fact that they are a publicly held company means that they are required by law to seek greater shareholder value above all else. That is their official mandate. Well, that's hard to do when you've already kind of mastered touring. The only way you can make more money is either to charge more money, or to add new services that haven't been a part of this before. They've sort of maxed out the services that we want: you've got merchandising, you've got parking, you've got concessions, you have venue rental, and then people aren't paying for downloads and exclusive web stuff, so what is there?

Clore: I guess the one thing maybe would be paying for a unique experience with the artist. Not that it's working for everyone.

Sure. Yeah, but it's not a billion dollar business. You're absolutely right – there's money to be made there, but there's a big difference between something that makes more than it costs to do, and something that adds a billion dollars to the bottom line to bump that stock price up. So when you talk about shareholder value, a VIP experience at a Bon Jovi show is good for Bon Jovi, but it doesn't do jack for your stockholders. And that's where we live. If I'm a brand-new artist right now, in some ways I think it's wise to just keep all of that out of your head – none of that is really important, work on playing your local clubs the best you can – and this is the most generic advice ever...

Clore: Not to everyone.

If you're fabulous, you'll be able to take it somewhere, and if you haven't gotten used to a quarter of a million dollars salary, it's all better from where you start – it's all bigger gigs and more love from this audience, and more opportunities – eventually there's a way to work that out. I think what Zac Brown Band has done is brilliant. In the context of the modern, suffering music industry, here's a guy who writes incredible songs with great people, puts on a hell of a show, he is attracting a bigger and bigger crowd, which is always going to be worth something. Ticketmaster can come and go. There will always be a way to make money if you can bring a lot of people to watch you play. Period. That cannot ever go away.

That's how I see all of this progressing from then to now.

Clore: Looking back, do you view Napster and Kazaa, et al. as detrimental to our industry?

I think they were inevitable. Yes, I see it as detrimental. I don't think it ever could have been avoided, so it's almost moot. I don't think that Sean Fanning is an evil guy.

Clore: I totally agree with you.

I do think that Morpheus was an ill-conceived business model. I think there have been shysters in the recipe. I mean, up until very recently, LimeWire was – they flew in the face of the entire industry, and then suddenly it was white flag, "No, we're great – you're doing yourself a disservice if we go away." Go away then. You can cry about it all you want – we don't care. But there's going to be something else in its place, and something else in its place, and this will forever be the state of affairs, with all forms of digital media.

Clore: How do you balance being progressive, but also staying within some sort of framework that allows an industry to exist?

That's a great question. To me, it is so easy to lose sight of the music itself, that you can. Watching what the ad agencies do with major corporate clients is a great way to keep tabs on new marketing methods, new ways to influence consumer psychology and spending.

For me, it's one part education, keeping in tune with what's happening in the world around me, through conversations with people that have this idea that may not be able to pull it off, but if we could figure this out somehow, wouldn't it be great – so you get that in real-time, but there's a litmus test in music, and that's the product itself – music itself. So, if you can't see yourself having a better time at a show because of some campaign or concept that was put together, you're probably off target. What is it at the end of the day that people really want?

Here's the trouble: the web is going to look different over time. It's going to get faster, it's going to be cheaper to do more interesting interactive experiences, but we've kind of gotten to a place where we get how it works and we get why people like it, and we know what a website is, and the basic information that was once unavailable, is now completely available in real-time and free: tour dates, news, biography, photos, videos, community features, message boards, social media, commerce – those are the core tenants, the pillars, of what an artist website needs to contain. And your social media profiles are just an extension of that – they're ways to communicate and deliver the exact same information.

We talk about being cutting edge, to some extent, it's sort of like the digital media thing, it's like are digital media files going to outpace the loss of physical retail? The only reason we ask that question is because we see that we're losing something over here, and we want something to compensate for it, as if there's some universal balance that needs to be maintained. The fact is, there is not such a thing as the universal balance that needs to be maintained, so progressing in digital marketing of an artist may not look the same in ten years as it does today. Progressive was, "Will your fans sign up for a paid portion of the website? Will your fans volunteer and register their promotions and marketing time through your website as part of a street team"?

That was innovative because we had these tools for the very first time. Now that's old school because these tools exist and there's not really the next level of thing that hasn't been satisfied. Social media was a gigantic leap forward because it took the conversation and made it the content – kind of like an old-school message board used to do, but Facebook made it about the conversation, so that's a huge leap forward – what's the next iteration of that? I don't know. I want to believe that there's still something beyond this, and I'm sure it will change and there will be this cool feature and that, but we've got all of the digital media that we can stand. Now it's just a matter of is it big or small or live on a mobile device or your computer? Is print going away? That kind of stuff, but it's all going to kind of come back to the same kind of stuff.

We understand metrics now. Analytics now. That traffic matters. That commerce matters. Things we had to learn about because it was a new invention, from the early '90s when the Internet came to be, to the early 2000s, when it kind of – you know, by 2004, when Facebook came around it had had enough time to become a common platform, from 2004 to 2014, it's really just been a refinement of what was already there. So, to get back to the original question – how do you stay progressive in the music space – if it doesn't relate to the music, you're off base. And a lot of times it's not a matter of reinventing the wheel, it's a matter of making great use of the tools that are available and accepting that music is music. Music is not a movie. A movie is not a video game. A video game is not a book. A book is not a puppy. They're different, and it's okay. [laughter]

144

Clore: Absolutely. I love that you and I both have this view, after the fat cats. It's almost like people in our age range have somewhat more of a pure view, of we're here for music. We're no longer here to make money because there is no money – to be a little cliché with that terminology these days. But still, really you're talking about it – the money has gone down and it's just not coming in like it used to. That doesn't mean the music industry is going away, it's just going to look different.

Exactly. And the fact is, there was never a time when everybody could be Bon Jovi. This is what cracks me up. [laughter] It's always been hard! That's why it's always been cool.

Clore: That's true.

So, it's not like I remember the good old days when you could learn three chords on the guitar and make a $60,000 a year income as a traveling musician. Like hell. That never happened, you know? And if it did, it's happening at the same frequency today. When we see a gigantic drop in touring revenue, it's because Dave Matthews Band and Kenny Chesney didn't tour this year. It's not because everybody stopped going to their local clubs. The economy had an influence on that, of course, but you're talking about the top 10 to 25 artists in the world. We're not talking about the overall music industry. And we talked about revenue falling out, and we're talking about units of CDs sold, we're not talking about demand for entertainment. So, I think it's funny, you know, you look at what Taylor Swift and Lady Gaga and Justin Bieber and The Jonas Brothers and Miley Cyrus and on and on and on, Hinder, and there's so many great examples of artists that are making tons of money and selling lots of records and of course selling out concerts that started after this supposed meltdown of the music industry, you know? I mean, I remember when Taylor Swift was 12 years old.

It's not going anywhere. When you look at what she's doing on her website, it's photos and news and community features and a store – it's not rocket science, it's just a matter of providing information that people want access to, but at the end of the day, it's the songs, it's the personality and it's what that represents to the individual fan – so, getting out of the way I think is the key. There should be as little distance between the artist and the fan [as possible]. All of us marketing types…need to always come back and remember that it has nothing to do with us. It has to do with where you were when you heard that song about that break-up that made you feel like Taylor was singing your heart. That's what they love. That's why I love Zac Brown.

Clore: I talked to Fred Buc from "Lightning 100" for this book and he talked about his theory of 15 to 18 years old being that time when you are malleable to music.

Amen.

Clore: I'm curious what those bands, groups, moments, songs are for you.

Well, for me it was incredible timing that the Grunge Revolution hit as I became a freshman in high school. I just moved to a new town. I had just started to kind of develop some competency with guitar playing, so I was just starting to play in bands, and for that musical revolution to occur right at that huge point of change in my life, it all came together simultaneously and there will never be a more powerful music experience for me than seeing Pearl Jam on "Headbangers Ball," in probably the winter of 1991. And I sort of became a student of the Grunge revolution: Nirvana, Soundgarden, Alice In Chains – I also kind of like the Pop stuff that came out of that – Counting Crows and Del Amitri…

Clore: Do you find yourself still mostly listening to those bands still? Even if you're staying current, which I know you do?

It's a little bit of both. I really love Pandora because it's a nice mix of what you know you like, and something new. I certainly have a bond with those artists that I don't think I'll ever have with another group of artists ever again, so I wholeheartedly agree with the point. It's frustrating though, to not be able to find something new, and I'm always sort of in search of that, and The Shins hit, I'm all about Phoenix. Because I work in this space I try to listen to everything all of the time. I know when Taylor Swift has a new song. Kenny Chesney and Brad Paisley. I also know when Usher has a new song, or Kesha or Kid Rock, and so on. So I try and stay up on everything, but it changes, too, when you make a living in music, I think, you receive music differently than when you don't. I stopped playing guitar because I stopped liking music because I was always analyzing the way something was created – it's like seeing behind the curtain. And I found that when I started working in the music business is when I stopped playing music because I was able to find some creative channel where I was really good at this strategy and communication – and I was never the best guitarist. I love playing guitar, but I never had the delusion, for one day, that I would have it as my primary source of income. Not ever. So, that was a blessing. A lot of people feel like there's nothing else they could do in this world, yet that's not working out.

When you work in the business, I feel you have a different perception of music than when you're just a music listener, or fan. As a fan, you don't have the hang-ups about whether or not you like Justin Bieber. So what? You like Justin Bieber. Music is not your identity, necessarily. Just because you like a song on the radio. Your identity maybe is as a doctor, or a teacher or a nurse, lawyer, whatever it is. So I think we in the industry are much more snobby and analytical about what's happening, and therefore it's harder to become a true fan to something new.

Clore: In no way, ever, have I thought of you as a music snob, and you could be one of those types...

You're much more in-tune with actual music that's going on.

Clore: I appreciate that. – How do you remain a nice guy amidst everything we're around? Really, you are a standout kind of guy. There are so many assholes. How do you wake up in the morning and think, "Back at it. And I'm actually going to treat people well in the process."

You know what I like about working with musicians, and I will also say entrepreneurs? I will say as I've gotten older, I've started to migrate towards the entrepreneur side of things. When you are working with people that have an extreme passion for what they're doing, it's easy to stay inspired and hopefully a nice person. If you're a mean person, you're a mean person. I know lots of those in this business. And if you're a nice person, you're a nice person. I think some of that is just genetics, some of that is upbringing, but I really enjoy the process. It doesn't mean that I don't have disagreements or that there aren't people who think I'm completely arrogant and way off base.

So it just depends. It's always easier to like somebody that you agree with.

I really love Nashville. I love the people I get to work with. I love having the fortune of having been in the right place at the right time, and I love the mentorship and teaching side of things, where when someone has so much drive to go create and do something. It's exciting to be able to help encourage them to do that. You can't do it for them, and there's no guarantee that if they did everything you did, it would work out for them like it worked out for you, but just giving people that, "It's okay. It's worth the ride. Take the leap" kind of motivation – that's part of what makes it fun and keeps it worth doing.

Clore: Speaking of which, you seem to come alive teaching at Belmont University. I'm looking for your thoughts on the importance of that: how you prepare, how you respond to students.

I gave a presentation a little while back that was called "The Best Job Ever" conference.

Clore: I saw part of that.

So, that was a fun thing to think about. They wanted to know why I had the best job ever, which is funny because I didn't apply and say, "I have the best job ever, let me tell you why." It was like, "Pinky has the best job ever. Let's have him talk about it." So I got to work through a lot of that stuff, and in addition to telling my story and my opinion on things. One of the key elements that makes a career worthwhile is the giving back, not because you need to donate your time to charity, but because I think one of the most effective ways to learn is to teach. There's the old adage: "Those who can, do. Those who can't, teach." Unfortunately you can take this too far, pretending you know something because you can talk about what it is, you can analyze it, but it doesn't mean you can actually do it. I like being right in the middle. There are good days and bad days to teaching. When I'm really in the zone and I have a command of what I'm talking about, and I have personal examples of how this plays out, and great statistics, and I can see that the students are engaged and taking notes and I know that this message got through today – I love it.

There are other days when I feel like I'm spinning my wheels a little bit. I'm trying to explain how something works and I'm still a little uncertain of how all of this comes together, especially because the course – it's "Digital Strategy and Community Management" – the digital side, these tools change all of the time. Facebook today is different than Facebook a year ago today. It's still Facebook, but the way I teach that is different because there are new features. There are new capabilities. There are new methods. Even with the same platform. So there are times that I feel like, "Gosh, am I as up-to-speed on this as I need to be?" But for the most part I think when you know a lot about something and you are excited to be able to do it, and somebody else shows interest in that, it's this natural thing. I think it's a lot like parenting. I assume, I'm not a parent, yet. What would be the joy of teaching someone their ABCs? That sounds terrible for me. I don't like the idea. Some 35-year old dude doesn't know how to read. I'm going to teach him his ABCs. That does not sound like it would be a good time for me, but, a small child learning their ABCs or how to read, it's so different, because you see them discovering life, and you get to project yourself through that experience, and you get to be a part of that fascination and wonder. I think it's similar in teaching. When someone has a genuine interest in what you love to do, you can't help but be excited and encouraging and fascinated by their perception, and that two-way dynamic teaches you something about what you thought you already knew. And there's always beautiful moments where you say something just off the cuff, and as it's coming out of your mouth. It's like "Yeah, that's exactly what I meant!" So, having to crystallize and formulate thoughts in a way that someone will receive, understand and be able to apply...I don't do it for the money. [laughter]

Clore: And that's so key. That's a great point and I appreciate you saying that. On a related note, I figured you'd appreciate this: I'm a huge fan of the piano. When I play at home, Harvey, my 20-month old, beelines for me and immediately wants up in my lap. He'll sit and bang on the middle keys and I try to play around him. It is such a special thing. To me, it's magical, because he really has no clue – the fact that he can already come and be there with me and be experiencing this...

So how primal is music that a 20-month old kid, who can't create it yet himself, still understands the connection that music is different than conversation or watching TV or playing with blocks? You know? I mean, it's that much a part of us. I think that's fantastic.

Clore: You're absolutely right. – Can you talk about San Francisco to Nashville? The companies involved and what that transition was like?

San Francisco, at that time, mid to late '90s, was a great place to be an aspiring Rock musician. Several really strong clubs. A really great, almost community spirit, where the booking agents knew each other. If you were persistent you could get a call back from a decent club and get a shot at playing a Sunday afternoon. For me, it was a perfect Petri dish to start from.

It all started when I had a friend that was in a band invite me out to a show. I came, and I saw them. I just flipped out, I thought they were incredible, and I wanted to do whatever I could to help, and the most valuable thing I could do was help get them more shows. So I focused on the city of San Francisco. When they were playing these shows, you would meet the other bands on the bill, and I was so infatuated with the whole thing – the whole thing was just magical and over-the-top and I couldn't believe I was so lucky to just be a part of the show. I always wanted to be behind the velvet rope, not as the groupie or the VIP, but as the producer or part of the band. So that was a really extraordinary experience and it gave me a lot of depth because I had all of my being invested in being a part of music. It was nearly impossible to make a living there, in terms of music. So that's why I went to Los Angeles, and it was miserable for a long time. I was only there for a year and a half, but it was a significant part of my early development, so it feels like it was a huge chapter in my life. The last year and a half have kind of flown by, but that year and a half took 10 years. There it was so much more cutthroat. There were so many more people that were specifically interested in the business of music, and my early biggest break was getting a job in the mailroom at the William Morris Agency, which is supposed to be how you're made. That's where David Geffen started. You start at the bottom and you make your way to the top. I hated that job, and that's kind of a long story, but I hated the agents, I hated my fellow associates in the mailroom, I hated the agent's assistants, I hated the HR guy. I hated everybody.

Clore: I appreciate your honesty. I really do. Most people wouldn't say that.

Oh, it sucked. And they would tell you it sucked, and there's very few people there now that were there then, because it sucked. It's a cutthroat world, and most agents are miserable – even if they're rich – I could name names.

So I ended up walking out on that job in the middle of the day, three months into it, and I thought it was probably the end of my career. I just couldn't stand it.

So that was my impression of L.A., that it was cut-throat, it was superficial, it was too expensive, it was too smoggy, it was dangerous – I hated it. So I came to Nashville because my girlfriend at the time wanted to be a Country singer, and we came out on a vacation just to check it out and I was dumb-founded. I had always envisioned Nashville as like Texas – dry, flat, no trees, cowboy hats and boots. And as the plane is getting ready to touch down, I'm looking out the window going – "Holy cow, there's forests and there's lakes and there's rivers – what is this magical place?" And the people were cool and it just was like, "We need to get away from L.A. anyway, this place seems magnificent, let's give it a try," and thank God.

So we moved, probably about six months from that time. July 1, 2000. My first job was with the Country Music Association, and that was kind of a corporate job within the entertainment space, but my boss then is one of my dearest friends now, a guy named Jeff Green, an actual genius. A memory unparalled. He not only remembers facts and information, but remembers maps. He can do math, complicated math equations in his head in seconds – he's just an incredible brain, but he's also a brilliant strategist, so under his guidance, we did a lot of consulting with those that wanted to get involved with the Country music space, either through one of our events, which is now CMA Fest, which was then Fan Fair, the CMA Awards, there were a lot of sponsorship opportunities, a lot of artists that wanted to be featured or showcased in some way, so we had an opportunity for what I now know as sponsorship activation. I did not know that term then.

We had an opportunity to combine marketing with money in effective and impactful ways, and I was still early in my career at that time, but those were the basic building blocks that I still use to this day. In the course of doing that, it was really obvious – nobody knew what was going on with the Internet. There was one other company doing it, they were very expensive and their service was very basic. Labor intensive, so I can't say that they were over-charging, I'll just say it was very expensive for very limited capability. So that's when I decided I would start my first real company, and that was Artist Media Group, which started at the end of 2001. What was great about Nashville, compared to L.A. or San Francisco, was that it was a smaller town, but it had big potential: lots of potential clients, lots of money, but a very small group of people that were really handling the day-to-day of everything. So it kind of just came down to being in the right place at the right time, willing to take a huge risk, but I had nothing to lose anyway. I was renting my house. I had no assets. I had a credit card with probably a $3,000 credit line on it. That was my world. It felt like a gigantic risk, but in the grand scheme of things, it was pretty manageable, and fortunately, it just worked.

Nashville then versus Nashville now is a different thing. Through the course of time, Artist Media Group became Echomusic, and Echomusic sold to Ticketmaster and all kinds of competitors sprung up around it, and eventually, and not just because of us, but because of the industry at large, began realizing the importance of the web, and the potential to not only use it as a marketing vehicle, but to make money on it. So, times changed. I went from being one of the only people in the region who was evangelizing the importance of an artist having a professional caliber website to artist management companies now having in-house digital marketing staff. Thank God. They should have had that a long time before that became the normal thing, because it became the primary focal point of the business – that's where your fans are, that's where your marketing should be done, you need an in-house expert. So it's changed a lot.

Now, I think, there's much greater appreciation for what "brand" is all about. Brand expectation, the way an audience wants to interact, what they want to interact with – what they're willing to spend and why and how. Because it's more established now, I think it's more competitive now – this specific space. As a musician, it's always been competitive. There have always been people coming to town with a guitar case and a hope and a prayer. I couldn't really speak to what it's like to be a musician in Nashville today versus other times. I will say it's never as much fun to be a musician in an industry town as it is to be a musician in a non-industry town. It's a lot more fun to play Portland, Oregon than it is to play Los Angeles, or Nashville, or New York. The audience is more receptive, more appreciative. There's a magic in the air that gets sucked out of the room when you have people there analyzing the performance instead of participating in the experience, so as a musician, you need to get out of town for your own sanity. You need to tour not because it looks good on the resume, musically speaking, but because you need to see the difference between an audience that lights up and an audience that has a strong, professional appreciation for what you're trying to accomplish.

Country has always been different than Rock. A Rock band has to connect, or they're irrelevant. A Country band doesn't necessarily have to have a following to get a record deal. They're going to sing somebody else's songs, which, not to bash it, it's the way our system works, you know? Lady Antebellum – incredible vocals, brilliant songwriting, great team of people, excellent record label – but they weren't out on the road until enough people were buying that a record label saw it as a low-risk opportunity. It was the right people in the right place at the right time. Linda Davis, who was Reba's back-up singer – Hillary Scott is her daughter. Lang, her dad, played for Reba. They're an industry family. It's a well-connected feel and they're fabulous. So that's just the way it works.

How does Nashville work compared to others? I think at the end of the day, there's going to be competition anywhere you go, but I think that the people in Nashville are proud to be in Nashville. We're a good group of folks. We're proud to have, for the most part, pretty strong family values, you know, it could be more culturally diverse than it is, in time it will be. Anyway, I really love it here.

Clore: As we sit here on January 19, 2011, what do you say to artists that still aren't using social media, and not that we need to make them feel stupid, but how do you try to help them see the potential that exists right in front of them?

Well, you've gotta have fun with it, or it's not going to work anyway. The way I grade the course at Belmont is one part coursework – you've got to show up. Of course there are tests, and there's a group assignment where, as a team, they will work with a local artist to apply these concepts, and that's always a great thing to watch them learn and apply to stuff. A big portion of the grade is a paper they write on a mainstream artist of their choosing. At the very beginning of the semester, they decide which famous artist they want to write three long papers about.

Last semester I had a student that wrote about Arcade Fire, and I thought – this is perfect. These guys are so innovative – they were certainly the biggest artist to utilize

HTML5 and its incredible interactive abilities – before any other mainstream artist that I saw. Extremely innovative, experimental website – I thought, "Wow, that's dead on." Well, as the student starts writing about it, the first paper was on the brand, which was easy for him – they're a vivid, almost cartoonish group of musicians – very animated, dynamic, great players, fun show, quirky, great people. Then he got to social media, how are they using Facebook and Twitter – are they using MySpace, other tools – but he was dumbfounded, as I came to be, by their lack of focus on it. They weren't updating, they weren't interacting. It wasn't current, it wasn't relevant, it was a completely wasted, missed opportunity – and he and I had several conversations about that because it's hard to write a paper when somebody is doing it wrong. It's easier to write about what they're doing right, but I hope he learned more as a result.

You've got Kenny Chesney out there who doesn't update his anything, so every post is going to be "This tour now on sale," "New single at radio," – it's all business speak. Fine, but that's just as much of a missed opportunity, in my opinion. Then you've got Taylor Swift, who's the cliché, go-to, how to do it right because she grew up on social media. She had a MySpace account because that's what she and her friends did, not because it was a wise thing to do marketing-wise, and she communicates through it, back and forth. She responds to fans. She has fun with it. For her, it's an intuitive, normal thing to do. I think the lesson to be learned from all of that combined – the difference between Arcade Fire, who doesn't hardly do it at all, which is a missed opportunity, Kenny Chesney, who thinks he's doing it, but isn't doing it at all, but something is better than nothing, and Taylor Swift, who completely gets it all, and is better off for it. If you don't use it, it's at your own peril, but to get back to the very first part of this conversation, if you don't have great music, it doesn't matter anyway. Unless you're going to be a stand-up comedian or a video performance artist, it doesn't matter anyway if the music isn't there. If the music is there, there are many musicians who wish they could just sing and play music all day long, and they really resent the hassle of being famous.

I get it, completely. "I don't mind being rich. I don't want to be famous. I'm not pursuing fame, because I don't want to deal with meet and greets – I want the respect of my peers, but I don't want to be the center of attention." If that's not what you want to sign up for, then you probably don't want to make your living as a professional musician. If you want to be there on stage, accept that this comes with the territory, and have fun with it. Experiment. If you don't get it, figure out why you don't get it. The fact that you don't get it doesn't mean it doesn't work. It means it's not connecting with you the way you think it should. You've probably got fans in the same position. How would you reach you online?

At the end of the day, some are going to get it, some aren't. Some don't care. As an aspiring musician, trying to draw the attention of people that are inspired by what you're doing and therefore want to work with you, and/or they see the potential to make a lot of money with you or have a wild ride. You're going to have a hard time being on their radar if you're not online. It's one of the easiest ways to get to see if someone is really doing a good job.

I got a lot of undue credit, as Rascal Flatts rose to superstardom. I was very fortunate to work with them from the very end of their first record, forward. They were amongst the first generation of artists in Nashville to have a high-caliber, professionally developed, fully-managed website. For that, I will take credit, and I'm proud of what we did. But, we got a lot of undue credit for their overall success. The fact is it came down to radio. Radio, radio, radio. They're a radio-friendly band. They have radio-friendly songs that resonated with a young female audience, that happened to be digitally aware, and so we did get a lot of traffic on the website. We built an enormous database of e-mail addresses and mobile numbers – their fan club was very popular, etc. But, the way we always talked about it at Echo was we don't make you bigger than you're going to be. We extend your career longer than it was going to be. We give you the opportunity to communicate directly, which means when you stop having as many radio hits, you can still reach people longer than you were going to be able to if you hadn't put that together. That's an important part of my philosophy on all of this, because you can do everything right online and if you're not worth listening to, it doesn't matter.

One of my favorite, least utilized strategies is to take the message of the individual song and build a campaign around that. The song, "Sarabeth," which is also known as "Skin," that Rascal Flatts did, is about a high school girl going through chemotherapy – she had cancer – incredibly emotional song, really impacted a lot of people. I mean, everybody knows somebody that's had cancer. So, that song really changed the direction of their career. They partnered with the Monroe-Carroll Jr. Children's Hospital. They've now donated over $2 million to them. Cancer research has become part of their platform as a band, and we had a lot of promotional activity around that song and how we could use that song as a vehicle to positively impact the world. You have to be careful in that specific case to not exploit something that is a very sensitive subject, but with every single you've got a story line – you should have a t-shirt for that song, you should have a strategy for that song, you should be telling that story through a marketing channel.

Those are ways that you can have a bigger reach, even if everything else is clicking – you know, you've got a song at radio, you've got a well-established band, your artist is interacting with fans online, there's always something that can be done to help reinforce that – maybe that's a better answer to what you were asking earlier about how do you stay on the cutting edge in this space. There's always something you can come up with that helps to tell the story, and it doesn't matter if it's a movie, a video game or a song – these are all stories and there are people that resonate with that story line, and there are ways to apply that story in unexpected ways to keep it interesting and fresh.

Clore: I want to get your thoughts on the entrepreneur side of things, especially as it relates to the music industry?

It's the exact same as the music industry. It's the same as being an artist, and that's what I found in time through a long, winding road. It's not different than being in a band, and, by the way, it's always going to be easier to be a band than it is being a solo artist. Same with being an entrepreneur – you can be a sole proprietor or you can be a co-founder. Be a co-founder – you have more parts in place that you don't have to pay for with every gig. Keep as much as you can, by all means, but, accept that it's worth giving a piece of the overall success to team members that will work for nothing for a long time.

Clore: Alongside of you, right? I mean, you're in it together...

Yes. So, I think it's not that there are parallels. I think it's exactly the same. A band is an entrepreneurial endeavor.

You're creating content, which is your business, which you are out to find customers for, that will pay you money to consume it. It's a service, as opposed to a product, when you're talking about concerts. It's a product as opposed to a service, when you're talking about a shiny little disc with notes on it. You've got a business. You need to think about your manager. Too many people see their manager as their booking agent. They're not a booking agent, they're your GM, your COO. They are your operations person, and while the bottom line is part of their responsibility, so is human resources, so is marketing, so is investment strategy, so is all of these other pieces – vendor relations and so on. This is not a booking agent. You've got a booking agent that's a booking agent, and they're easy to replace. An agent just knows people at venues that buy entertainment. So, anyway…

Being an entrepreneur, I started in 2001 and didn't know what the word entrepreneur meant at the time. It was probably 2004, 2005 before I started hearing that term a lot, and probably 2006 before I took ownership of that title.

"Yeah, geez, I guess I am."

Now it's probably one of the things I'm best known for, certainly in Nashville. I think some of the lessons I've learned are: you've got to have the idea, just like you have to have the songs, and it's really difficult to know when you have the right idea. There are two different schools of thought when it comes to how you get started. Some people say keep your ideas a secret, that creates a pent-up energy, sort of like not having sexual relations prior to a big football game or boxing match or whatever – sort of, the more you keep it inside, the more powerful it will become, and there are people that are just more secretive and that's just how they work. They won't tell you what their plans are until they are ready to go. The challenge with that is that you will never be perfect. You'll never have everything where you want it to be, and a lot of people never get off the ground because it's never perfect, and they think it has to be perfect to begin with.

Usually it's a messy start. My preference, personally, is to talk about what I'm excited about, which usually it's going to start as just an interesting conversation with a friend that puts that little nugget of information in your head, or it's going to be a blog post that you read, or a book that we really got a lot out of – and you start thinking about something and it really becomes a common theme for you. That's how you know you're probably on the right track for something. At that point as you start talking to other people about what you are thinking about – "I think this is really cool," or "I could see somebody doing that," or "Why isn't there such and such?" or "I really think that I could do that if I just had a programmer" – that's how it kind of starts. I find that the feedback from my friends and other professional associates, not only helps to give me the encouragement I need to keep going on it, if it's a good idea, but a lot of times they have the missing piece for me, or they have a piece I didn't know was missing in the first place. It's this relationship or that, or, "Have you thought about applying it in this way?" That goes a long way.

Eventually, if you're on the right track, I think there is a universal law. My favorite quote is, "Be bold, and mighty forces will come to your aid." I think that happens as an entrepreneur, as a musician. When you're on the right track you create a magnetism that attracts other people that are also in-line with that concept. It won't attract people that aren't. They just won't be interested in it. If you have some brilliant idea for some new line of fashion accessories, "Dude, that sounds awesome for you. I have no interest at all," but if I was way in to fashion accessories, that would be a very dynamic conversation we would be able to have. So I find that people who are meant to be part of it, find their way into it, and that's how you start the band. Getting to ground zero, getting to the starting point, is have a team together that's going to be able to create what you have in mind.

Next, you have a new challenge, and that is, how do you pay for it? If you can do it with just sweat equity, you're so much better off, but chances are good that you will quickly create too much work for yourself, and that's where I'm at with Carazel right now. I've got three other partners. We've got a seed investor that's given us $50,000 and is waiting to give us another $100,000 when we finally cry uncle and need it. But, because there's four of us, we each have only a quarter of the company, and every time you take investment dollars, more of that goes out, and now we have to start paying initial developers and customer service people, because we're committing to work that needs to be delivered in certain windows of time. We've reached a very difficult juncture, which is, "How do we keep moving this thing forward without giving so much equity away that it's not worth doing?" And that's a tough spot to be in, so you're going to reach a point where you either have something or you don't. And just because you were on the right track to begin with, it doesn't mean your final product will end up looking like what you envisioned on day one.

When I first started talking to my partners about this whole concept, I thought I was going to be able to charge $20,000 for a six-month campaign, with a licensing fee on top. Not even close to correct. Not even in the universe. Way off. It doesn't mean it's not a viable business. There's a famous term for this called "pivot." You have to pivot. You have to change direction. You have to be a nimble football player. You're a running back now. You've got the ball in your hands and you need to get it down field. You have to be able to roll around the tackle – you can't just expect to be untouched. So that's kind of where we are. We know that our competitors are seeing what we're up to, and are able to do what we've done because we did it. We don't own a patent. Patents are fairly worthless in most cases, anyway. So we have to move further and faster with bigger clients if we're going to survive. So we are now at a place where we see pressure on the technology, but opportunity with the service and the strategy, so that's kind of how we're morphing and evolving. All of us have other day jobs, which makes it challenging. And at the end of the day, there's going to have to be enough passion to keep this thing going to keep us working nights and weekends, or it's going to die.

The final chapter for me, and I'm advising a would-be entrepreneur, is it's okay to put it down if it's not working out. It's okay to leave the band sometimes. Sometimes there's a specific window of time that you know it's going to work out in this window of time, or it's not going to work out. It's okay. There's more long-term risk, people will see you as flighty or flaky, or not committed enough to really see something through, so you want to be careful not to do that on such a regular basis that you develop a reputation for doing that, but it's okay to let something go if it's not working out, and that's part of your personal path and your long-term identity.

Me, I spend the majority of my time working with other people, simply to be of help to them. I have two paying clients, everything else I do is volunteer, and that's part of how I'm able to survive a change of opinion, what's hot today. "Pinky, what have you started and quit at this point?" And I've done lots of stuff: I have a business brokerage in the Caribbean. I've done everything from writing copy for websites to running adwords campaigns to inventing new technologies altogether. Some of them make money, some of them don't. Very few of them become Echomusic, which became a team of 80 people, providing high-pressure services for 300 well-known accounts. The same thing that got me there – I'm just interested in a lot of what I see around me, and I like the conversation, and when something really stands out, I'm typically not afraid to take the risk of going after it. But, most songs don't work out. Most artists don't become famous, but you just keep going. You explore the things you like to explore. You have your good days and your bad days.

Clore: Professionally-speaking, what has been your highlight?

Selling Echo was a big deal. It changed my financial situation completely. It's funny because it wasn't enough that I could retire, and I'm glad that I'm not in a heavy amount of debt and all of that, but I went from being really desperate and out of energy and worn out, to feeling like some things are worth taking a risk on. I'm so proud of what we built as a team at Echo – it was not one person that was responsible for how it happened. There were five co-founders, and there was the entire staff. There was not a single person that made the difference. Without the whole ecosystem, it would not have worked. So I'm looking forward to doing something like that again. I would say, professionally speaking, that was the highlight because it gave me the credibility to give other people the inspiration to go take a shot at their dreams, and I think a lot of musicians that achieve a level of fame feel the same way. On the one hand, you're still doing the same thing you always did. You're writing songs, you're playing your music on stage, you've got to do the meet and greets and the hustle and all of that stuff, but to have been able to say, "I've made it," gives you some way to give a new level of encouragement to people, beyond the, "We're all in this together and isn't this great?"

It's like, "I've been to the mountain."

I don't think I would be happier with 10 million dollars than I was with 1 million, and so I think for that reason I feel like that was, early 2007 was kind of like the big event, but I like my life more now than I did then, by a lot. I feel more comfortable in my own skin, I feel more confident. When I do see an opportunity, I feel good about being able to take a shot at it. Part of that comes with age – I'm in my mid-30s now – I wasn't then. All of those are contributing factors.

The things I'm looking forward to: if I had 10 million dollars, I would do exactly what I'm doing now. I feel great. Just like I was saying before, it doesn't make every day rosy. You know, the weather sucks today, it bums me out. I drank too much last night, I feel like crap. You have your good days and your bad days. The days you feel like a Rock star, and days you feel worn out. I think being an entrepreneur, being a musician, sort of feeling like you've got a roll in your own destiny – it's worth being a part of, and I think you could be an accountant, a plumber, you could be an administrative assistant, and have the ability from where you are to be where you want to be if you apply pressure over time. Pressure on yourself, which is as much a state of mind as it is on daily actions, but you've got to be serious about it. That's where passion makes all of the difference. If you don't have passion, you're probably not going to do much with life, in general.

Clore's Summary:

- I really appreciate Pinky's attitude and approach. He has been in both good and bad working situations and has learned plenty from both. He has found financial success, but also points out that he would continue to do what he is doing now, regardless of money. I hope you can say the same about your current situation, and that you love and enjoy what you are doing, or that it is at least a worthwhile step towards your bigger goal.

- Pinky points out that it has never been easy to be successful as a solo artist or band. This is a huge point. Regardless of the industry's business model of the time, it never has been, or will be, easy. Before you even start, know and understand this. The same goes for behind-the-scenes types. Above all, you must have passion. As Pinky said, "When you are working with people that have an extreme passion for what they're doing, it's easy to stay inspired and hopefully a nice person."

A few more points not to miss:

- The music has to be good.

- Online marketing will not necessarily make you bigger, but will make your career last longer.

- Brand. We all are our own brand. Artists are brands. Be strategic in how you represent and communicate your brand.

- Authenticity is key in online communication.

- Do not be afraid to walk away if something is not working.

I Saw Paul McCartney

On our walk to the car after the show, I told my dad that Paul could have come on stage by himself, stood there, maybe played at least one song, and it still would have been one of the most amazing concerts I ever have, or will, see.

Along with some 17,500 people on the night of July 26, 2010, I had the tremendous and rare honor of seeing and hearing Sir Paul McCartney play a nearly three-hour show at Nashville's Bridgestone Arena.

Special only begins to describe the man.

I will never forget the feeling that came over me when Paul and his band started to play "All My Loving." It was literally as if in that moment, time reverted back to February 9, 1964 and I was participating first-hand with all of these people around me whose lives and culture were literally changed by the music of The Beatles that night as the band appeared on CBS' *The Ed Sullivan Show.* "All My Loving" was the first song performed on that show.

Not only was I able to experience this concert with my beautiful wife, but it was absolutely priceless to me that my parents, who both remember that night in 1964, were sitting to my right during the entire show.

During the set, Paul paid separate tributes to his dear friends John and George, performing the song "Here Today" for John, and "Something" for George, as pictures of Mr. Harrison rotated across the video screen, plenty of them including a much younger Paul.

Although Paul's touring band is spectacular, I felt an incredible sense that something was missing at times throughout the night. Do not get me wrong, I live in a reality where only half of the original line-up is still alive, but regardless, it is not quite the same. I am certainly thankful to have seen Macca in-person, but nothing will ever replicate The Beatles. Life does go on, however, and Paul is doing an impeccable job of respectfully performing and sharing these precious treasures of music.

Paul spoke of how he and his band were able to be the first Rock show to play in Moscow's Red Square, and how he learned from multiple Russians that they actually started learning how to speak English from listening to Beatles albums.

The impact of this man and his music is nothing but unfathomable. There is absolutely no way to try and comprehend the impact of his writing, recording and performing on the world. He did not find success in The Beatles alone, but he was essential to its genius. Paul continues to write and record new music, thankfully, but even more thankfully, he continues to share the timeless music of The Beatles in a passionate and genuine way, with people who are equally as passionate and genuine with their love for it.

I was born 17 years after The Beatles took over America. I am completely honored to now have the distinction of saying I saw a Beatle in concert.

I should probably consider no further concerts; there is nowhere to go from here.

E. Michael Harrington

You're not born knowing how to do this stuff well. And a lawyer could lecture you on it, but until you really do it, you don't know.

D r. Harrington is one of the most gifted individuals I know. His knowledge of music is ridiculously vast. I know a lot of people that know a lot about music, but Dr. Harrington always stands out in my mind. Not only does he keep up with popular music, he is also extremely knowledgeable in the areas of classical music, music business, legal issues, political issues, social media – and it is likely the list does not end.

I have always felt a sense of excellence in his work, studies and general approach to life.

E. Michael Harrington holds a Doctorate in Music Theory and Composition from The Ohio State University, a Master of Music in Music Theory and Composition from the University of Miami and a Bachelor of Music in Music Theory/Composition and Performance (Guitar) from the University of Massachusetts at Lowell. He spent twenty-three years as an outstanding professor at my alma mater, Belmont University, in music theory and composition, musicology and ethnomusicology, in addition to music business and intellectual property classes. As of the writing of this book, he is a professor of music business and intellectual property at William Paterson University in Wayne, New Jersey. Harrington serves, or has served, on several boards, or has been actively involved with: Drapkin Institute for Music Entrepreneurship, Nashville Composers Association, College Music Society, Journal of Popular Culture, Brevard Conference on Music Entrepreneurship, Music and Entertainment Industry Educators Association and Leadership Music.

My time as a student at Belmont was nearly single-handedly made worthwhile by Harrington. I was fortunate to have him for copyright law in 2002, which was a very interesting moment in time considering the dawn of the digital age as it related to the music industry. From the first day in class, he had a way of simultaneously encouraging and challenging us, which to me is an important and necessary balance for all of life.

Professors see so many students over their years; it is no surprise at all they rarely keep up with former students. I am thankful to have the relationship, and the access, to be able to interview one of my former professors in this manner.

To encapsulate Dr. Harrington in two words: music expert.

He has been interviewed by *The New York Times*, CNN, *The Wall Street Journal*, Bravo, *Associated Press*, PBS, The TODAY Show, NPR, Radio Canada, *PC Magazine*, *Billboard*, *USA Today*, *Salon*, XM Radio, *Rolling Stone*, *Money Magazine*, *Investor's Business Daily*, *Mergers & Acquisitions*,

People Magazine, Life Magazine, Reader's Digest, The Washington Post, The Boston Globe, Miami Herald, and others.

He has worked as consultant and expert witness in hundreds of music copyright matters involving: director Steven Spielberg, producer Mark Burnett, the Dixie Chicks, Woody Guthrie, Steve Perry, Keith Urban, Ne-Yo, T-Pain, T. I., Akon, Snoop Dogg, Collin Raye, Tupac Shakur, George Clinton, Mariah Carey, Patty Loveless and others; delivered more than 100 lectures to more than 70 law schools, organizations, universities and music conferences/festivals throughout North America, including: Harvard Law, Yale Law, George Washington University Law, Cardozo Law, Brooklyn Law, BC Law, Loyola Law, the Boston Bar Association, the European Film Commission, the Experience Music Project, NEMO, Future of Music Coalition, Miami, Berklee, NYU, UCR, McGill, Carleton, Eastman, Emory, and others; and been a consultant to the Electronic Frontier Foundation, Columbia Law School, UCLA Law School, Mel Bay, St. Jude's Children Hospital, and others.

He knows his stuff.

Clore: I am convinced that you know more about music than pretty much anyone in the world. How do you remember it all, while always being so current?

Thank you for such a kind compliment. I don't know if I have a better memory than most people or not, but a lot of music does come back to me and often when I need it. I think one of my strengths is that I am curious about what I don't know: musically, culturally, philosophically, politically – and want to understand things better when I am clueless, as I usually am about new experiences, people, sounds and sights. I am a xenophile – I am extremely attracted to foreign and unusual matters: people, music, food, etc.

Clore: What moments in time do you consider to be most important in the history of recorded music?

The first date that comes to mind is not the earliest, but it is something like a "Big Bang" when it comes to pop music and culture – February 9, 1964 – the day The Beatles first appeared on *Ed Sullivan*. Everything in the U.S. stopped that Sunday night as the entire nation watched in either wild bliss or shock. I doubt there was much middle of the road, moderate type reactions. William F. Buckley, Jr., the most prominent of political conservatives back then, stated that they were the "Crowned heads of Anti-Music," and more – this was proof that society and culture had sunk as low as it could. Caligula and the worst, final depraved days of the ancient Roman Empire were shiny bastions of high culture compared to how desperate things had become with these four frightening young pseudo musicians who were not quite women or men in appearance. Funny, funny times how the conservatives freaked out. It marked the first huge divide between generations (one that later got worked out), and more importantly, it marked the end of business as usual, at least in terms of music that could be pushed upon kids. This music was incredibly exciting, vibrant, new and high quality.

The biggest proof of this huge chasm was seen in what musical acts were big before February 9, 1964, and after February 9, 1964 – very few survived. It marked the end of almost every artist. The only artists who had hits before and after The Beatles were a few Motown acts: The Miracles, Marvin Gaye, Stevie Wonder – and The Beach Boys. Elvis had 14 number one hits before John, Paul, George & Ringo, but only one (1) post February 9,

1964. There would be much less soft stuff and adult created stuff aimed at us kids. Millions, including four or five boys in my neighborhood, would immediately start imitating The Beatles.

The next day, after my incessant begging, my dad and mom rented a guitar for me. For that month, I only stopped practicing that guitar to go to school or sleep. I was a professional musician two years later when I was 12, as I was paid to play (and sing) live and teach guitar, piano and organ. My dad made a great deal with me – he would match whatever I earned and would help me buy as many instruments as I could! In 1970-71, they put me on an equal keel with Stevie Wonder, as we both got the brand new electronic keyboard from Fender, the best sounding damn thing you ever head – the Fender Rhodes. It was quite cool being in high school with a brand new 1969 red Gibson SG and a Fender Rhodes, as well as acoustic six and twelve-string guitars, percussion instruments, and an upright piano and a church organ in our basement. (Our church was being torn down, and a new one built, and they gave away the downstairs organ with its pedals and large noisy motor – way too cool a toy as a kid!!)

That was a revolutionary year unlike any, in terms of a musical assault.

The next biggest year in my opinion would be 1999, and that was more of a technological assistance, or euphoria, for music fans with the launch of Napster and easily accessible music, and the Diamond Rio (the first portable MP3 player, a now stone age type of device). The dream of the Internet got fulfilled that year. Also in 1999 (June 14, 1999), the federal court ruled that the Diamond Rio was not a recording device and that it could be sold. This stubby gadget led to the iPod, the iTunes Store, Planet of the Apps, social media and life as we now know it.

I can think of some other big years – '67 was amazing. They call it the "Summer of Love," but I think they missed out on the summer of just great music and new bands. In '67 is when San Francisco really hit, beginning, as far as everyone knew, and first albums of The Grateful Dead, Jefferson Airplane, Moby Grape, Quicksilver Messenger Service – there were some fantastic bands, and every label had to have theirs. RCA had the Airplane, Capitol had Quicksilver, and Columbia had Moby Grape – and I think the bands were really great. The Beatles' *Revolver* had a big impact on those bands, and that of course led to *Sgt. Pepper*, which changed the world, too. That's '67 as well, *Sgt. Pepper* was a serious earthquake, like nine on the Richter scale. Everyone got influenced by it.

Also, Summer of '67, Hendrix – "Geez, what was this? A guitar can make these sounds?" One thing people overlook with Hendrix is how well he wrote. He was a great, great composer of music. I don't even want to say songwriter, I say composer, as in, there are more things involved than, "Here's a little love song," you know, "Here's a little message." It had compositional facets that were intricate and developed. Janis Joplin. Again, that was just an amazing time.

I also think '77 was quite a year, because Disco was raging, and art music, that stuff was going on in England and other places. I love what occurred then, if you look at bands who started, that was the year of Sex Pistols, The Clash, Elvis Costello, Talking Heads, Prince – I mean, there were a lot of things that occurred right then. I don't think it got noticed as much as the Summer of '67 did, because the times were different. There wasn't a war raging in '77. We were out of Vietnam. There was no international event as significant as Vietnam.

'91 was a good year too, because of Seattle, and all of those bands all hit at once.

What Napster did, and partly the Internet – it's computers getting cheaper, and getting better. What that's led to is interaction among people. You interact with almost everyone you've ever known, as opposed to you just have a handful of neighbors and a few friends, and you make some long distance calls – that's how you used to connect with people. Now, the fact that I usually don't even have to say "How are things going?" because, you know what I've been doing because of Foursquare, that links to Twitter and Facebook, and everyone knows where you're at, and that is so neat that you really keep in touch with everyone. It feels like you're not apart anymore. And if you're in this much serious, quality contact with people, then what's to stop you from saying, "Well, let's collaborate"? And I read people, I see what people are doing, and it influences me. So now, the number of influencers I have in life has gone crazy. And the opportunities I have to work with other people, learn from other people, is great. And bands and so forth. Between Reverbnation, Lou is a friend of mine – Lou Plaia. I'm having lunch with the head of A&R at Grooveshark, and all of these things just interactive. If these people don't know each other, as soon as I might mention a name, they will know each other. Everyone can know. The dissemination of knowledge and of contacts of people is astounding. This of course leads to music being heard by so many more.

Now, you could of course start with nothing, and at the end of the day – I mean, you write some music, you record and upload it, what a simple matter it is to have a thousand people hear it within ten minutes. Whereas in the past you couldn't do that. Also, the idea I'm big on, and I know you are too, is blogging, and the printed word, because as I tell young musicians when I speak at conferences, "Yeah, do everything musically right, but you're overlooking the importance of the printed word." The printed word, I can do a search of me, or you, or anyone, and find a lot. Or if there's little, then not much of where you are in print. But can I hear your music? If I do a search for this band's music, I don't get tons of mp3s showing up, I get the other stuff. I get the printed word. So I think in what you say, and how you brand yourself, like Twitter is incredibly important. With Twitter you can, of course, post your little tweet – it's short, everyone can see it, and read it. You can retweet, which does fascinating things. You can say, "I am with this kind of person. I am with this movement, this style of music." All of those things. And you can contact the most famous and important people. They may or may not read it or respond, but suddenly you are linked in with them. Oh geez, to use another name – LinkedIn.

[laughter]

The world, it's just astonishing how things have changed, and how widespread everyone's information and identity, which is brand, how that now just goes everywhere. And a few years ago, who's thinking, "I'm a brand. And I'm this and I'm that. Why would Facebook be important?"

I remember when it began, 2004, I'd get these emails from students that say, "They want to be your friend" on something called Facebook, and I'm thinking, "Someone wants to be my friend? Well that's as nice as can be. How terrific? I love that idea. So yeah, we're friends." So, whatever Facebook means, and I don't know what this thing is. And then what it became was just amazing.

So, how this can help, and does help musicians get known and think outside the box, and think of things other than just "my chords," or "the song I'm writing," or "the gig" – you've got to be a person now, too. And those of us who follow bands, and like certain artists, well, we'd like to know more about them, and now we can know more, and the artist has more responsibility. I really think this would make you behave better, too, because, what's private anymore? You know, if someone sees you, they take a picture on their phone, they upload it, it's tweeted, it goes everywhere and the smart artists interact with their fans, and the ones who don't are going to have fewer fans, I think. Because we like to feel like, "Oh, I have some say in this." Like, so and so retweeted me. Or I get a response from something I've written. In Facebook you can see that this person thinks this way, and I might interact with someone really cool, and then my friends decide that they then want to meet that person because the fact that I know the person, and vice versa. I mean, I now have met some really cool people because of who my friends know. I mean, this stuff is just incredible – what this leads to.

Clore: I will never forget you wearing a Napster T-shirt to class when you taught my copyright law class at Belmont University. I know you received some criticism about that. Can you share your view about transitional technologies and times, especially as it relates to the music industry?

Oh yeah, that Napster shirt! I was such a black sheep in Nashville in those days, and caught so much hell for wearing it everywhere in Nashville. I also lived in Midtown Manhattan for most of 2004-07, and wore Boston Red Sox clothing daily, so what's so bad about wearing a Napster shirt in "Copyright Heaven," aka Nashville?

I saw Napster as the coolest damn thing. I was convinced that this was the best thing that had happened to music, that this could not be stopped, and that opposing Napster was like opposing the sunset. I understand why people would be opposed to sunset, because, like it or not, there is more crime at night, which sunset heralds, but...

And it was the nicest thing – I loved meeting Milt Olin, the COO of Napster. When he came to Nashville to speak, it seemed like an atmosphere similar to Obama coming to speak to a gathering of the Ku Klux Klan, or Hitler speaking to B'nai B'rith. A few years later I also became friends with Wayne Rosso, the CEO of Grokster when he came to Nashville and spoke at Vanderbilt. The CBS News magazine, "60 Minutes," was also there to film it. It caused quite the ruckus.

Clore: Can you give us a big picture view of what a copyright infringement court case is like, regardless of the side? What is the preparation like and how does the case usually play out in the courtroom?

Usually it doesn't go to the courtroom. It's under one percent of the time that it does go to the courtroom, and the reason for that is, because, by the time you actually get into a court, I would say, both sides, individually, have probably spent between three or four hundred thousand dollars, to a million dollars – it's so expensive – because you've already had depositions and discovery, and so forth. And when you get to a trial, there are going to be intelligent people on both sides. And at depositions they've scored really good points. I'm showing this now with my students. We had a moot court the other night, and one student is dying at how the other student, this woman, is asking incredibly good, pointed questions, and I'm having to remind them, "No, you just answer the question. You can't go on."

So, both sides score their points and you really don't know the outcome, how the judge thinks, how the jury thinks, how you look. There are so many factors and there is so much money, so you always want to start before it.

But how it begins is there's often a song out there that's a hit, and a friend of a songwriter says, "That sounds just like that thing you played for me the other day," or words like that. Lonnie Mack was at dinner with his son one time and they hear a song coming in the speakers called "Little Miss Honky Tonk," by Brooks & Dunn, and Lonnie Mack's son said, "Hey, that's you're song." It was very close. So it's often someone points out to a potential plaintiff, "Hey, someone took your song."

So the next step is to get a music attorney, or someone like me, an expert witness, who can really – I really shed light on it more than the attorney does. The attorney is an advocate, I mean they're always an advocate, and they'll want to say, "Well, some of them have really good scruples and principles," and they might even say, "Before we do anything, let's hire an expert to get an expert opinion." Sometimes they'll just cut in and say, "No, it's not." And some attorneys are smart enough to understand music, and they'll say, "Well, why is it not an infringement?" But if they file – so, then at that point the attorney either has to file the case, file the lawsuit, agree with the plaintiff, or hire someone like me to give an opinion as to whether we should or not.

So, say if they do think it's an infringement, they then proceed and they give notice to the other side, "This is what we want." They state the facts that, "Your song infringes our song, and we need to discuss what to do about this." What to do means how much money has to change hands. For instance, "Give us money and co-ownership of the song," or depending on how similar they are, they might even say complete ownership and cease and desist – "Quit selling it and having this thing played." Those things play into it.

And then if you keep going, the defendant's likely to say, "Well, it's not an infringement," and they'll find someone like me, get an expert opinion, to agree with them. Those are how things often begin. And then what happens is it's often the quality of the expert witnesses. You can always find a hired gun. I've been in cases before where the expert who was approached, you then bring in the expert for questioning, after you have discovery of his credentials and so forth. You do all of that, you read his report thoroughly. You prepare a rebuttal of it. What will happen is, one of the best questions to ask is, "Okay, this expert's been involved in 75 cases. Now let's go through. In the first case, Dr. Jones, you were approached by a plaintiff, and your opinion was for whom? The plaintiff or the defendant?" And he'll say, "The plaintiff." So, if you find out in 75 cases, 75 times, whoever approached him, he agreed with them, and took their side, then that looks dreadful – he's just a hired gun. He works for whoever contacts him. If you can find someone, on the other hand, who says no plenty of times – like my situation – I'll just charge someone a flat fee, say $900 to give an opinion, a very brief opinion, but it's a big yes, or a big no. If I say no, then all I get is that $900. If I say yes, then I could get anywhere from ten to 50 thousand dollars. So, if I say no 10 times, that's potentially a half a million dollars I'm out on, and I would make $9,000. It's a big difference. So that's a big deal then, also, as to what's the strength of your expert in this, because the lawyers are generally going to be good to great, most of the time. Sometimes not even good, but usually they're smart people who go at this well, and they really take their training and their oath very seriously, and they're doing a very good job, you know, most people. It's easy to diss lawyers, but you often have to take the side of what the company is, you know? You see this in the record label sometimes. Like, I wish I didn't have to sue a student, but I'm paid well, and I'm the lawyer, so they do it. A similar kind of thing goes on with this.

The case goes on for a period – a year, or three, or five. It depends, it can be stretched out. There are counter motions. The first case I was ever in, the other side does what I realize now is standard. You immediately say, "This expert's not qualified." If it's their first time, then yeah, they could be better. You're not born knowing how to do this stuff well. And a lawyer could lecture you on it, but until you really do it, you don't know.

The expert should be paid upfront, like a retainer. Like 10 or 20 hours in advance, then you work down. After those hours are done, you should be paid another chunk.

Let me add something really important, and this is how this should go for plaintiffs and defendants. The best way lawyers should do this, and I feel really strongly about this, is when you contact an expert, you tell the expert that there's a copyright matter between the songs. You don't even have to mention the exact songs or artists. Better yet, don't. And don't even say who you represent. Just say you'd like an opinion whether song A infringes song B. That's exactly how it should be done. Don't say who you represent. And try to not even tell them who the artist is, maybe just the title of the song. But that's what's called doing it blind, and it's completely fair, objective and honest. That's what I prefer. And there are certain attorneys in Nashville I love to work with because they never tell me who they're working for, and they know that they're going to get really straight from me.

Say, for example, there are two songs, and one of them I could work for Keith Urban, or against Keith Urban. Well, say if it's an unknown versus Keith Urban, some expert would rather be on the side of Keith Urban because there's a lot of money there. Where this unknown guy might be getting a young lawyer who maybe doesn't know this stuff well, and you may not get paid. But if you're working for some major artist – Keith Urban, Garth Brooks, Sting – then, you know that's more of a big deal. So it's best to keep that information away from an expert, so they're really blind, honest and fair about it. That's really important. That's what I prefer. I don't want to know anything else. I never want to meet the artist. Never, I just think that's crazy. Otherwise, because if I wanted to, what am I, some little fan of the band, or the artist? Like, no! I'm treating this just objectively. These are interesting intellectual and musical questions. That's all.

Clore: What are some of your favorite copyright infringement situations? For example, mine is Neil Young's "Borrowed Tune," which I learned about from you.

I'm glad you remember Neil Young's "Borrowed Tune." I would argue that he has not *infringed* the copyright of The Rolling Stones. Yes, he was surely inspired by them, imitated and copied from The Rolling Stones' "Lady Jane" – *I'm singin' this borrowed tune / I took from The Rolling Stones / Alone in this empty room / Too wasted to write my own.*

He even comes out and says [paraphrasing], "I'm wasted, and I took this tune from The Rolling Stones. Like, I did take it." And I would argue that he didn't, because that is a little descending, four-note part of a scale. "So fa re ma, fa re ma do" is what it is, and of course The Stones didn't create that originally. They sing it with those words, "My sweet Lady Jane, I've done what I can." That thing, I mean, their notes are insanely unoriginal. Of course they're not original. There's thousands and thousands of examples of that. Now, had he taken the exact words and the melody, then there's a problem. But, he actually says he took from The Stones, but he even changes the little melody. It's not identical. It sounds like it, but he did a couple of cute little changes at the end. I mean, I think it's one of the ultimate tongue-in-cheek kind of jokes. If I ever met Neil Young, I wouldn't want to be like an idiot and ask that question first, but I would like to say, "You know, I would be on your side on this one."

I don't know if I'm making this clear, that the melody that The Stones did is in their song, and it's okay to use, but it's not original. Like, all of the words – you and I have known each other for ten, twelve years or whatever. And say in all of the years we've known each other, I've never known you, and you've never known me, to say an original word. I mean, we've conversed, and clichés come and go, and that's a nice little cliché – [hums the tune from "Borrowed Tune"] – that's just a nice little cliché. So even if he says he's taken from The Stones, he's acknowledging that that's a great song and my melody is like it. And he's trying to get across this idea of emptiness and gloom and loneliness and despair and drugs. So, he even goes further to call it "Borrowed Tune." [laughter] The guy's brilliant to pull all of this stuff off, you know?

Clore: He really is. I'm so glad you pointed that out, because I may have missed that had you not brought it up in class that day.

Oh cool. Yeah, when I play it for students, everyone laughs and has the exact same thing, "Well, he's guilty. He says he did it." And I try to encourage them, "No, think this one through a little more here. What about this and that? A., it's not original to begin with, and he changed it. And he's not using the words." If you're using the words, okay, now there's way more of a problem, because I'm sure there's no example in the history of our civilization of those lyrics, with those notes. I am convinced you can't find that earlier than The Rolling Stones. It's an original statement, because once you add words, suddenly – you know – when words line up with notes, it's way more significant than if it's just notes. Just as a general statement.

Clore: You're right. I can even remember my reaction in class, "Oh man, guilty." [laughter] And The Rolling Stones probably liked it, but still, he's guilty. And then the more you talk about it, I'm like, "Okay, I see. It's a lot deeper than you would think."

Well, the first time I heard that song in the 70s, I was like, "Geez, Neil Young's career has gone to hell. What is the matter with him?" Because when it came out, I was heavy into classical music and computer music, and I said, "Geez, I'm glad. I mean, my heroes of the past, I realized, what a bunch of…" – see, I left that stuff because it was too simple for me in terms of chord structure. I wanted deep and complex, and then I did enough of that, and I said, "Nah, this other stuff's good, too." Now you know me to be really open-minded, like, "Give me anything. I can see the value in all of this stuff."

Clore: Sure. Absolutely. – I am a fan of Girl Talk. How does he get away with mashing up so many songs? Does he get proper approvals? How do these types of situations typically play out as it relates to legality?

It could be that he hasn't made very much money on selling these CDs, and that suing Girl Talk would not bring about much relief.

Suing him would also likely bring about a lot of bad PR.

Most importantly, I think it would be great to defend him based on how music and culture has evolved. Bach, Handel, Haydn, Mozart, Beethoven, Brahms and all of the other "art music composers" were doing what they are supposed to do – take preexisting music, credit the composer, and then re-work it. It's part of the "theme and variations" tradition, and more, and has been a revered and taught practice in Western Music for centuries. It is what we classical music composers HAVE to do. Every great composer studied music this way. The way to create music is to think about it, create it, re-create it (as many times as necessary), and perform it. In the case of an artist who improvises, the creation process has much less time. One has to think and create and immediately perform it. It cannot be re-created, unless the performer wants to repeat and change a previous musical gesture she already played.

Copyright law, it's a great law. And it's a wonderful purpose. The purpose is twofold. The most important part of copyright – I mean, there's two interested parties. One is the creators, then there's the gigantic group called the public. And it's supposed to be a balance. You want to give the creator a monopoly, and only that creator can exploit the work in many ways, and that's really good. That creator makes money, and maybe tons of money. And the public's enriched, because the public created the law, to allow this to happen. So you wouldn't want the public to always have everything and never have to pay a creator, because there would be fewer people creating, probably.

On the other hand, if the creator could control, "Oh, I can't even sing my song out loud in my house, because they could hear it, and I need to pay a royalty," you know, like every little apartment would have to pay a royalty, a license to ASCAP, BMI, SESAC. That would be dreadful. So, in the balancing act, what's been determined by the courts, is that the most important party is the public. That's something in Nashville they don't know. If they do know it, they don't want anyone else to know it. So it has to benefit the public. Now, then you take copyright back to its original purpose into what composers have done, I mean, in classical music, of course, you borrow, you don't ask permission. Mozart writes a theme in variations on some other composer's music. Bach takes pre-existing music, puts it into his own, and changes things. And on and on.

There's thousands of examples of this throughout classical music. And classical people don't sue. Jazz people hardly ever sue. Blues people don't sue because they all fuse everything they hear. It's a cultural way of looking at copyright. The culture says, "Well, of course, we're all in this together. We're all borrowing. We're using the pre-existing words and chords and melodic snippets, and things, you know?" No Country song is going to be a hit if it's got very original chord progression. In Country, they want just a few chords, very simple usually. It comes down to the culture. As you see like in Rock, in Country, even in Christian, there will be lawsuits...in Hip Hop, Urban and R&B – because there are several reasons for it. Sometimes the creator doesn't know that this is how a lawsuit works. For example, someone goes to a club, and you hear songwriter A performing at the club, and writes a song called "Sweet Melissa," and plays "Sweet Melissa." And then, someone comes home and is filled with this idea and writes a song called "Sweet Melissa."

Well, the songwriter at the club who did "Sweet Melissa" first, beforehand, shouldn't be mad that so-and-so takes the idea, "Sweet Melissa," and writes a song with the same title, but they might be. Or you pitch a song to someone, and they take a few words.

I was involved in a case where a guy gives famous Hip Hop artist a recording, and his song is titled, "Been So Long." And then the Hip Hop artist, without giving the guy any credit, uses the phrase "been so long" in a few places in his song, but with different melody. And I was asked to determine whether the famous Hip Hop artist infringed the guy who handed him the song with "been so long" all throughout it. And I said, "No. What he took were the words 'been so long,' but he even sings them differently." So, "been so long" is not a significant enough phrase to get copyright protection. It's three common words. If you said, here's four common words: "Flintstones, meet the Flintstones." Well, geez, that's extremely original. That's not an old folk song, it's an old TV show. So, that person's entitled to some copyright protection, to some amount. But the person that wrote "Been so long" isn't. So that gets to be important, is to how cultures, different groups of people – that's why I keep calling it cultures, because that's what it is. How the culture will view the material and value it legally, and in terms of financially, the business-sense of it, too.

Clore: How do you feel knowing you are a professor with often-profound impact on people's lives? What is your teaching philosophy?

I'm kind of amazed that people would want my advice or opinion. I never take that for granted, that I'm in an interesting position. And I think it's an honor to be able to help other people, either with a flat tire, or fix your flat, or give advice, or give love or caring – those are wonderful things. And there's nothing that makes me happier than helping someone with some problem. A question about music and copyright. Or whatever. What key this would be best in, and what chords you should use here. So that's stuff I always love. And the fact that, I guess I've been good enough at it to keep getting hired and keep getting asked questions and consult in cases for different companies – I just view that as the greatest honor, and I'm absolutely thrilled.

I treat every day as just another great, great day is coming. I'm going to be surprised all day long. You know, students ask questions and I don't think anything like they do, which is perfect. That's how I want it. And I prefer to be in the unknown. You know, that's why I'm so glad to be away from some of my past musical things, because it's like, "Well, I did a lot of that," but a lot of things I didn't do while I was doing these other things. It's like, "Well, now it's time to – I want to get good at social media or different technology things." Assume I did everything perfectly yesterday, if the same things came up, the exact same day came, I'd want to do that day completely differently – I want to try a different approach to it.

My approach to teaching is just love and be thrilled with the newness, and I think it's very important to be an outsider. If I was speaking at a business conference, which I have, I mean, I've never taken a business course. I've taught them, which is strange. I've never taken a law course, but I've taught law classes.

I think when you're an outsider looking in, you have a freshness that can't be beat. A good thing, a Bostonian, like me, I came to Nashville, rather than just someone local. And good thing that all my influences and Nashville and my students have had on me, now I plunk down in New Jersey and I'm way different than anyone here.

And this idea of being the outsider, and being amazed at what's new, being a xenophile, you know, someone who loves what's foreign and different. That's been really important to me. Stuff I learned from seeing how my father reacted to new stuff. He just always wanted to do things that were new. So, I think it's just great that I've been able to be around students. If I've done some good for them, well boy, what good they've done for me is amazing, in terms of how I think better, and how I'm not old and bitter. People in their 50s can often be in their second or third decade of being bitter, because life didn't turn out well, for whatever reason. Mine just keeps getting better. You know, I have trouble believing I'm this old, chronologically.

Clore: Right, and it shows. It shows in your attitude, and that's something I'm really big on, is to try – well heck, that's what the title of this book is…

The preceding interview took place in April of 2011.

Meeting Heroes

I used to think I wanted to meet all of my heroes, including people like Billy Joel and Elton John. I am not so sure I feel that way any longer. Now, if the opportunity presented itself, I would go, but I am done looking and hoping for ways to make it happen. I know it is unlikely to help how I view them. I have met enough "famous" people during my career to fully understand that they are simply people. They may have ridiculous musical abilities, or great looks, or had the right song at the right time, but I promise you they have emotional ups and downs just like the rest of us. In many cases, theirs are worse.

I still understand the excitement around meeting heroes, and always will. All I am saying is as you spend more time around people in the spotlight, you often see that "meeting" them is usually not that big of a deal. Nine times out of 10, you have a better chance of preserving your positive view by never meeting them.

There is a reason keeping "the mystery" around celebrities is important. We are all better off knowing them from a distance.

Chris Hauser

When I left that radio station, I made $12,500 a year, gross. My part timers were minimum wage employees, and they were mostly friends of mine.

I am a passionate person who loves to tell others about things of which I am passionate. I don't know how to turn it off.

Chris Hauser makes me look like I don't care.

I have never been around someone so positive, so full of life and so visibly excited about a multitude of things in this world – specifically music. He's always ready to share it. I don't mean just mentioning in passing. Hauser will make certain you know where to find it, or let you borrow it, or take you to the concert. As you read the following interview with him, you will meet a genuine and fearless promoter who loves and believes in what he does.

Chris Hauser has been involved in Contemporary Christian Music (CCM) radio to some degree since the early 1980s. When it comes to the world of CCM, his passion and dedication have played a vital role – not only in a big part of CCM's development in the 1980s – but in CCM being the successful genre it is now, some 30 years later.

The list of artists he has worked with during his career is admirable. To name a few: Amy Grant, Phil Keaggy, Randy Stonehill, The Choir, Steve Taylor, The Winans, Dave Barnes, Newsboys, Mat Kearney, Bebo Norman, Michael W. Smith, Waterdeep, First Call, Andrae Crouch, Derek Webb and Flyleaf, among many others.

The guy is truly remarkable, and is certainly one to learn from.

The following interview was conducted in Chris' home office on February 3, 2011.

Clore: I would love to hear you talk about the CCM market when you were first really around it. What the radio audience was like. How people were responding to this new genre.

I started really being introduced to Christian Rock music around '79 when I got to Syracuse and went to college at Onondaga Community College. I fell in with a group of believers who already were well versed in Larry Norman, Randy Stonehill, Keith Green, Phil Keaggy, eventually Rez Band. They just had a vibrant faith that captured me. I wanted to be like them, so I found the music and it lit me up.

Dallas Holm as well. Dig this, my mom took me to a David Wilkerson crusade in the Spring of '76. I was a new Christian. It was the same Broome County Veterans Memorial Arena that I saw KISS in in December of '75. I'm a new Christian and my mom takes me to this David Wilkerson Crusade, and Dallas Holm and Praise are playing the music at this thing. I think she bought a record that day. That was kind of an introduction to something that was starting to become Contemporary Christian Music around then. But again, it was just about my surroundings. So I get to college, find all of these kids who are already in to Christian Rock and Roll, I find *CCM Magazine* and I'm off to the races. I'm starting to buy records, and I'm making tapes for people, and I didn't even understand anything about copyright laws or anything like that. So I'm making tapes and it's my ministry to make tapes for all of my friends. And I'm sure that people bought a few records because of all of those tapes I made. That's another reason *High Fidelity*, the movie, is such an intrinsic part of who I am, because that guy's making mix tapes for girls that he's breaking up with, and Jack Black's got his Top 5 Monday morning depression songs, or whatever, in that movie. It's so wonderful.

I was noticed by one of my college professors…The Christian radio station in Syracuse, WYRD. Now, on the air we called it, "Word Radio," but really, it was "weird." It was weird radio. He said, "So, I've got one of those reborn again kids in my classes, Sue Boehner, you should interview this kid and see if you have a slot open." I reached out to her and they hired me part-time in 1979. So I started getting around records more, and getting around that culture, and I'd sit in this radio studio for eight hours on a weekend and I'd just pore over LPs and liner notes, just getting to know people in the music business that way. The day that I interviewed for the job was the day I picked up my first *CCM Magazine*. Seawind was on the cover. It was the Fall of '79, and by then, I also had a Christian Rock radio show on my college radio station there, so I was hauling in Larry Norman and Randy Stonehill and Rez Band records and playing them on this college radio show. I was in this high evangelism mode kind of position too, so I was really trying to get other people involved in the music that I was listening to; the music that was changing me, really having such a positive impact on me. So I went full-time at the radio station in 1980. I almost got fired a couple of times for sleeping in when I missed my alarm clock.

The early '80s, with CCM and the records that were coming, labels were sending all the records to the radio station so I was well-aware of what was coming in, what was being pitched. And my PD at the time, who I'm still in relationship with, through Facebook, he would let me sit in on music meetings and let me discuss which songs we were going to add. I was so into it, and I became the PD at that radio station by '83, around the same time we became an AC reporter to the national charts. Charts were monthly. I had a Rock show, probably by '84, where I was playing two hours of Christian Rock on Saturday nights and reported my charts. Being a promoter, being a lover of great music that was impacting me, I began to go out and do speaking engagements talking about Christian music to any youth group that would have me, any parents group. Eventually, when Christian videos were getting made, I made sure that they had a VHS machine and a TV, and I would show Rez Band and Larry Norman videos and whatever I could get my hands on from record companies to start playing. It was all about getting people excited about what was happening for music.

I also remember how I would plead with people over the air about the concerts that would come through Syracuse, "Just come to this show. If you come to this show, more great artists will come through Syracuse. But if you stay home, if you find something else to do, then [concert] promoters will not be as tempted to try and take a risk." The thing that hurt most is when a concert would come through town and it wouldn't do very well, and the next day, somebody would call the radio station, "Hey, when is this artist going to play? When is that happening?", and it would make me crazy to say, "That was last night, and we didn't have a good turnout." Ahhh! It was horrible, but I got to go out and MC these concerts. It was a huge deal to be out in front of a couple thousand people. When the big shows were coming through with Petra and Mylon LeFevre (early '80s, Syracuse), it was just a very exciting culture.

I found out afterwards that because of what we were doing in Syracuse with the radio station, promoters were beginning to go, "You know what, we can count on Chris Hauser. We can count on Syracuse delivering a fairly good crowd." Where Syracuse was fairly forgotten for years and years, with the radio station in place, and using our radio station as kind of a hub…DeGarmo & Key, Mylon LeFevre, Petra, Amy Grant came a couple of times.

I'm working a Smitty [Michael W. Smith] song now, my first ever. So I'm telling the story all day long to radio stations right now, that I played the first Michael W. Smith record in 1983. He was on "The Age to Age" Tour. He sang to tracks, ran back and forth across the front of the stage. I interviewed him. Debbie [Michael's wife] was there, pregnant with their first kid. When he asked, "Now, do you have the whole record?" I said, "No, I just have a 45." [I have the 45-RPM of "Great Is the Lord"!] He sent Debbie out to merch to bring me a full LP.

And then I played him all through the '80s. Already by '83, Syracuse, New York didn't register for an Amy Grant interview. I couldn't get an Amy Grant interview in the spring of '83.

Clore: Really?

Yeah, so they threw me a bone with Smitty. [laughter]

Something I want to bring up relevant to this time period: The Bill Gothard Seminars. He had these seminars on how to have a proper, Biblical family, though he was never married and lived with his mother. Part of his daylong seminar was a very convincing message about anti-Rock. Beat on two and four, the missionaries with the kids playing Christian Rock and the natives coming and saying, "You're drumming up evil spirits. Stop that, stop that." All of that kind of stuff.

In the early '80s, I was in a bit of a defensive mode against people who didn't like hearing contemporary music on the air. I would argue with people at churches when I'd go make presentations. I'd argue with people who didn't feel like a Rez Band video had the Gospel presented well enough in three and a half minutes. There was a certain element of defensiveness that I constantly was in because I was trying to say, "No, this is good. This is good."

Look, in the early 1900s the Salvation Army Band with the "oom-pha" – that was all bar music. That was scandalous for that time period. Martin Luther's "A Mighty Fortress is Our God" – that's a melody that came out of the bars. That was scandalous at the time. "Now, all you people who think Rez Band and Petra are of the devil, you're fine with a trumpet and a bass drum and 'A Mighty Fortress is Our God,' but if you could transport back in time, you would not have been."

So there was that element where I was constantly having to explain and defend, and that's probably another theme in my life, of maybe feeling a little bit embattled. I get on that phone every day, and I talk to people who are overwhelmed with the amount of music they have. They're trying their best to make it manageable, so they're trying their best to get as many songs off that pile as possible into the "no" category so that they can concentrate on this. One reason for that is that they're underpaid, over-whelmed, have too many other jobs, and by and large, aren't really able to spend the proper amount of time concentrating on the most important thing that's happening at that radio station, which is the music that goes out over the airwaves. So, I'm in an adversarial relationship to a degree with people all day long, and I've been doing that since 1987.

But I really don't see it as adversarial, though there's disagreement all day long. People will say, "I'm not going to play that song." And I say, "Whoa, whoa, whoa. Hang on. Let's uncover why you would say that. Why you would say that now? Why you would say that so early in the process? Let's unpack this a little bit and see if we can come to an agreement that maybe in two months I can surround you with a great cloud of witnesses and if you'd be willing to say, 'Well, maybe I missed it on this, and, yes, I'm going to try that'."

That's happened countless times. So, it's still a funny little dance. I call a radio station because I need something from them, I want something from them. And they are in a natural position to try and say "no" to a number of songs so they can make their lists and their pile more manageable, and thus their lives more manageable. But somehow, in the midst of all of that, I've been able to have great relationships with people, and love people well. They know that I do have their best interest at heart. In my relationship with a radio station, if they can win with their audience, their staff, if they can win, then I win. When a promoter looks at them as the enemy, and not as a friend, not as a co-laborer in some way, when a promoter looks at them as, "I've got to wear this person down, or beat this person into submission," nobody feels good at the end of the day in that kind of a way.

I'll never forget, you know, with Amy Grant's *Unguarded* hitting in '85, the Amy Grant record, where all of the sudden she had a song on pop radio, "Find A Way," which even the bridge has like a Christian lyric, "If our God His Son not sparing came to rescue you/ Is there any circumstance He can't see you through?" is the line in the song. Again, the church was scared of getting too close to the big, bad world. Amy Grant was such a lightning rod for controversy and all of that stuff.

I'll never forget in early '86, turning on MTV and there's an image of Amy Grant and a song, I'll never forget, the first three notes of the song I was like, "I don't know this song, but that's Amy Grant." It was her duet with Peter Cetera, "The Next Time I Fall." Even at that point I was like, "Okay, this is going to be so big. She's transcending anything that we've experienced in the Christian music business. When she's on MTV with Chicago's lead singer, and I'm in the music business, and I didn't even know what this was – I'm seeing it on MTV for the first time!"

I'm somewhat glad to be over it, probably. It was just an amazingly growing time for the Christian industry.

Clore: Well, considering your passion, I'm convinced that you helped play a big part in getting the CCM marketplace to what it is today. We're talking about the era where it was either going to make it or break it, and fortunately it survived. And you defending it out of the gates is phenomenal to look back on.

I remember the guy who managed DeGarmo & Key at the time came through town and told my boss at the radio station, "Hey man, your station sounds great. I'm all over the Country and your station sounds wonderful." Now, here's the interesting thing though, is that I tell people I had to get out of radio because I was a horrible programmer. I was not great on the air. I played way too many songs. You know, people have done it so much better. Almost everyone has done it better than me. I approached radio like a true fan. I would get on and I would play Tonio K, I'd play all of this alternative music, I would read interviews on the air, I was so into it. I did horrible radio, but I loved it so much.

One of the jokes in the early days, when the station would get knocked off the air and the phone would ring, I'd jump up and go, "Oh, there's our listener!"

[laughter]

"Hang on, ma'am. We'll be okay. It's coming back."

In '87, at the radio station, I worked in a doublewide trailer in a swamp, in East Syracuse. When I left that radio station I made $12,500 a year, gross. My part-timers were minimum-wage employees, and they were mostly friends of mine. There was no such thing as automation. You can program a radio station from your cell phone now. I know guys who do it. People have been stuck in snow-storms – they're programming their radio stations from their cell phones. Back then you needed somebody with a beating heart, and some kind of brainwave activity, to push buttons at the radio station. A lot of the part-timers were friends of mine who felt sorry for me because they knew if they didn't take a shift, it would be me working the weekends. I'll say this, radio people are the hardest-working people in show business. They are. Especially commensurate to pay and appreciation. They work all day long, then they're out doing station promo things at night. They're doing remotes on the weekends. It is hard, hard work. I think that's part of the magic for me in my relationship with radio – I did it. I get it. I understand. And I feel for them.

A promoter working the White Heart single called "He's Returning," with Steve Green on lead vocal, Dan and David Huff were in the band, and the box this came in – it was a metal box, locked, and the 45-RPM record was inside the box. It was '84, and a week later we got the key to open it and it said "Radioactive Material" on the outside. You open it up, there's the 45-RPM by White Heart. It was a Myrrh release. So, I felt like it was too heavy for my radio station. I felt that the power chords were too big, too hard, and so the promoter calls me, he says, "Are you going to play White Heart 'He's Returning'?" I said, "I don't think I can. It's too Rock and Roll for me on the AC side. I can't play it."

He'd probably heard that 10 to 20 times that day, and he took it out on me. He said, "How dare you? How do you even add records?!? I'll bet you stand at the top of a staircase and throw a bunch of records down the staircase, and whatever gets to the bottom, that's what you play that week. Is that how you do it?" I was so embarrassed and hurt and angry, and this rush of emotion happened where I blushed to the point that my glasses fogged up. That's only happened to me like four times in my life, where the blood rushes so fast. I just want these people to be happy. It was hard for me to say to this guy, and I thought, "If I ever get in to that position, I'm never going to treat somebody like that."

And another guy, a year later, he called, I said, "I've been so looking forward to telling you this. Your song is number one this month for me!" And he said, "Yeah, that's great. I'd rather talk to you about something else."

By that point, I was thinking, "I want to get out of radio and I'd like to go work for a record company." This was

'85. I thought, "If I ever get into that guy's position, I'm thinking any time a radio station chooses my song over someone else's song, I'm going to turn inside out for that person. I'm going to be thankful, I'm going to be gracious and appreciative, and not treat them how I was treated."

So in '87, I'm ready to leave the radio station. I am done getting crapped on at that place and I've got people in my church offering me jobs – selling shoes, selling furniture, selling cars – any of these places I could be making more money. I was overwhelmed. I chose to go to GMA of '87. I pay my way there. I pay my way because I am going to do everything I can, if I have to walk up and down Demonbreun or Broadway with a sandwich board advertising my credentials, I'm going to do it. I want to get a job in the record industry.

My boss at the radio [station] says, "You're paying your way down there? That's amazing! Let me get a flight for you. You're going down to better yourself and learn more about the radio industry. That's wonderful." So he bought my plane ticket to go down there and I met all these people for the first time, and I was putting a name with a face. That was April of '87.

Then in September, Myrrh Records called and said, "We've got a job opening for radio promotion in L.A." And the entire Myrrh office had just moved from Waco [Texas] to L.A. that year.

My wife was pregnant with our first son – called him the "Bicoastal baby" – conceived in New York, born in L.A. She was really nervous about moving away from family. Neither one of us had ever lived more than two hours away from our parents, and here was the potential of us moving from Syracuse to L.A., pregnant. This was the golden ring for me, this was the thing I was so excited about. Myrrh Records – there was no hotter label in the land. It was Amy Grant, Russ Taff, and The Imperials – and Phil Keaggy was coming out. It was just an unbelievable array. Benny Hester and Sheila Walsh, too.

So anyway, my wife and I ended up in an argument about it and she was emotional, being pregnant, but it was a very heavy thing for us. So I said, "Let's just go to our separate corners and pray for a couple of days and see if we can come to some agreement here." After two days, I came back to her and I said, "You're the most important thing to me. If you can't feasibly see being away from your family, with a baby on the way, then God has something else for me and I'm just going to trust Him for that, and we'll plan accordingly here." She said, "I can't live with myself, thinking 10 and 20 years in the future if we never took this chance."

I get emotional thinking about it.

We did it, and it was the greatest thing we'd ever done. We struck out on our own. Her dad said, "If it doesn't work out there," – which he didn't really think it would – "If life gets to be too much for you out there, I just want you to know, we'll move you back here. We'll find a place for you and take care of you." We got out there and life opened up for us: spiritually, emotionally, my job. All of the sudden, I was in the greatest job in the world, on the other side. I was the first guy hired out of radio to work for a record company in the Christian industry. I was in marketing meetings at Myrrh and they'd say, "Well, we're going to do this for radio," and I'd be like, "I can tell you right now, that would mean nothing to me if I was in that position." They're like, "What?!? It always worked before." I'd say, "Ahh, it didn't really. It didn't really work before." So it was like a foreigner coming in and changing the dynamic of how record companies even viewed radio stations.

Clore: Were you ever around Keith Green?

Yep. I almost worshipped the dude. I was a huge fan. He had a huge impact on me. "The Last Days" newsletter, his records – yeah, he and all of those other artists. It was very, very big. He was so into evangelism, it was so inspiring. I saw him [perform] live once. It was at Houghton College. A bunch of us – probably five carloads of kids – in the fall of '79, drove from Syracuse to Houghton College, in Western New York. We got back at like five in the morning, but we all went to see Keith, and the crowd was so huge that they considered making it two shows and keeping a bunch of us outside. But they ended up breaking all the fire codes and I ended up sitting up on the stage at his feet, with my girlfriend. I was about 10 feet from him, sitting next to the piano and that's where I watched him.

Clore: That's ridiculous.

Dude. It was really, really something. So I met him that night. Never anything more than that. But I played him like crazy on the radio. I remember exactly where I was when I found out that the plane went down, and he died. July 28, 1982.

Clore: Among those that know you, you are known to be one of the most consistent, joyful individuals around, especially on the radio side in the Christian music market. First of all, thank you. And secondly, how do you keep that up?

That is a great question, and I've read that question, with tears, to my wife and my men's group and a couple of different people. It really, really touched me so much, that you would say that to me. I think one of the things that keeps me really fresh is that even though I've done the same thing for so long, and so many other people burn out on this kind of thing, a couple of things keep this job fresh for me. First, there are radio people. There's a high turnover rate of radio people, and so I'm constantly being challenged to learn new ways of finding in-roads, commonality, with radio people. So that keeps me on my toes. There's nothing boring about meeting new people and finding out the points that we both touch on. I also would like to say I'm glad I haven't bailed out on this, because in the last five years some of my favorite radio people of all time are people I am calling every week, or two weeks, and talking about music now. So I'm glad I didn't bail out. I would have missed the blessing of meeting these people.

Secondly, there's always new music coming. I love that I worked Amy Grant and Russ Taff records in the late '80s to Dusty Rhodes at WPIT in Pittsburgh. I love that I worked records to him, for Myrrh Records, and there was a teenager in Pittsburgh, growing up then listening to WPIT, named Aaron Shust. Aaron Shust [Christian recording artist] used to listen to that radio station, to songs I used to work, and think, "My gosh, could I ever grow up and be one of those people?"

And then, Wes Willis of Rush of Fools, grew up in Montgomery, Alabama, and had already been to part-time auto mechanic school. He also was a star high school pitcher in baseball. People expected him to go on to college, probably on to the pros in baseball. And he heard a song called "Ocean" on WAY-FM, in the spring of 2001, and God completely stopped him in his tracks, and said, "I want you to do this." Wes had never written a song. He had never picked up a guitar, but that song, "Ocean," that I worked to WAY-FM, so changed the direction of his life that he eventually picked up a guitar, eventually started writing songs, eventually started leading worship, eventually started a band, eventually got a record deal. And I got to work Wes' record for Rush of Fools, called "Undo," which was the number one song of the year at Christian radio in 2007, as was Aaron Shust, "My Savior, My God," number one at Christian radio in 2006. My imprint is on those songs. You could follow the thread through that I had an impact on each of those guys. And Wes Willis' song has saved people's lives. There were people who were going to kill themselves. They were so despondent, and they turned on a Christian station and found the song, "Undo."

So, the joy that I feel, John, of being a part of these kinds of stories, and having an impact on both those guys' lives when they were teenagers, and then being able to have an impact through their music as they got signed, I just can't describe the joy and the honor that I feel in God's big picture, and God's big plan of His story.

Clore: That's beautiful.

So, there's always new music coming, and there's always new artists coming, and that keeps it fresh for me as well. And then new radio people keeps it fun and challenging. In addition, there are all of these great radio people that I've been friends with for two decades plus, that they've been on my back porch. I've been in their homes. I've met their wives and kids, I know a lot about their stories and they know a lot about mine. And I get to do this with friends. I'm a people person and love people a lot, so that's the other thing that keeps me so energized and excited.

Secondly, I would say that I've kind of come in to this new position in my life, and in my career, where I'm somewhat mentoring some younger promoters, and helping them get their start. I'm being a sounding board for label people, and then I'm also mentoring and fathering and being a big brother to some younger, independent promoters and seeing some success in their lives, and that's incredibly gratifying to be that kind of a voice in to these people's lives.

Clore: Can you tell me some specifics about how you encourage these people, especially the ones that are artists, and whether these are brand new artists, or maybe artists that had success years ago, and aren't finding so much these days.

I would say managing Waterdeep for two years, between '99 and 2001. That was something that had a huge impact on my life, because I think in the label world, I ended up lying a bit to cover my assets here and there with artists and managers, because I would drop a ball or something. I look back on that time period and after I got out of the label world and realized some of the wrong priorities that I had – managing a band and getting close to a band, and really fighting for them everyday, and knowing the heart of the artist has changed the way that I approach life, the way that I approach the artists, and ultimately, I believe that the most important thing in this whole entire process is the heart of the artist, the gifts that they have from God, and the preciousness and the vulnerability and the super-sensitivity that they have. That's why they can write songs that make thousands of people cry, and I can't.

That's where I care very, very much about an artist, and for 10 years now as an independent promotions person if I can get close to an artist, I always want to be up-front and very, very honest with them and not sell them a bill of goods, and really honor them and the gifts they have, because without that, radio stations have no great music to play. I have no great music to promote. People have no great records to go buy – it really has always got to be about the artist and their heart. I would say that if anything does frustrate me a little bit, is that at times a radio person can be somewhat cavalier about the gift, and can be cavalier about, "Oh, that's not a hit," or, "Well, that guy used to deliver hits, but no more." I understand that they have to approach all of this differently because they've got 75 records coming at them every week, and I'm not working 75 records. But they've got so much coming at them, and they have a very, very hard job to do. I think that through the '80s when I was working in radio, and I was not good at it. It's a good thing I got out of radio and got to the other side of the phone. Radio people are the hardest working people in show business, but they have to approach the art and the music differently. But at times it feels like it's a little bit cavalier, and a little bit dismissive, and I wish radio people could stop and maybe get to know the artists and their heart.

Clore: What's your number one professional highlight?

I have to go back to Amy Grant in 1988, to the *Lead Me On* record. *CCM Magazine* put out a book, *CCM Presents: The 100 Greatest Albums in Christian Music*, and *Lead Me On* was their number one pick. I was fresh in the label at Myrrh Records. And they hired me, and very shortly thereafter, the person who hired me in radio left, so I was on my own. The Word bigwigs came in and gave me a cassette to cram on, overnight, of the *Lead Me On* record. And so I probably listened to it four or five times, and I was a big Amy Grant fan already. Had seen her numerous times in concert and played all of her records through the '80s, and of course I had a crush on her before I was married, like all able-bodied, red-blooded American Christian men had.

Clore: Certainly.

I came in with guns blazing the next morning into that meeting and said "Saved by Love" needed to be the first single from that record, and everybody was aghast. They disagreed, and I stuck to my guns. I think "Saved by Love" was the song of the year that year, the number one song at radio that year. And my point was that people at radio needed to be reminded that Amy Grant was one of us – she'd been on pop radio. She had somewhat of a controversial interview in *Rolling Stone*. She had music videos that all of a sudden didn't look so "Christian" anymore, per se, and so I felt like if we could just deliver a song where she said "Jesus" in it, and it was about being a mom and a wife, addressing exactly who was listening to Christian radio – it would be the right thing to do. And it was the first of four number one songs on that record. The song that everybody else wanted, "Lead Me On," ended up being the second single and another number one. So that was four number ones and just a pivotal, monumental, watershed record in our industry. And I got to be the radio promotion person for that.

I've had lots of great experiences in my career, but I still go back to that one as being a real magical moment in my life, and the week the single, "Saved by Love," shipped to Christian radio, was the week our first kid was born. It was just a really, really sweet time for me.

Clore's Summary:

I don't know how to teach you to love and be passionate about music, but if you are reading, it probably registers with you somewhere. Take to heart the general energy of a man like Chris Hauser. Do what you can to spark this level of excitement in your life. If you have never had it, it will change you. If you used to have it, I deeply hope you can get it back soon.

Quality Communication

Proper communication in today's music industry is very important. Not that it hasn't always been, but it is more important than ever, and by "proper" I do not mean formal.

Consider the unending messages transmitted in today's world. Think about how you receive the information that is coming your way. What stands out to you? What actually causes you to stop and interact?

Think through what you are saying, *before you say it*. If you have nothing to say, do not force it. Find your rhythm. Keep it natural. Let people in. Use common sense. Some information was never intended to be shared online.

These thoughts apply not only to those in the spotlight, but also business-to-business relationships within the industry.

Communication is vital, and communication is synonymous with content. Quality communication is quality content is quality communication.

Be present, continuously, but please think ahead about the messages you tell the Internet.

Mark Hollingsworth

*I believe that the many "creative types" have been put
on a pedestal, or at least catered-to when they needed to
be learning additional abilities beyond just their artsy/
creative sensibilities.*

We all need mentors – people we can look up to.
Those we can watch and learn from. This interview is with one of my most important mentors.

Mark Hollingsworth is a guy you need to know. The
wealth of knowledge he contains is intimidating, but he
is not. He is the kind of guy who has experienced more
of the music industry, and this world in general, than me
and you (and a few other people) combined. Mark has
managed artists (Petra, Sixpence None the Richer, Steve
Taylor, etc.), worked at record labels, worked at retail
chains, booked/promoted concerts (nearly 2,000 combined), been a published writer in over 25 magazines,
has been music/program director at four different Rock
radio stations and was even the GM of a minor league
hockey franchise at one point. Mark released his first

book, *Embracing the Gray: A Wing, a Prayer, and a Doubter's Resolve* (Wheatmark Press), in 2010.

Mark spends his time as Manager of Radio Marketing, for an amazing organization called Compassion International, a Christian, third-world child-development ministry that assists one million kids in desperately poor situations in 25 countries.

Referring to him as a "renaissance man" does not feel adequate.

I had the life-changing opportunity to intern for Mark at Compassion International in 2002.

Clore: After nearly three decades as part of the music industry, what aspect of it still piques your interest? What challenges you?

Actually, I started in 1973 during my freshman year in college where I promoted shows and began writing reviews in the campus paper…so it's been 36+ years.

I am still passionate about quality live performances… whether it's the bombast of U2's 360 Degree Tour in stadiums, or Muse or MUTEMATH tearing up a packed theater. I can also be moved by David Wilcox's storytelling or Monte Montgomery's guitar wizardry in an intimate club setting.

As far as challenges, I think we're all more than a little curious about how to find a reasonable financial platform from which to mass-market music. The traditional record label-based model is obviously deteriorating. There are many ideas being tried on the Internet, but there doesn't seem to be any systems that are working consistently to break new artists. Twenty years ago, an artist was probably competing against 1,000 other new acts per year. A decade ago, it was more like 10,000, when the Internet was really starting to click. Now, it's probably 10 million or more. There's just an awful lot of competition for people's eyes, ears, and most importantly, their passion. Every year there seems to be a few that break out like Sufjan Stevens or Sigur Ros or Death Cab For Cutie, but there are millions that can't seem to get anyone's attention, and, honestly, how could they? There's just so much noise to cut through. It always comes back to having great songs, delivered with passion and skill before people who can help carry your torch for you. The web certainly helps level the field, but there are so many people packed onto that grid it's hard to find room to move and really garner momentum-building attention.

Clore: During your years in management, what were some of the most important things you learned about handling the business side of a creative type?

I believe that the many "creative types" have been put on a pedestal, or at least catered-to when they needed to be learning additional abilities beyond just their artsy/creative sensibilities. Artists not only have to have talent, but also be driven, have common sense, and people skills. All are necessary to make it these days. I guess in my many years managing artists, I tried to bring all those out in artists. They may have kicked and screamed about it sometimes, but ultimately, they were glad to learn more about staying on a budget, taking care of vehicles, sending "thank-yous" out, doing tons of interviews, etc. All of those Dove and GRAMMY Awards didn't just come about because they wrote catchy tunes.

Clore: What historical segments of music do you look to for inspiration and/or lessons? How has understanding, and having a strong knowledge of history impacted your career?

Like I mentioned earlier, I've always had a deep respect for artists who honed their craft through lots of live performance. That's where you really figure out how to connect with an audience viscerally through the songs and what you communicate in other ways.

As far as managers go, I always like guys who were committed to their artists for a long time: Paul McGuinness (U2), Brian Epstein (The Beatles), Herbie Herbert (Journey), Cliff Burnstein (Def Leppard, Metallica, Muse), Ray Daniels (Rush), Jon Landau (Springsteen), and Tony Smith (Genesis, Phil Collins) all come to mind. They started with their artists and helped lead them through their initial lean times, amazing growth spurts, and then partnered with them through (in most cases) some good longevity.

As far as music that still moves me, I'm still fascinated with the romantic era of classical music from the 1800s. To me, it is still the highest, most passionate, form of music ever created. Rossini, Mussorgsky, Debussy, Liszt, Tchaikovsky, Wagner, and Dvorak are a few of my favorites – very influential in areas of Rock (the Progressive movement of everything from Yes to Muse), Broadway, and cinema scores.

From a historical standpoint, in CCM [Contemporary Christian Music] I am chagrined by lack of acknowledgement, let alone understanding, of where it all came from. Whether it's the call-and-response Gospel music from the cotton fields of the deep south that then melded into the Blues, then Rock and Roll; or even just being able to trace the beginnings of the Jesus Movement in the late 60s that was anchored in many ways by the heartfelt music from converted hippies. For Pete's sake, very few Christian radio music directors today even know Larry Norman, or Petra, or Amy Grant. This lack of heritage also means lack of deep catalogue, and hence, there [are] diminishing returns when it comes to ongoing sales and touring capabilities for artists longer than about a decade (at best). When you look at *Billboard* you see so many classic artists still selling in the millions of units, but there is absolutely no correlation in CCM, and it all starts at the feet of Christian radio, which allows no room for playing any of those heritage acts that paved the way for where we are now. It's sad.

Clore: How has your current role with Compassion International been influenced by your preceding professional years?

In my role as Radio Marketing Manager for Compassion, I've been able to stay in touch with lots of folks that I grew up with in the '70s and '80s. Many of them are now GMs of stations, or even heads of entire networks. By being friends so long, we can talk in shorthand about what might work and not work in creating creative campaigns that will inspire their listening audiences to get involved with helping poor children around the world. Since '01, we've been able to raise about $140 million through these partnerships, and just so you know, I bring the idea to these folks all the time for giving heed to those classic Christian artists. It generally falls on deaf ears because they claim the research doesn't back up the idea. I respectfully tell them their research is skewed and wrong, but they are so far down that path now, they don't think there's any way to put the toothpaste back in the tube now (if I can mix metaphors).

Also, because I know many artists and managers from years gone by, it's great to be able to commiserate with them on concepts that could work with radio like tour tie-ins with stations/networks packages, overseas trips with listeners, new audio/video testimonial campaigns, and so on.

Clore: Your travel has always amazed me. Please share with us an updated number of countries you've visited, along with any other "fun facts" you may have tracked over the years.

I've been to 50 countries, many of them numerous times. More than 1,600 flights covering over a million miles. I'm blessed to be able to see the world through the perspective of so many beyond our borders. It has helped me become even more of a "citizen of the world" and not seeing things through the often narrow lens of Americana.

Clore: What's one "claim to fame"?

For years I know many people cursed at me indirectly whenever they would open an album, or cassette tape, or CD package and a paper insert would fall out with artist tour/merch info on one side and an appeal for helping the poor on the other. I came up with that while I was managing Petra in '82. Within a few years it became industry standard. Hundreds of millions of dollars in child sponsorships and t-shirt sales came from that.

Clore: Any good book recommendations? Any tips for those of us looking to learn from you?

I read about forty books a year, so there's a potential of a huge list. Here are a few that I think will help broaden one's perspective and inspire: Donald Miller's latest *A Million Miles in a Thousand Years*, Philip Yancey's *Soul Survivor, City of Joy* by Dominique LaPierre, *Traveling Mercies* by Anne Lamott, *Rich Christians in an Age of Hunger* by Ron Sider, *Irresistible Revolution* by Shane Claiborne, and *The Great Divorce* by C.S. Lewis come to mind.

In Ecclesiastes, the wise teacher states that, "There is nothing new under the sun," and I think that's just as true today as it was when written nearly 3,000 years ago. I think most ideas are just variations on previous themes. That goes for a lot of art, music, and literature, and certainly is true of marketing. Sometimes the best concepts are just recycled and repackaged from a previous generation or two. Don't be afraid to look back for intriguing ways to let people know about what you've created. When blended with new technologies you may come up with something that is fresh for this generation.

The preceding interview took place in January of 2010.

Unmet Expectations

I was watching "Metal Evolution" on *VH1 Classic*. The "Grunge" episode. There were musicians ripping on seemingly Grunge-influenced bands like Candlebox, Creed, etc. Whatever. My point is not to defend a particular band or era of music – that is all extremely subjective. What I do want to address is how angry people can become when their careers don't quite turn out like they had envisioned. Be very careful not to get caught up in their negative energy. It is not good or helpful, and only makes people more cynical and asshole-ish.

Look, I fully understand there are myriad reasons to hate the realities and confines of the music industry on the whole. That is why I wrote this book. But, we all must try and get beyond crushed dreams and the shrapnel of dubious lies, and live life to the fullest.

Things rarely work out as we hoped, expected or built up in our minds – just like Clark Griswold in *Christmas Vacation*. We often build things up in our minds to a point where if they don't work out, we have absolutely no idea how to respond, other than ripping on everyone else that did make it.

Taylor Swift is one of the most talented and engaging entertainers. One cannot deny the incredible "thing" she has going. She is spectacular. But I consistently hear people taking jabs at her. Why? Jealousy. Plain and simple. Taylor Swift has blown up to utterly gargantuan proportions, and she continues to make the right moves. But I still hear that she isn't a good singer, her songwriting is shallow, etc. Have you heard Bob Dylan "sing"?

Stop being negative.

It is one thing to not be a fan of something. It is another to simply try and tear it down because it is not you.

I don't like the New York Yankees or the New England Patriots, but I cannot deny the stellar legacy of both teams and their consistent competitive play.

Accept the fact that very, very, very few musicians will ever be rich and famous. If that is your dream, please check yourself. Don't give up, but do your best to not unintentionally tear everyone around you down because it didn't quite pan out like you hoped.

Michelle Tigard Kammerer

You have to be driven and never stop. Sometimes it takes years. You just CAN'T give up. Basically, find a way to make enough noise that someone listens.

Behind the show, there are some amazing people that you will never hear about. There are people that put in hours upon hours of unglamorous work, and they are often the people that keep it all moving.

Michelle Tigard Kammerer is a great example of this type. I hope you have the chance to meet her. She is one of the good ones.

At the original time of this interview in 2009, Michelle worked for Creative Artists Agency (CAA) in Nashville. CAA is one of the top talent agencies in the world, working with everything in the entertainment industry, including: music, television, movies, Broadway, marketing, literary, branding, gaming, etc. Michelle worked in the music department and more specifically, the Country Music Department where she worked with a roster of over 500 artists worldwide, but specifically focused on one hundred plus of CAA's Nashville Country Roster.

During her time at CAA, under Stan Barnett & Marc Dennis, she personally worked with: Lady Antebellum, Shania Twain, Willie Nelson, Alison Krauss, Montgomery Gentry, Billy Currington, Rodney Atkins, Joe Nichols, Kellie Pickler, Bill Engvall, Randy Travis, Travis Tritt, Keith Anderson, Trent Tomlinson, Heidi Newfield and The Lost Trailers. She helped book shows in arenas, coliseums and amphitheatres in the Midwest and Western Canada, plus fairs and festivals throughout the entire U.S.

In June 2011, Michelle accepted a position at Country Radio Broadcasters (CRB), as Director of Brand Marketing and Strategic Partnerships.

The story of Michelle and her husband Lucas is where you begin to find the real magic of a genuine and loving soul such as Michelle. Two years and three months of their overall relationship has been spent half a world away from the other.

Lucas served in the United States Army Reserve for two of his college years. Following the events of September 11, 2001, he decided he would become active and spent five years as part of the 101st Airborne Division, Infantry, United States Army. He was apart from Michelle for two tours of duty: Iraq for fourteen months in 2007 to 2008, and Afghanistan for more than eleven months in 2010 to 2011.

While Lucas was away, Michelle started an email blast to some of her closest family and friends where she updated those individuals about Lucas' day-to-day activities. It served two purposes: to attempt to share her burden with those that cared for and loved both of them, and to help those around her truly understand the realities of military combat. I am honored to have been one of those recipients, and it did alter my view of my compatriots abroad.

Michelle also threw herself wholly in to work during this time, but anyone that spent any time with her at all knew exactly where her heart was.

Clore: How about a quick intro, in your own words?

I'm a twenty-something (emphasis on the "something") country girl from small-town Kansas, who's been in love with Country music since I was old enough to listen. I had a dream to work with the music I loved and help get that music to as many people as possible. So after college, I packed up everything I owned and without knowing a soul in Nashville (or ever actually having been to Nashville), moved here. Sounds like a Country song, doesn't it?

Clore: During your time in the music industry, you've seen (up close) artists with huge teams around them, and artists that no one seems to care about. Especially considering personal relationships you have with artists of both sort, how do you mentally and emotionally approach working with these different types of artists?

Personally, I work with every artist the same way. Whether they are making a million dollars a night or playing for tips, they're all talented and special or we wouldn't be working with them. One of my mentors once told me, "Follow the music and the money will come." That's one of the coolest things about the music business – the guy who was working for peanuts one day can have a hit song and be the biggest thing in town the next week. So, I guess it goes back to the golden rule: "Treat everyone the way you'd want to be treated" (whether they're making you money or not).

Clore: When a musician has the urge to "make it" in the music world, what are your recommendations on where to start? Do you need to be in a particular geographic location, know certain people, have certain talent, have a certain drive?

Everyone's journey is different, but I would say use every resource you have. If you have something to say musically, go find a place to play in front of an audience. If you know people in the music industry or radio, go talk to them. If you have Pro Tools on your computer, record some stuff. If there's a talent competition, enter it. There's no set "career ladder" to climb. I've seen artists become huge overnight because of MySpace and YouTube, so use those too. You have to be driven and never stop. Sometimes it takes years. You just CAN'T give up. Basically, find a way to make enough noise that someone listens.

Clore: For the younger generation of music industry types, what would you say to them is the most important topic/subject to be knowledgeable about today?

I think the digital media world is a MUST right now. It used to be a side note in the music business blueprint, but now it's front and center. Know how to use iTunes, Facebook, YouTube, Twitter, cell phone ringtones, and anything else you can find. As an artist, using those digitals tools, you can build a fan base, sell your own records & merchandise, and, if you're going after a record deal, can show the label you have a loyal following that will purchase the music you're wanting to make with them. As a music businessperson, you need to know the best way to market your artist and that is digital media, hands down. The game has changed and it's going to be the most creative and digitally savvy that are going to win.

Clore: You have been involved with creating and/or implementing many great events in the Nashville area (where you call home). What have been some of your highlights, and learning moments, during said events.

I think working with Lady Antebellum from day one was a real learning experience. The first night I saw them, there were about 12 people in the room. Being part of the launching process, and watching them grow as artists has been a true honor. Seeing them sing in front of thousands of people now just makes my heart smile. Also, I've been blessed to work with a company that believes in giving back. I've headed up the "CAA Supports Our Soldiers Campaign," where CAA and our clients send care packages every month to U.S. soldiers overseas; Red Cross Blood Drives, where managers, promoters, clients and others in the music industry donate their blood to make a difference; and the Young Nashville Party, which is an annual charity event hosted by CAA for Nashville's "most influential young industry professionals," including CAA clients, music industry executives and young entrepreneurs. Being able to help artists give back to their fans and show the same love they are given is a true highlight.

Clore: What is it about music that keeps you going? Did you always "know" you would land in this industry?

Music is in my soul. It's the language that brings us all together. It's the song that comes on the radio that makes whatever you're going through okay. I've had music in my head for as long as I can remember. It's a part of me. There was never really a choice whether I'd go into the music industry or not. I came to Nashville not knowing a soul, but knowing I had to be a part of what I loved. So, I worked hard, networked my way in and have been learning and growing ever sense. Truly,

I don't know where my road will lead, but I know there's way too much good music out there, and as long as I'm here, I'm going to try it.

Power In Representation

We are only as powerful as what we represent.

Yes, our skills and knowledge increase and compound over time, making us more marketable as we go along, but, the older we get, the less appealing we become (in *most* circumstances). So, on the continuum of our finite lives, the window for success and power is pretty limited.

Consider why people want to talk with you, or why you want to talk with most others. Usually, it's for what's on the other side, giving the temporary delusion that the person in the middle has power. Yeah, they technically do in that moment, but what happens when their representative power ends?

I started my career working with very independent artists. More often than not, no one cared. It's amazing how some of those same people responded (usually for the first time) differently when I was able to attach a major record label after my name. Those first few years of my career have, and will continue to, provide my personal motivation. Motivation to do better than them.

Motivation to treat people better, no matter their role. Motivation to win.

Winning can mean a lot of things. I want to make money as much as the next person, but there are plenty of things not worth sacrificing to achieve monetary success and fleeting fame. It all eventually fades away anyway.

The great Jim Foglesong once told me, "John, someone is always watching." I can think of few lessons in my life that have impacted like that one. It was a seemingly simple thought, but it is not. It is powerful.

Whether discussing horse racing, selling paper or the music industry, if the profitable performance has ended, so have the hangers-on, and it rarely ends respectfully. The once-successful artist may eventually receive much-deserved acclaim, like Johnny Cash did, but when the success runs out, normally the party is over.

When you start to think you are an invincible badass, think about why people even care about you to start with.

Sage Keffer

We really don't need you here. There's thousands of you coming in here every day, and when you leave, no one's going to miss you.

Spend any time in the entertainment industry, and you will know that sentiment is true. That sentiment is exactly why I will never understand, and always have an incredible respect for, all artists with a dream.

Sage Keffer is one of those artists, and the above line was told to him within 10 days of arriving to Nashville.

Incredible belief in yourself is the only thing that can keep you going in moments like that one and the countless similar moments that comprise the life of an artist trying to "make it." Exactly what "making it" is, is a whole other topic unto itself, but for our purposes here, we will just assume it means being signed to a major record label, having high-powered management, receiving regular radio airplay, playing big shows all around the country – and having a team of people around you that help pull all of this off.

Going it solo is a different ballgame. Going it solo is typically harder because you are likely receiving far fewer ego boosts that fuel you when times get tough. (I realize some artists are far happier remaining "solo," and for that I can't blame them one bit, but you see the point).

I personally know a number of people who continue to pound the pavement with few true signs of encouragement along the way. If you spend five minutes with Sage Keffer, you will be overwhelmed by his absolute positivity, and it is no wonder the dude stays at it despite the utter BS he encounters from fake people, with fake promises in a generally fake town.

In early 2010 I had the opportunity to chat with Sage about his time in Nashville, his dreams and what keeps him moving forward.

Clore: Did you have a moment in time where you knew music is what you would pursue at all costs?

When I was a little kid, I wanted to be all kinds of different things. All kinds of great, wonderful things that we all dream of as little kids. I've wanted to do music ever since I was about five or six, especially after my dad took me to see Neil Diamond. I was amazed at the presence that was on stage; I was really blown away, and thought I'd really like to do something like that. I grew up singing, acting and doing a lot of live theater. Live performance is where I really get my thrill. It's where I've always drawn my inspiration to do this kind of thing.

Clore: How has your upbringing, combined with your time in Nashville and your time on the road, shaped you in to who you are today?

Quite a few things helped shape me. My dad was real tough on me. In terms of any kind of rejection one may face in a place like Nashville, let's just say they haven't faced my dad. But, along with the encouragement I received from my mom growing up, it helped me have a tough skin while not becoming too doubtful. I've always been able to see the hope. I was able to still be inspired and still dream, and recognize there are people that may not believe in you, but that doesn't mean you can't do unbelievable things. Not that I have, but I know that if it wasn't for the encouragement from my mom, I would've gotten nowhere.

When I first moved to Nashville, I was awestruck by the size and lights of the city. Before I made the move, a former girlfriend helped connect me with someone she knew in Nashville who gave me a place to stay for a few nights, plus some work with their construction company.

I had taken a couple of music business classes in college, which didn't inform me about the music business all that much, but that was the knowledge I had. Within my first couple of weeks in town, I was very fortunate to meet with some good people.

Through some connections, I got a meeting with some-one at SESAC [a performing rights organization] in Nashville. During the meeting, the guy proceeded to tell me, "Well Sage, we really don't need you here. There's thousands of you coming in here every day, and when you leave, no one's going to miss you." I hadn't even been heard yet, by anyone, including the man behind the desk.

Like anybody, it took me a couple of days to get past that one, but I got right back at it.

I've realized you need to have both doubters and encour-agers in your life so that you can realistically take a look at what you're doing, and try to accomplish all that you can.

Clore: What is your biggest challenge as an artist in 2010, and if you could change one thing about how the music industry currently functions, what would it be?

The biggest challenge as an artist is that it takes a lot of money to be invested before you get a return on that money. Personally, I'm about to finish up my sophomore album, and trying to figure out what comes next is definitely a challenge.

The biggest challenge as an industry is how to make money off music in the digital age. As an industry, we have to figure out how to create a new business model. I'm guessing that the model will be something like on-demand streaming, used as a loss leader to sell other things. Either way, we have got to get our hands around this and make some decisions quickly on what this industry's going to do so that it doesn't fall apart.

Clore: What do you consider your greatest accomplishment(s) of your music career? How have these accomplishments propelled you forward, or perhaps changed the course you were on at the time?

There are quite a few things I feel very fortunate to have been a part of. First thing that comes to mind is being a part of Tin Pan South, which I consider to be the most incredible festival that Nashville has. This year marks my eighth consecutive year to be a part of it.

The second thing is having made it to the finals of "Nashville Star," seasons one, two and four. I never made it to the TV portion, but to experience the finals – those three seasons gave me an iron stomach. I'm not as concerned when I play in front of people anymore. And through that experience I learned that no matter how you do, you're going to still wake up the next day and be fine.

"Nashville Star" changed my course as much as anything. I learned a lot about how the business works through that show, especially because the show is only concerned with ratings. They don't really care about your career, so it teaches you to not take anything personally.

One of my biggest achievements is being a part of the CMA Music Festival. June 2010 will mark my sixth year to be a part of it as an independent artist. I've always had one of the busiest booths at the festival. The last two or three years I haven't even had lunch because my line has been non-stop, and for that I'm so thankful. I feel a lot of artists don't recognize just how thankful they should be for their fans. I make it a real point to let my fans know just how wonderful they are.

My latest highlight was being a part of a reality show with Ted Nugent called "Runnin' Wild...From Ted Nugent." I won. I was promised major prizes and money throughout the process of auditions and filming. None have been received. So, it was a highlight, in that I learned much. It was hell being hunted by Ted Nugent while being deprived of food, water, sleep and experiencing hypothermia, none of which was revealed on the show. There is a lot to learn in a situation like that.

Clore: How do you stay in touch with your fans, and what types of things do you do to keep them engaged?

I need to do more of this. I stay in touch through e-mail, Facebook, Twitter, etc., but there's only so much I can do in the course of the day when I'm handling everything for myself: booking, marketing, songwriting, performing, practicing. I have a few people helping me out, but boy do I need more, specifically people that know more about it than I do.

Clore: To the new artists out there, what's your biggest piece of advice?

A fan of mine recently called saying she wanted to become an artist. I told her about the guy from SESAC and what he said. I told her I have not faced rejection in Nashville, but that I've faced people who said they were going to do one thing, and then never got around to it. I told her that she's beautiful just like everyone else, and that no one's going to miss her. I told her you've got to plan on being here at least 10 years, and if you're not willing to sacrifice at least that, don't even bother.

You've also got to believe in yourself more than anyone else does. Don't be unrealistic. Don't be dependent on others for approval.

Clore: If you had it to do all over again, would you change a thing?

I would liken that answer to seeing an overwhelmingly good looking woman that you want to ask to dance to any 20/20 hindsight I have in the music business. I would have been more courageous. I would have acted a little faster. All too often we all let fear tell us we don't have a snowball's chance in hell. Yet, sometimes a girl will say "Yes." But you'll never know if you don't ask. Like the music industry, I wish I'd asked a few more girls on that ol' dance floor.

Other than that, I feel pretty good about what I've done.

Clore's Summary:

Tenacity. Courage. Commitment. Bravery. Mental toughness. – Learn these things from Sage. He is an amazing man with a bigger heart than most people can even imagine.

An Anti-Piracy Rant

The more time goes by, the more frustrated I get on the music-piracy issue. I have tried again and again to be cool about it and tell myself that it will be okay. That it's just part of the "new school" way of doing things and it will all work out.

But it isn't. Not even close.

I am all about sharing my stuff and passing my interests off on others, but it never crosses my mind to copy all of my crap and let them have it, music or otherwise, and they should not feel entitled to it.

Piracy is nothing new. Let's be honest about that. Not even in the music industry, but its deep, deep impact is now being felt in a way it never has. Ten years into the digital age, I see evidence all of the time that the industry I love is drastically changing. I realize many apart from the industry love that. They are "sticking it to the man" and "getting what is owed them after buying all of those terrible songs packaged with the one good one." Trust me, I get that sentiment, but goodness gracious, at what cost?

It baffles me that people steal music (and other digital data) at far too many corners and carry on with life thinking it will all keep coming like it always has.

Let's be clear: music will continue to be written and recorded no matter how much the music industry of the past 40 years continues to devolve. I am not naïve enough to think the mass of society cares about said devolvement, but in more ways than most want to acknowledge, it will affect what music they ever become aware of.

I certainly have issues with the whole of the music industry of which I currently make my living. It is not close to perfect. One thing I can say with absolute certainty is that I am one of those who loves music so deeply that I am not in Nashville striving for filthy riches. There is truly no other industry that remotely interests me. For a while, I thought I would try and work for an MLB team someday, but I realized I don't love that industry enough to simultaneously work in it, deal with the problems, politics and injustices, and remain a true fan. I am not here to work for free, but I assure you my passion for music will sustain many a less-than-ideal salary.

The Internet is the new radio. The thing is, it is far more powerful and with many more tools. Either way, it is a tremendous marketing vehicle where we learn about all sorts of new things, including music. As I write this, I am listening to a free download sampler from *SPIN Magazine.* Hopefully there will be a song or two that will really grab my attention. Then, I will very likely engage and transact with that act on some level (buying a CD, t-shirt, concert ticket, telling my friends, etc.), but for the rest that do not grab my attention, at least I was exposed to them.

Yes, one must get a product out into the marketplace through sampling, etc., but at some point, free has to run out. You may get a free sample at Costco, but if you want to take more home, you have to give them your money.

Just because a transfer of (any) information can take place on the Internet, that does not mean it should be free. What is the deal with people thinking Internet equals free? Few things bewilder me more. I am not saying every single product in all of creation should cost something, but the bulk of products and services are not free.

I realize music needs to get better in a lot of ways, but there are plenty of absolutely amazing songs and artists coming out every year. (Have you heard The National, MGMT, Manchester Orchestra, Kopecky Family Band, Florence + The Machine, The Head and The Heart, The Avett Brothers, Ryan Adams, Fitz and The Tantrums, Dawes, Mumford & Sons, Foxy Shazam, Jamey Johnson, etc., etc., etc.?)

If you are getting off on sending a statement to the "evil music industry," fine. If you don't even realize that stealing music is wrong, get a freaking clue. Either way, keep in mind that the very artists that provide the soundtrack to your life are, and will continue to be, impacted if you never send any of your money their way.

Please consider not being paid for your work. Trust me, it sucks.

Brenda Lee

*I was always welcome at Graceland if I wanted to go,
but I never would infringe on his privacy, because he
had so very little of it.*

Brenda Lee's story reads like a fairytale. Sweet, young,
not-rich girl from the Deep South with an excep-
tional voice encounters great opportunities, takes
them and works super hard along the way. Eventually
performs at The Ryman Auditorium on the bill with
Elvis Presley, and becomes a member of both the Rock
and Roll and Country Music Halls of Fame.

The more I consider the life of Brenda Lee, the more I
absolutely adore her. Her history and accolades hold up
against nearly any other musician in the history of popular recorded music, and she has been married to the
same man for a long, long time. She is not strung out on
drugs, or on her way back into rehab. She still has great
industry relationships and is far from desolate.

The Beatles opened for Brenda Lee in the early 1960s,
multiple times. Most are confused by this, including

Brenda. She tried to get them signed, but the label passed.

Little Miss Dynamite is best-known for her recordings, "I'm Sorry," and "Rockin' Around the Christmas Tree." Two absolutely timeless classic songs in popular culture.

Her first recording contract was signed in 1956.

She counts among her friends: Elton John, Keith Richards, and the late, Elvis Aaron Presley.

John Lennon said of Brenda, "She has the greatest Rock and Roll voice of them all."

The following conversation took place Thursday, February 3, 2011. I am thankful that Jackie Monaghan, the wonderful person who connected me to Brenda, was part of the conversation. Jackie became head of Brenda's fan club when she was 15 years old, and has worked directly with Brenda for many years since that time.

Clore: Brenda, I wanted to share with you that Mr. Jim Foglesong is also part of this book.

Oh, I love Jim. What a great guy. He had a lot of input on my career in those days and was just a very, kind of like Owen Bradley in a way, with his loyalty to his artists, which a lot of times today you don't find. That's not to say that that's a bad thing, but back then, I feel like in the upper echelons of the recording industry, artists really meant something personally to the labels. Sometimes I find that missing today, maybe I'm wrong, but sometimes I find that personal aspect missing.

Jackie: John, just to show you the difference – when I started working with Brenda, and this would have been early '70s, Brenda would take a large shopping bag full of tapes, and in those days they were the reel-to-reels. She would carry the boxes of reel-to-reels of songs that had been submitted to her from all of the top writers in town, because everybody wanted a Brenda Lee cut in those days. So Brenda would load up the shopping bag full with the tapes and carry them down to Owen Bradley's office, down on Sixteenth [Avenue, in Nashville] when it was Decca. It was Decca in those days. Owen would have a stack, like a mile high of reels that had come in to him. They would take the afternoon and sit together and go through the songs. Now, how unusual is that?

Clore: Was this at the Quonset Hut?

It was right across the street at the offices, but that's where we recorded everything, was at the Quonset Hut. And then we went on to the barn, when Owen had the barn. But yeah, you had a real personal relationship with your producer and it wasn't like, "Get this in, get this out." He really took time and trouble to find the right songs. Owen did, at least. And it was a joy – it wasn't work. It was just a real joy to go through that process, and I think that's somewhat missing today.

Jackie: Plus you didn't have to record everything Owen published.

No. And then too, of course this has been around since day one, of artists just putting their names on songs that they had nothing to do with, and I'm sure that still goes on today. But I was one of those artists that said, "You know what, I had nothing to do with that, I don't need a part of that. I just want the song to sing. Hopefully it will do well for me and in turn it will do well for you."

Clore: I'm assuming you are glad at this point in life that you did that?

I am glad that I did that, because I had nothing to do with those. I was offered so many times, "If you'll do my song, I'll give you half." I said, "You don't need to give me half, I'm going to do your song anyway, because I love your song. Your song is good." I've had that happen to me so many times. I had nothing to do with that process, that creativity, so I certainly wasn't going to take kudos for something I didn't do.

Clore: You are a rare one. – I want to go back to early, early in your life at church. I know that was part of your earlier, maybe your only, musical influence. Can you tell me about that – what it was like at church? Did you sing in front of everyone early on?

Like Jackie said, and I don't know how she knows because she's a Yankee, [laughter] but she says, "When you're a poor daughter of the South," which I was, "You don't have many outlets to hear music," or I didn't, and the church was our social life, as well as our spiritual life. It was our social life, and that's where I heard music. That's where a lot of my roots and heritage come from, and that's where, I guess without even realizing it, I honed a lot of what my voice became to be, and my style.

And then there was an old black man that set up at the end of the dirt road where I lived, at the candy store where I used to go and stand on the counter and sing. And people would give us money for that. Pennies and nickels – what have you. And this old black man used to sing outside and I was just mesmerized by him even though I was only four, five, six years old – whatever I was at the time – I was just very young. I didn't even know what he was singing. I know what it is now. I know it's Rhythm and Blues, but I had no idea what it was called then, I just knew that I liked it. Between listening to Gospel and getting a touch of that every once in a while, I think that's basically where and how I started my musical life.

Jackie: Brenda, didn't you tour with a little quartet, too?

I did. I toured with a quartet called The Masterworkers Quartet, and they were a wonderful Gospel group out of Georgia. We used to sing in churches, and VFWs, and high school gymnasiums and wherever we could sing.

Jackie: And you would have been how old?

I would have been six, seven, eight. Somewhere along in there.

Clore: Wow. – I saw an interview where you were talking about not knowing where your musical influences came from. Now, you just talked about the guy at the candy store and church – but really, other than that...

No, because I didn't have a record player or anything so I wasn't subjected to any other talent. I didn't know about other people. I just thought that people sang in church and that's how you sang, and that's what you did. Then we did have a radio at one point and we could only listen to it at certain times because we didn't have a lot of money to buy batteries. So, our listening time was kind of doled out between daddy's baseball games and the Grand Ole Opry. So then I learned that there were other singers, but I didn't know who they were.

And then when I was little, my mother would sing me to sleep at night. She was a pretty darn good little singer herself, and she would sing Hank Williams songs, because I guess that was her favorite. And then of course I didn't know what she was singing. I just knew that I liked the song – and then when I started singing I started singing those songs. Then I learned who Mr. Hank was, and my first record, of course, was "Jambalaya." And I always loved his songs.

Then I met my manager, and through his worldliness – for lack of a better word – he introduced me to people like Bessie Smith and Judy Garland and Sophie Tucker and Billie Holiday and Sinatra and Tony Bennett...Édith Piaf and people like that that I really sort of, kind of had a history of knowing these people when I was 10 years old, 11 years old, 12 years old.

Clore: How about Mahalia Jackson?

Oh, well she was my favorite. Yeah. I adored her.

Clore: Where were you first introduced to Mahalia?

Mahalia came to Nashville and played The Ryman and I went to see the show. I was just absolutely mesmerized. She just became one of my heroes because she just stood up there as bold as day, with just an organ behind her, and just opened that mouth and that glorious, big bois-terous voice came out and I thought to myself, "Now, that's what I want to do. I want to be on that stage some-day and I want to sing good and loud like that."

Clore: I would love to hear you talk about what you were really thinking around age nine, 10, 11, when things really started happening. It seems like it was the most natural thing in the world to you. Is that how you felt?

Singin' was the most natural thing to me, and I wasn't frightened. When I came to Nashville to record I wasn't frightened of the musicians. I wasn't frightened of the studio. And God love 'em, even though I was young and green, they respected me and respected my talent. I've always thanked all of the guys for that. A lot of them went on, of course, to be on "The A Team," which recorded all of my hits, just about. It was a lot of fun to me, but the stage was always like my second home. I didn't have to take off one hat to be Brenda Lee and put on another hat to be Brenda Tarpley. I was just the same everywhere I went.

Clore: How about Red Foley? What are some of your primary Red Foley memories?

Red Foley discovered me in Augusta, Georgia. At that time – I think it was 1954 – he had *The Ozark Jubilee* network television show and believed enough in me to let me be on that show, which was unheard of because he had an offshoot of that show called *The Junior Jubilee*, which was just for children, but he put me on the adult portion. I was seen by a columnist in New York – Jack O'Brian – who wrote me up stellar, and from that I went on to do, without a record or anything, just *The Red Foley Show* that had kind of catapulted me in to the homes of America. I went on to do *The Perry Como Show, The Steve Allen Show, The Ed Sullivan Show* – and I did that all without a record, which was unheard of back then.

Mr. Foley was a mentor personally, as well as professionally, and I loved him dearly. I would probably be singing somewhere, because that was my dream, was to sing. I didn't have an agenda. I wasn't worried about selling records. Didn't know anything about that. Wasn't worried about having hits. I didn't know anything about charts. I just wanted to sing, and because of him he gave me the opportunity to break out of my little hometown of probably where I'd still be, singing somewhere, but he gave me the opportunity to further my dream in life. I tried to respect that gift. I tried to do the best I can with it, and always think about him whenever I do anything because he was such a driving force back then of introducing me to the world.

Clore: How was your mom through all of these early events? It sounds like she was supportive.

My mom was the most supportive mom, and she was not a stage mom, but she could be if she thought I was getting the raw end of the deal or getting taken advantage of. She didn't want to manage me. She didn't want to do any of that, but she wanted to make sure there were good, honest people around me. And she saw that there were good, honest people. She was always in my corner and gave up a lot for me.

Jackie: Brenda, tell John the story about how every week you and Grace would get on the bus and go to Springfield.

Oh Lord. Yeah, every weekend, mom and me, we'd get on a bus on Friday in Augusta, Georgia – on a Greyhound – and ride however many hours it took to get from Augusta to Springfield, Missouri, at that time. We would ride and get there sometime Saturday morning, go right over to the theater, rehearse, do the show, get back on the bus, get back to Augusta and I'd be in school on Monday morning.

Clore: Oh my goodness.

And we did that weekend after weekend after weekend after weekend, until we finally moved to Springfield [Missouri].

Clore: That is absolutely amazing.

Jackie: That was quite a trip. That had to be, what, 10, 12, 15 hours?

Oh, at least. And, no interstates.

Clore: I think that's what amazes me as much as anything else. When I think back on this era of touring, how spoiled people are today with flights and the interstates – what you all did back then is phenomenal.

Well, you know, back then, truly, you truly had to love it because there were barely any creature comforts. So it truly had to be a passion, and you just had to love it to be able to stick to the grueling schedule that was presented to you.

Clore: Do you know how old you were the first time you made that trip?

Probably nine, going on 10. Somewhere along in there.

Clore: I'm trying to think what I was doing at nine. – I'm not trying to jump away from that part of your career, but I'd love to talk about Owen Bradley. I'm curious where you think Brenda Lee's career would have gone, what direction, without Owen Bradley?

Without Owen Bradley, you know, whatever sound that people say – "That's the Brenda Lee Sound" – that's Owen Bradley. I think we were a great pair because I needed him, and he needed me. We gelled the first time we ever met even though I was a little girl. I respected him, and he respected me. I knew that he could get the very, very best out of me, in the best way possible, and he always did.

I could do a song, and he and mom were just alike. I could do a song and I could think, "Oh, that was really good, I really think I did a good take of that," and both of them would say, "Yeah, that was good, but you can do that better," and nine times out of 10 they were both right.

He was just a magical man when it came to music, choosing songs for his artists. He was very loyal, very honest, just a good, good friend and a good mentor. Helped Ronnie and I a lot with business decisions, and really cared about his artists – really cared if they were saving their money, were making the right decisions, really cared about the material he gave to them. It wasn't just a job to Owen. It was much like me, I think, a passion. It was just something he had to do. There was no way that he could not do what he did.

Clore: At that time in your career did you feel more comfortable on-stage or in the recording studio? Or did you love it all the same?

I loved all of it, but I've always loved the one-on-one with the audience. I love that. But I loved recording, too – because it wasn't like recording, it was like getting with a bunch of my friends and getting in there and, you know, back then we didn't write up the arrangements. Grady Martin would say, "Well, I think this lick would go good here," and Floyd Cramer would say, "Yeah, I think I'll tinkle the keys here." And Boots Randolph would say, "Yeah, I can put this little riff in here." You know, everybody had their input, the Anita Kerrs and everybody. And before you know it, we'd have a record.

Clore: I want to talk about the December night in 1957 when you were on the bill on the Opry, at The Ryman, with Elvis Presley.

Yeah, yeah, that was quite something. That was quite, quite something. Nice man and remained a real nice guy until his passing. Cared a lot about his roots. Cared a lot about his family. Cared a lot about his fans. And that's the tragedy of it all – that the people that he cared a lot about were not there in the end to help him. But he was always very nice to me. Couldn't have been any sweeter, and that was something, you know, for me to have my first appearance on the Opry and it to be with Elvis – I mean, how much better does it get?

Clore: It's phenomenal to hear even you be excited about that.

Oh, I was so excited! I was so, so excited. Just to be on The Opry was exciting enough, but to have him on it – it was like, "Oh, my Lord."

Jackie: Have you ever seen the picture of them together?

Clore: The dancing picture?

Jackie/Brenda: Yes.

Clore: I have. That is wonderful.

It's pretty cool, isn't it?

Clore: It really is. Was that from that night?

That was from that night.

Clore: Did you spend much time with him after that night?

We never worked together after that, because Elvis usually worked alone. But I saw him after that. I was always welcome at Graceland if I wanted to go, but I never would infringe on his privacy, because he had so very little of it. And if he invited me to Graceland, I would never go, because I thought, you know, I know he's doing that out of the goodness of his heart, but he never has time to do anything. I just didn't want to infringe on that privacy. We went to see shows in Vegas. A lot of the shows that we went to see we never even told Elvis we were there – we just wanted to go see him because we were fans.

Jackie: John, when I first went to work for [Brenda], I was probably 18. Elvis called the office one day. Brenda happened to be up there in a meeting with her manager. Elvis called the office and I answered the phone, and it was like the highlight of my life. He was calling to get some Brenda Lee records for the jukebox at Graceland.

Clore: Oh. My. Goodness.

Yeah, "Sweet Nothings" was his favorite song.

Clore: Speaking of that, how about Keith Richards allegedly listening to that song often before Stones shows? Have you talked to him about that, or ever heard that?

A friend of mine who used to work for Decca, who's now, he works with Elton, and The Stones, and various people. Tony King is his name. Great guy, lives in London, and he was telling me that Keith always listens to "Sweet Nothings" on his iPod before his show. I said, "Oh, you've got to be joking." He said, "No, I kid you not, he always does that." I said, "Oh, please get me an autographed picture" because, unfortunately, with all of my European travel, and with all of my work in England with all of the groups, including The Beatles, I never met The Stones. I never worked with them and I never met them. When he sent me the autographed picture I was so thrilled and across his forehead he wrote "Sweet Nothings." It was cute.

Clore: And I don't think that many people can say "I was always welcome at Graceland." That's quite an honor.

No, probably not, but I always was. And I've been to Graceland, but like I said, when you're just somebody like that that's bigger than life and every minute somebody's pulling at you and all – if you're truly a friend, you don't infringe on that time.

Clore: Yes. Absolutely. – I'm really interested in your time at The Hollywood Professional School.

Oh God, that was a blast.

Clore: What was that like?

Well, it was great and weird all at the same time. I mean, it was like, you'd be sitting in class and a casting director would come in and your teacher would stop class, and he'd say, "Okay, I'm looking for a girl, 5'2", blond hair, blue eyes, blah, blah" – and all of the sudden, "Okay, you'll do." "Pardon me, but we need her for a shoot," and she'd get up and leave class. I was used to normal school, and that was anything but normal. It was what it said – it was for professional children.

Clore: Did it change what you were doing on stage or in your media relations? What impact did it have on you?

Well, I met a lot of great folks there – a lot of great friends. Kurt Russell went there, a lot of kids went there that I met and was able to get to know and have relationships with today. One of my best friends, Sandy Ferra, who dated Elvis in the early days and is now married to Wink Martindale – she's one of my dear friends, and she kind of took me under her wing when I went out to California to go to school there. Here I was, I was what, fifteen? Looking twelve? And dressed in my little clothes. My little Mary Jane shoes and my little clothes that fit my little body, and there they were all looking like Annette. Needless to say it was a big, huge awakening for me. So she kind of took me under her wing. We went out shopping and got the correct clothes where I could sort of be in with these kids. But Mickey Rooney Jr. and all of these kids that go there, they were all hip...and it was just crazy.

Jackie: And Sandy looked like she should be dancing in Vegas...

[laughter]

Yeah, Sandy looked like a Vegas showgirl, and there I am in my little felt skirt without the poodle on it. Thank God I didn't have the poodle on it, and my buckskin bucks, with bobby socks, and they're all in hose and heels and God knows what else...

Jackie: Push-up bras...

Oh yeah, and filled them out, that was the most amazing thing. You know, it was a wake-up call for me. Is this how the other half of the world lives? Oh my God. I never knew there were girls like that until I went to California.

But we've remained friends all these years and talk to each other all of the time and reminisce about our days out in California. I'm just who I am so it didn't change me, it didn't make me grow up anymore, it was just...my eyes were wide open though, I'll tell you that.

Clore: How about today, as you reflect back on The Beatles specifically, knowing the impact, culturally and across the world they've had since back in '64 and prior. What are your thoughts about that, especially knowing you pitched them to Decca and they passed.

When I first worked with them, when they opened a show for me, I knew they were special. I knew they were special and I knew their sound was special. And I certainly knew their writing was. They were as different as night and day. They had four very distinct personalities, which should have never gotten along, but they were just precious. And to think that they opened shows for me…I don't even know how to talk about it. When people ask me, I'm like, "Yeah, they did." I was really huge back then in England, but to think that I took those guys their demo and all, and my record company passed up on 'em, and a year later they were just huge, huge, huge on the scene – but I knew they would be. I never had a doubt.

Clore: So this was '63 or '62, or both, when you were with them?

'61, '62 and maybe part of '63 – if I'm remembering correctly.

Clore: And The Who – did they open for you as well?

No, The Who we met over there on a TV show – "Battle of the Bands" – and I was a judge, and they were one of the bands.

Clore: My goodness.

Yeah, I think it was called – it might have been called "Battle of the Bands" – I can't remember if it was that one or "Ready, Steady Go." I can't remember, but yeah, that's how we met.

Clore: Do you listen to The Beatles today?

Yes, I do.

Clore: What are your primary musical interests?

I'm all over the place. I love Elton John, and I loved him from the time I discovered him in England as a fan and record buyer, to this day. We remain close and very good friends. But I'm all over the spectrum with voices and music and what have you. I try to listen to a little bit of everything, cause I think you can learn from everything, or at least dissect and figure out why that's doing what it's doing and why who's buying it and the reason they are. That's interesting to me.

Clore: Of all of these duets through the years – from Perry Como to Kris Kristofferson – can you share some of your favorites?

Well, Perry – Perry was such a laid-back guy, and just precious. And the thing that I remember about Perry and Steve – and I never called them that, I called them Mr. Allen and Mr. Como – was their respect for a little girl. They respected my talents and I certainly respected theirs. They didn't treat me like a child, and I think Jackie will agree with that. Even when I was a teenager and I was doing things with Tony Bennett, and Sophie Tucker, and all of those people, they never treated me like I was a child. So, I had great experiences with all of the acts that I've ever met and worked with. And I think I've met just about everybody. Sinatra I didn't meet, and there are some that I haven't met, but I've met my share, and I've learned at the feet of some great people. It's just been a wonderful experience.

Clore: What do you think is the reason you are able, to this day, to be able to have a semblance of a normal life? How are you still so together? Is it your faith? The people around you?

I think it has a lot to do with the people around me. I think it has a lot to do with my faith. Jackie will tell you that on a daily basis nobody ever told me I was good. Nobody ever said, "Hey, you're great. Hey, you're just so wonderful. You're this, you're that." That just wasn't said, so I wasn't spoiled. I knew that what I wanted to do was sing, and I was being allowed to do that. I was so grateful for that chance and to get to sing that I was willing to put the hours in, be disciplined, learn, listen, be good to my fans and I never wanted to be a star. That came sorta to me, out of the blue. I wanted people to hear me sing, but I never thought about all the trappings that went with it, so therefore I wasn't expecting anything, and everything that came my way I was very grateful for.

I've had very grounded people around me. I've had people like Jackie – who have loved me as a person, and not just as a product. And I think when you're just treated as a product, it really scars you. But when you're loved as a person and all of the other comes with it, and everybody's proud, and everybody's happy, I think that's what makes it to where you're not sitting in a corner crying because you don't have a number one record. I always say that's why there's numbers under one – you can't be number one all the time.

Clore: What do you hope for your legacy? Musically, professionally, whatever. What is it that you hope people remember about Brenda Lee?

Oh gosh. That's awfully hard to say. Musically, I would like to be remembered for my dedication to my craft and that I didn't sell out for commercialism's sake. I was very diligent about what I recorded and what I put out there, and the image that I portrayed to my fans, which was my image. And that I loved my fans, and still do to this day.

Personally, you want people to respect you and you want to obtain a place in the industry to where people do respect you and what you've given, and I think that I've achieved that to some extent.

Clore: Oh yes.

I have chosen to have a life outside the industry, and sometimes, I think, when you do that, you pay a little bit of a price for that. Because in the early days you're living, eating, breathing and sleeping it – and that's what you have to do if you want to attain in the industry what you need to attain. But at some point I said to myself, "I want a family, I want a husband, and I want to devote some of my life to that." So sometimes, I think, when you do that, you give up some things in order to do that. But those are the priorities that I wanted, and that's the road that I took and I'm not sorry that I did it.

Clore: How do you encourage and talk to younger people?

Just be true to yourself. Make sure whatever your aspirations are in life that they are your aspirations. They're not what somebody else wants you to do, because especially in this industry, it's very hard even if you love it, and it will be even harder if it's somebody else's dream. I can only speak to what I know. Make sure it's your passion, because there's going to be just as many valleys as there are mountains, and you're going to have to learn to navigate both.

Clore's Summary:

- The next time you complain about your work or travel conditions, think about Brenda Lee riding that Greyhound bus from Georgia to Missouri.

- Integrity. Brenda had countless opportunities to take co-writing credit on a song she had not written. She never did.

<u>Quotes not to miss</u>:

- "When I first worked with them, when they opened a show for me, I knew they were special." (referring to The Beatles)

- "I had great experiences with all of the acts that I've ever met and worked with. And I think I've met just about everybody."

- "Personally, you want people to respect you and you want to obtain a place in the industry to where people do respect you and what you've given, and I think that I've achieved that to some extent."

- "I always say that's why there's numbers under one – you can't be number one all the time."

Harrison in Benton

A long Interstate 57 in Southern Illinois there is a town called Benton. It is the home of the Rangers, and John Malkovich, and Rich Herrin. It was also the home of a lady by the name of Louise Harrison Caldwell, who happens to be the sister of one George Harrison, late of a band that went by the name – The Beatles. George paid a visit to Benton in September 1963. Louise was living in Benton, at the time, with her husband who had landed a coal mining manager job for Freeman Coal.

I grew up in another coal mining town 30 miles to the southeast of Benton, called Eldorado.

So the story goes that in September 1963, The Beatles took a vacation. John, Paul and Ringo went their own directions while George opted for Benton, Illinois to visit his sister, Louise. At this point in time, The Beatles had not appeared on *The Ed Sullivan Show* – that would come around four months later. In the meantime, George Harrison could wander the streets and square of Benton and go relatively unnoticed.

While in the area, Harrison made a visit to WFRX-AM in West Frankfort, Illinois – a town seven miles to the south of Benton. He met with a 17-year old female disc jockey by the name, Marcia Schafer (Marcia's married last name is Raubach). Marcia is widely believed to be the first disc jockey in the United States to have played a Beatles song on the air, "From Me To You."

Cindy A. Lee wrote about Marcia's experience in the February 11, 1995 edition of *Williamson County Life*. "It was during the summer of 1963 that Louise Harrison Caldwell would come to the station with records that had been made by The Beatles, which included her brother, George. 'She literally hitchhiked out to the station to bring his music to us,' Marcia said in recalling the numerous visits Louise made to the radio station in trying to promote her brother's music in the United States."

Around the end of 1994 and the beginning of 1995, plans were underway to demolish the former home of Louise Harrison, the house George had visited some thirty-one years prior.

Enter one of the biggest-hearted, and biggest Beatles fans, you're going to find. Bob Bartel was in the Benton-area on business in December 1994, and decided to look up the house he knew George had visited. "When I arrived, the backhoe was in the back, and I looked in the house and I thought, 'Well, there's nothing wrong with this house. It doesn't look like it had ever caught on fire. The house next door is empty. The house next door to it is empty.' I was like, 'Well, what's going on'?"

Bob Bartel's discovery began a mission in him that continues to this day – to save that house. He did save it at that time, but not without hundreds of hours of work, including extensive research, promotion and gathering of the right political figures that could ultimately make the call to save this historic landmark. The house still stands as of the year 2012. Bartel has officially become part of Beatles history as a result of his labors of love.

On the night of September 27, 1963, a Benton-based band by the name "The Four Vests" had a gig at the VFW Hall in my hometown, Eldorado, Illinois, a town with a population around 4,000 people. Harrison was in attendance that night, and what occurred is believed to be the first-ever performance of a Beatle on U.S. soil.

I grew up just a couple of blocks from that VFW building.

"Last fall, a young man from England named George Harrison visited his sister and brother-in-law in Benton," wrote Leslie G. Kannon in the February 9, 1964 edition of Evansville, Indiana's *The Sunday Courier And Press*. "While there, he went to the Veterans of Foreign Wars Club in Eldorado where a small combo was playing. He was asked to sing a few songs, and the response was enthusiastic – so much so that one man slapped young Harrison on the back, and commented: 'Son, you're pretty talented. You know, with the proper backing, you might really go someplace'."

Ebie McFarland

All of a sudden, the days of preparation and hours of standing meant nothing. The people that came to my "rescue" were there because somewhere along the road, I had helped them or made them feel as if they could trust me, and vice versa. In that moment all the work and stress made perfect sense.

Ebie McFarland is a fantastic publicist. I had the honor of being her co-worker for about a year in 2005, when we both worked as publicists for Kirt Webster's PR firm, Webster & Associates PR. I immediately knew she was a remarkable soul, and over time, that has been continually confirmed.

She has now started her own PR firm, Essential Broadcast Media, where she works with artists such as Darius Rucker, Eric Church, Clint Black and Ronnie Dunn. I cannot say enough good about Ebie. If you get the chance, work with her.

Clore: The world of PR and publicity is often invisible to most people. Can you give us a brief rundown of what publicists do?

Most simply, I would say that publicists assist clients in generating a message to the masses – through electronic, digital, or print media, primarily. Lately, in my experience, that "umbrella" has expanded to encompass all messaging from blogs to client-catered website items to beyond! It's a fantastic feeling to develop and design a brand and work hand-in-hand with the marketing teams to get that brand awareness.

Clore: Some seem made to handle the world of publicity; you are definitely one of those. Have you always known this would be your segment of the entertainment industry? Have there been "aha" moments along the way?

I truly enjoyed the challenge of "selling" people on ideas while in college, whether it was a new band or a special event. I wanted to share that enthusiasm as to why they should care. To be honest, I had no idea that the profession could be lucrative. I thought, "I'll do this for a few years then have to get a real job." I had that mindset because I feel like in college you have the flexibility to really put your creativity to good use, but at my university, I had no idea that it would become my full-time occupation.

I did have an "aha" moment. I was afforded the opportunity to work on the publicity for a speaking engagement in Nashville with Dr. Maya Angelou. The promoter of the event was not familiar with the market and asked me to assist in the production of the event. Suddenly, I was handling the catering, staging of the green room, the book signing (and subsequent satellite bookstore at the venue), AND booking the opening talent. The night of the event, I had worked since 5:00 am calling in every favor that I could to make the evening perfect: flowers, assorted cheeses, photographer…I even had our church use the seat-filler tickets to help a local outreach program as to not waste a single seat. I had previously met the leader for the Fisk Jubilee Singers and was representing Montgomery Gentry at the time and somehow managed to get them both to perform "Some People Change" as the opening act at no expense.

I was literally standing on the side of the stage to a sold out audience shifting my weight from left to right because my feet hurt so bad, and Dr. Angelou said, "People may forget what you say or what you do, but they will never forget the way you make them feel." All of a sudden, the days of preparation and hours of standing meant nothing. The people that came to my "rescue" were there because somewhere along the road, I had helped them or made them feel as if they could trust me, and vice versa. In that moment all the work and stress made perfect sense. To this day I have a series of eight photos from that event framed on my office wall directly to my left so I am reminded of that moment every day.

Clore: What has been your career highlight(s) so far? Is there a particular artist and/or band you aspire to work with someday?

There have been too many moments to count. I think there's a new one everyday, honestly. Watching my staff take ownership in the company and truly care for the artists is probably the best part. I love that their music inspires not only myself, but the talented women that work with me. I hope to work with all the acts on our roster for years to come.

Clore: What keeps you motivated amidst the thankless hours?

Obviously the continued success of an artists' career motivates us, but I think the team members and their creative juices and energy helps keep us from getting stuck in a rut. Surround yourself with great people and you will continue to be inspired and motivated!

Clore: How important is proper, strategic and thought-out communication over the course of an artist's career? And, as artist's careers ebb and flow, what role does publicity play in maintaining momentum?

Publicity, when used effectively, can absolutely propel a campaign into the limelight. Communication is a huge part of that. When the label, management, marketing team, radio staff, etc. are designing a campaign, it's imperative for them to share that timeline and overall goal with the publicity team in order to garner as many new eyeballs as possible because hopefully those impressions will translate into fans. If you know your audience, then you should be able to effectively create a campaign that targets them while allowing room for growth. There are so many great media avenues now, and I think knowing who your key "fans" or "tastemakers" are, for that particular act, can aid in the initial impression that audiences take away. If you lead with positive reviews and support from those key people, most avenues will follow suit, or at the very least give it an honest and fair listen before jumping to assumptions based on previous messaging.

Clore: What are some basic points that all of us can keep in mind as we work to improve how we communicate?

PICK UP THE PHONE! [laughter] I think some great points are the following:

1. Be present in your own life. When you're talking with someone via phone or in-person, be attentive and pay attention. You might learn something.

2. Treat people how you want to be treated. Back to what Dr. Angelou said, "People will never forget how you made them feel."

3. Care. If I call you because I have to, then that sets the tone for the entire conversation. But, if I call a reporter with a first listen and genuinely ask him/her to listen, that careful attention to detail is transferred and can only benefit your client and your company.

4. Don't overpromise. Commit to what you know you can get and then grow upon that.

5. Don't be afraid to ask for help. I am the first one to say "help me" when I have too much on my plate, or am feeling overwhelmed.

The preceding interview took place in November of 2010.

You probably aren't that cool

I live and work around relatively cool people, but I am often amazed at just how "awesome" some people think they are, including myself sometimes. When you are, or work around those that are remotely "famous," it is really easy to start thinking you really have it going on. People come to you for free tickets, free drinks, party invites, job hook-ups, whatever, and you really start to think you wield some pretty rockin' power.

And maybe you really are that cool, but I doubt it. And, when you start to "know" that you are cool, that is probably when it is going to quickly go off the rails and people will begin to despise you and your arrogant attitude.

There are plenty of people I feel this way about, not only in Nashville, Los Angeles, New York and Chicago, but many other locations.

By the way, not only right now, but throughout this book, I am including myself during these sarcasm-laden rants. I have spent plenty of time as the underdog, and have had just enough time as a "go-to guy" to feel what both ends of the spectrum are like. They are very different. I hope you are able to have enough of a balance of the two to know what they both feel like. Do not forget what it felt like on the other side. It is important to know how to approach those with some power, and it is important to know what it is like to have absolutely no access. One minute you may have access, but do not forget, it could be gone the next.

Who you are associated with plays in to this – big time. Put thought into who you closely associate yourself with. We often group reputations together. Make certain you are positioning yourself in a manner consistent with who you are. Of course there are people we would like to associate ourselves with but simply do not have access to. Continually ask yourself if that person or company or group of people are worth the effort and potential compromises you would have to make to achieve access.

Treat people well. My goodness, I have seen some real jerks in my time, and for no good reason whatsoever. Stop and consider how you are treating people, how you are sharing your opinion and whether or not you helped make their day better. Do you really like it when people treat you like crap?

Be consistent. You want people to know what to expect when they call on you for whatever reason. Do not be a different person when you are out late at night as opposed to who you are at home or in the office. I will never understand people who one day are super nice and bubbly, but the next seem to not even know me.

Do not meet someone two, three, four or five times. Remember them after the first time. I am not saying you are necessarily going to remember their name and every talking point about them, but for the love of God, pay enough attention that next time, you aren't "meeting them for the first time." I can think of multiple people I have met on numerous occasions because the first, second or third times, I was not in a position of power, or did not have access to the right artist(s). When they finally do allow space for me in their brain, I often harbor resentment towards them for being such an ass. Do your best to not treat people this way.

You may know a lot, but that does not mean you have to be a jerk about it. Sometimes it is for the betterment of all if you just keep your mouth shut. You may know this and that and whatever, but do not be the guy always spouting off and annoying the bejesus out of everyone. Over time, people do not like that person, regardless of knowledge.

Look, you are cool in some way. We all have something special we bring to this mess. Just be self-aware. In an industry and lifestyle where every single person is seemingly clawing for their own version of fame, know that your words and actions are still important, no matter the setting or context.

People are watching. Do not be an idiot.

John Ozier

Young artists have to really want to be an artist – it's not all glitz and glamour – in fact, it's the opposite.

In early 2010, I had the privilege to spend a day with an amazing individual: John Ozier. John and I tag-teamed the record label panel at a GRAMMY University educational event at a high school in historic Muscle Shoals, Alabama.

John Ozier is an A&R guy at Nashville's Curb Records. He is one of the nicest, most genuine people I have met during my time in the music industry. If you ever have the opportunity to engage with him, do not pass it up.

Clore: Tell us about the role of an A&R person in an artist's career. What is A&R? Why is it important?

A&R is essential in an artist's career. A&R, which stands for Artist & Repertoire, is in charge of signing new acts and finding songs for those artists. Everything involved in the creative aspect, musically, is the A&R department's responsibility. We help match artists with producers and help find a sound that will separate the artist from everyone else. Everything in an artist's career begins with A&R – without the music, artists don't exist. "Everything begins with a song," to quote NSAI [Nashville Songwriters Association International]. A&R is also responsible for recording budgets and making sure we create a quality sound within the given budget. Essentially, we provide creative direction for the artist, and oftentimes, serve as a liaison between the artist and the rest of the record company.

Clore: Looking back, how did your career path bring you to Curb Records?

When I was a sophomore in college at the University of Georgia, I called a friend, Drew Alexander, who was, at the time, running Curb's publishing department. He was nice enough to set up several meetings for me that summer. I was able to network and make a few relationships on Music Row. When I finished UGA, I moved to Chapel Hill, North Carolina, where I worked at Sugar Hill Records – for free. I told Barry Poss, the owner of the label, that I would do anything – scrub toilets, stuff envelopes – anything I could do to get my foot in the door. Since I was working for free, I obviously had to take several more jobs to pay my bills. I worked at the record company in Durham from 8:00 am – 12:00 pm; then I drove to Burger King, where I changed into a suit in their bathroom; then worked the front desk at a law firm from 12:30 pm – 5:30 pm. I then left Durham, drove back to Chapel Hill, where I waited tables until 9 pm. After that, I played music out to make a few extra dollars. This schedule lasted for about five months when Drew Alexander called and asked if I was interested in interviewing for a position at Curb. I agreed and was hired on the spot. I moved back to Nashville a week later and have been at Curb ever since.

Clore: Where do you look for new talent? What is that process like?

We look for new talent everywhere. We attend showcases, take meetings with publishers, managers and anyone who is in the artist development process. You never know where you might find the next star. There are so many artists out there that it is impossible to listen to all of them. So, it's easier to take meetings with managers and publishers, or attorneys, who have a reputation. Writers are also a great way to meet new writers and artists.

Clore: Can you talk in general about the artist/label timeline, i.e., once a new artist is "discovered," all the way until their first project comes out?

There is not a specific timeline for any artist – they all vary. Rodney Atkins, for example, was on Curb Records for nearly 10 years before his first big hit, "If You're Going Through Hell." Lee Brice, who is a Curb Records artist and writer, has been signed to the label nearly seven years and is experiencing his first top 30 success with "Love Like Crazy." Essentially, "Overnight successes" are extremely rare. There is artist development, in which most artists are writing a ton and demoing songs. This helps the artist shape their sound and figure out who they are and what they want to tell the world. There is a radio tour, photo shoots, recording, etc. It is a long process, but is shortened by a hit song!

Clore: I know you've felt moments of genuine job satisfaction. Can you share a little about that, especially what it means in context of your time invested?

I love my job. If I weren't married, I would sleep at the office! One of the most rewarding experiences I have had since being at Curb is watching the creation and release of Tim McGraw's top 20 single, "Still." I was lucky enough to pitch this song to Tim who cut it shortly after. Hearing it on the radio never gets old.

Another great experience was handing Garth Brooks a number one plaque for the song we publish, "More Than A Memory." I walked into the writing session when that song was only halfway finished and I got chill bumps all over my body. When it debuted at number one, for the first time in Country music history, it was pretty incredible – not to mention handing Garth a number one plaque. When songs change people's lives, it makes you remember why we got into this business to begin with.

Clore: What do young artists most need to do to garner your attention?

Be great. Write great songs. Play out a lot. The more attention you can create for yourself, in terms of web presence, independent record sales, radio play – the better. Young artists have to really want to be an artist – it's not all glitz and glamour – in fact, it's the opposite. Being an artist means traveling in a van with four other guys to play a show in the middle of nowhere, but that's what it takes. You have to love music and you have to really want to share with other people – the rest will fall into place. Be different – separate yourself from the other artists out there because there are a lot of them, and I bet they're working just as hard, if not harder than you are.

The preceding interview took place in March of 2010.

The Innocence of Guilty Pleasures

Have you ever thought about the social behavior being acted out when we talk about our "guilty pleasures?" Have you ever fully thought about why you feel the need to disclaim something you love into this hidden-in-the-open category?

I don't get it, and (at least in my world) I want to claim all guilty pleasures innocent.

If your love has actually committed a crime, disregard this. If your love is awaiting sentence because your culturally-adapted frame-of-reference deemed it such, then I think you need to grant it a stay.

Chances are you're just trying to be cooler than you already are. You tell your friends that Britney is your "guilty pleasure" because her pop(ular) music has fallen to the category of "Can't really like that; too many people are enjoying it that don't really *understand* music. I need to keep up my own image by dumping Britney into my (all-forgiving of what people think of me) 'guilty pleasures' category."

Screw that. Enjoy what you love and be proud of it. No matter who you are trying to impress.

Alan Parsons

I'm grateful for what the music industry has brought me.

When it comes to the world of music production, Alan Parsons is among the best ever. He has been integral to recordings by The Beatles, Pink Floyd, Paul McCartney, The Hollies, Ambrosia, Al Stewart, and many others. Following his work on Pink Floyd's *Dark Side of the Moon*, Parsons, along with Eric Woolfson, started The Alan Parsons Project, opting out of Pink Floyd's invitation to return and work on *Wish You Were Here*. The Alan Parsons Project subsequently released 11 successful studio albums between 1976 and 1990.

Alan has been nominated for 11 GRAMMY Awards over the course of his career, has been the studio manager overseeing London's Abbey Road Studios, and in 2011, released a 10-hour educational video project, entitled *The Art & Science of Sound Recording*.

I first had the honor of meeting Alan Parsons in August of 2004 when I escorted him down the red carpet at the Latin GRAMMY Awards' MusiCares Dinner, honoring Carlos Santana as the 2004 Latin Recording Academy Person of the Year. That day, and ever since, Alan has stood out to me as one of the most gracious and caring individuals I have encountered in the music business.

Clore: What keeps you motivated to continue working with and around music?

I am still motivated, but I'm not the guy who is a workaholic, when I really was a workaholic right through the '70s and '80s. I thought nothing of working all night – dropping one thing to accommodate another, and things like that. Music's been good to me, and I continue to be motivated by it, but I can't say why. I'm pushing towards when most people would be thinking about retirement. I can see myself retiring from live performance because, you know, I'm simply too old and wrinkly to stand on a stage. I can't see that I would ever really, totally give up what I do with recording. I think that will always be there.

Clore: Can you describe the good and bad in transitioning from a behind-the-scenes person to a performing artist?

I was the exception to the rule, having grown up through the ranks of tape op to engineer to producer, then to recording artist. When I became recording artist with Eric Woolfson, we kind of made the decision that we would never perform live, because, we were essentially a recording outfit that did not have a live act. We joked at the time, "How does a record producer perform on-stage? Does he just go and warm up the audience with a few jokes?" [laughter] But thankfully my music career did start with playing guitar, and learning piano and flute – so I had some musical ability. I was no virtuoso. I have never professed to be a virtuoso, but going to the live stage was a post-Alan Parsons Project thing – something that we decided to do having made my first Alan Parsons album, the first album without Eric. And we just wanted to give every possible boost to record sales that we could. And the other two – Ian Bairnson and Stuart Elliott – the guitar player and drummer that I collaborated with on the first Alan Parsons album, called *Try Anything Once*, we just said, "Let's put a band together. Let's do a tour. Let's promote the record via being on the road, which is what everybody else does."

Until that time, it really hadn't been practical to put a band together because the keyboard sounds were so adventurous. Keyboards in the early '90s had just become sophisticated enough to be able to program a whole bunch of sounds and save them and record them. It would have been an absolute nightmare for the keyboard department to play live before that time. In fact, when we first went out live, we had two keyboard players to handle everything, and now it's gone down to one.

Playing live – I didn't think it would ever happen – it did happen, and I'm now very comfortable with it. I've even started singing quite a bit. I never thought I would do that, I thought I would be sort of a passenger in the band. As I became more experienced, I became more comfortable with playing the part of Rock star.

Clore: When a band is in the studio working on an album, what do you suggest they do to remain friends and bandmates?

That's an evil question. [laughter]

I've been reasonably fortunate with the people I've worked with, remaining friends. Eric [Woolfson] and I through spending so much time together – writing and recording – it's a bit like being married to somebody for too long – you know, friction starts between you and things become difficult. So, you know, you just have to work hard to compromise – and see things from the other person's point of view.

Pink Floyd were the best of friends when I was working with them, and they grew more and more antagonistic towards each other. When I was working with The Beatles, they had already reached that stage – it just seems to be a function of spending too much time around each other. Just like a marriage growing stale. There are good marriages and bad marriages, you know? Sometimes they last forever. Sometimes they don't.

Clore: Can you talk about the importance of education in music?

It seems to have become much more important. I think the reason is, I mean certainly in recording technology, there is so much technology to absorb now. There was so much less to absorb when I was growing up in audio. You essentially just learned good sound, you learned mic technique, you learned about tape machines, good balance – and that was about it. Now everything is computer controlled. There's hundreds of new plug-ins every month. It's just really hard to keep up.

I think education has just become a process of figuring out what you're good at, and what you want. I think there's no such thing as a person who can handle every job in music these days. You can't play *and* record *and* engineer *and* produce all at the same time. I mean, there are people who do it, but they would do their job better if they specialized more.

For jobs in audio, I think employers would now almost automatically look for someone who is a candidate of a sound recording college, or music college – whatever it is. It's become like joining an orchestra. You can't join an orchestra without having been to a music college – there's no question. And I think you can't get a job in a recording studio – the few that there are left these days – without having attended SAE or Belmont, or wherever it is.

It has become more important. But the sad thing is, commercial studios are becoming fewer and fewer, and most jobs in audio center around broadcasting and cable TV and film these days.

It's not to say there's not lots of music being made, but it's being made in people's houses, not in the studio.

Clore: At this point in your career, when you consider what really matters to you, what is it you value the most: professionally, personally?

I value my past success, honestly. I don't sell records anything like that quantity I used to in the heyday – which was mid '70s to the '80s – and that success has dominated my lifestyle. It's because of that 10 years that I enjoy the lifestyle that I have. I live in a beautiful house in California, I have a beautiful American wife. I'm grateful for what the music industry has brought me.

I've kind of separated my personal life from my professional life, more than I used to. My entire existence, probably until the mid '90s was entirely based around the music industry. Now, in my old age, I value my private life a great deal more than I used to. I'm eternally grateful for the success and the financial rewards that it brought me. And I'm completely broke now. [laughter].

All of my friends used to be in the music business. Every sort of social occasion seemed to be centered around the music business, but it's not like that anymore.

Clore's Summary:

You can eat, sleep and breathe the music industry while still maintaining your private life. Pay close attention to not let these become too mixed up – to the detriment of either.

The preceding interview took place in September of 2011.

It's Not Worth It

I have stood at the precipice of divorce, and later in life, entered its lonely confines. I do not like that, but I am thankful for the perspectives they brought me.

As I write this, there are two little boys asleep in their bedrooms about fifteen feet away from me. We share last names. They hang on my every action – the older one usually imitating my words and movements. There is not a single thing I would not do for either of them, but more than anything, I cannot imagine walking away from them. The thought of purposefully leaving confused little eyes crushes my heart. Not to live motivated by fear, but consequences are good to keep in mind.

The entertainment industry can be a dark and dangerous place, and I am not referring to physical safety. The limitless temptations are baffling. Are they present everywhere else? Probably. But there is something altogether different about an industry built around mostly attractive people performing for people who idolize them. Add in long days, weeks and months on the road, in the office, or out at shows, and the issues are amplified.

I am not above any of the topics of which I write, and this is not a holier than thou discourse. Where do you think a lot of this motivation comes from? I simply want to call it what it is. When is the last time you saw an affair go well? When have you heard someone on their deathbed wishing they had spent more time in the office? When is the last time you talked with a child that enjoyed living amidst a broken mommy and daddy relationship? Rarely do temporary pleasures turn in to permanent joy.

This is difficult stuff. Let's be very honest. In one way or another, each of us are tempted towards flashing screens that seem to light the way, but are nothing but the opposite of where we should be going. I have lived up-close with those that have taken the bait, and they will be the first to tell you it did not satisfy. All hell usually breaks loose. It may appear okay on the surface, but I have had enough conversations with those on the backend to be fully convinced that it rarely is.

Consider what this means for you. It is different for all of us. Whatever you may be silently leaning towards, it is not worth it.

The following lyrics from one of my favorite artists, Andrew Osenga, have pierced my heart many times. The song is called "The Man of the House."

You should have seen how I first saw her

Should have seen the way we danced

The bar became a ballroom

The haze became a trance

She kissed me like a serpent

And squeezed 'til my heart broke open wide

She told me that she loved me

Guess that's when she crawled inside

Dolph Ramseur

We try our best to treat the fans with the respect they deserve.

irca 2004, I had the tremendous opportunity of working with what came to be one of my favorite bands, The Avett Brothers. If you have never listened to this outfit of blood brothers, Scott and Seth, plus their friend Bob, please put this book down right now and look them up online. Start with "Salvation Song," "Paranoia in B Flat Major" and "Offering."

During my time with The Avett Brothers, I was fortunate to meet this amazing behind-their-scenes guy that deserves significant attention. His name is Dolph Ramseur, and he manages The Avett Brothers. I assure you you would want Dolph on your team if you could have him. He is the founder of Ramseur Records, based in Concord, North Carolina, and is one of the nicest, and most effective, guys in the music industry.

The following interview took place during the Summer of 2010.

Clore: Your genuine, honest and true love and passion for music is evident in all you do. How do you maintain that spirit when you're actually part of the music industry?

First and foremost I am just a fan of music. My love of music is always the first thing I take into consideration. So if you love something, you try to take care of it, and treat it with respect. I try and always treat music like a lady. I also don't even think I am in the music industry. I just represent music that I have a passion for, but at Ramseur Records, we do things totally different than the norm.

Clore: Can you give us a brief history and overview of your company, Ramseur Records?

I started Ramseur Records in the year 2000. I started helping English singer-songwriter Martin Stephenson. He was my guide. I learned from him what to do and what not to do. From that relationship I discovered that I could start a label and management company.

Clore: How did you originally connect with The Avett Brothers and what were some early stages of determining you would work together? What did you see in The Avetts that drew you to them?

My mother told me about them first. She read an article in the local paper. The Brothers and I are from the same town. I contacted the guys and they invited me out to a show. Since we are from the same town we connected on lots of levels. We both came from blue collar families, so hard work was just something that came naturally to us. It was expected, not something we strived for. I saw in the Brothers a lot of talent as artists, performers and songwriters. From day one I thought they were one of the best bands in the world.

Clore: It has taken years of work, furniture moving jobs and countless miles on the road to get to where you all are now. What has kept you going through it all?

Just believing in the artists I work for is a big inspiration. Wanting to share them with the rest of the world – my love for their music. Kind of the philosophy of them being a mix tape I am making for the rest of the world.

Clore: It is nearly impossible to put The Avetts in a single, musical category (a good thing). How have you dealt with this in your years of introducing the band to everyone you meet?

This has been a tough thing. I am at the point where I just call them Rock-n-Roll. We have had Folk Rock, Rock, Grass in every possible way (Punkgrass, Grungegrass, etc.....). The guys can take music so many places.

Clore: How important are core fans to The Avetts? How do you all interact with, and reward, them?

Very important. Besides the songs and the performances, the fans have helped make the band what they are today. We try and give them the old NASCAR approach. When I was a kid, Richard Petty would sign autographs until nobody wanted one. So we went with that kind of approach. We try our best to treat the fans with the respect they deserve.

Clore: What is your favorite moment/highlight during your years with The Avett Brothers, and/or your career in general?

With The Avett Brothers, seeing the joy they bring to the fans. I have had so many great moments like that it would be hard to single one out. With my career in general... seeing how much my kids have been exposed to music and the arts. They are only seven and 10, but are way beyond their years with music and art knowledge. That is something you cannot put a price tag on.

<u>Clore's Summary</u>:

- Work Hard.

- Respect everyone.

- Love the music.

Tandy Rice

The bottom line is, when I was 30, I was a handful. I don't think you would have liked me at age 30, and I don't think I would have liked me.

If there is one thing about Tandy Rice you can always count on, it is that not only will he be on time, he will be early. On the cold day in early 2011 that we met for this interview, it was of the utmost importance to me to arrive before the man, and be prepared for his willingness to sit and share with me. I will never forget looking out the window in that Starbucks and seeing this classic man walking across the parking lot, wearing a sweatshirt with the letters RICE great big across the front.

Few people have had the level of impact on my heart, soul and overall behavior in the music industry that Tandy Rice has. He is a special man, with a beautiful charisma that cannot be topped. He possesses a caring spirit that knows no end. He cares deeply about every single individual he has the privilege of crossing paths with.

As you will see during my conversation with Tandy, he did not necessarily always approach life in such a way, but that is the beauty in time, experience and wisdom. A man like Tandy has lived life to its fullest, and has seen many a result of such living. His experiences continue to culminate, and he continues to learn what works, and what does not. He is overjoyed to share these results with anyone willing to listen. Mr. Rice knows what matters, who matters, and when it is time to stop. He understands the importance of treating everyone with respect, care and admiration.

In May of 2008, The Citadel, Tandy's alma mater, awarded him an honorary doctorate degree. He originally graduated from The Citadel in 1961 before spending time in the United States Air Force as information officer of the Strategic Air Command at Loring Air Force Base, Maine. A chance meeting in a grocery store with a family member in the early 1960s introduced him to what ultimately became a lifetime as an integral part of Nashville's music industry.

Tandy was a publicist early in his music industry days before becoming owner of one of Nashville's strongest talent booking agencies, Top Billing, Inc., in 1969. He was president of the Country Music Association in 1981. He has been featured on ABC's *20/20*, in *Newsweek* and *Playboy*, hosted sixteen annual United Cerebral Palsy telethons helping raise millions for the organization, is a former agent for President Jimmy Carter's brother, Billy Carter, has been a judge at two Miss America pageants and was a professor at Belmont University. Rice has been the keynote speaker at over 500 conventions in the United States. He was the long-time manager of comedian Jerry Clower, and was instrumental as a booking agent in the careers of Dolly Parton, Porter Wagoner, Jim Ed Brown, Tom T. Hall, Helen Cornelius, Jeannie C. Riley, and many, many others.

I had the tremendous privilege of sitting under Dr. Tandy Rice in his artist management class at Belmont University in 2002, an experience that changed my life. Since that first day in class, Tandy has been one of my biggest encouragers and supporters – something I do not take for granted.

Listen to the words of this wise man. There are years and miles and hours of experiences that have brought him to how he views the world today.

Clore: I would love to hear about your skydiving experience, and what lead to you doing that.

I'll tell you exactly what lead to it. It was a crying daughter. I was being a daddy. My daughter had a broken heart. My youngest daughter had a broken heart and she was really in low cotton. I basically said to her, "Baby, let's go out and do something fun. I don't care what it is – you name it and we'll go do it." At that point she said, "Well, let's go skydiving," and at that point I couldn't back down. I had given her my word, so here we go.

We called Tullahoma, Tennessee, which seems to be the capital of skydiving around here [Nashville]. To make a long story short, we drove over there on a Saturday morning, the weather was glorious and it rained for a while so we just kind of had to sit around and look at each other. We went through a morning briefing, and after you walk through that door with all of those people – have you heard that Christian song, "No turning back..."?

So there we were, we're all outfitted up, we're all processed and the guy said, "Okay, this group of six, we'll be taking off in about fifteen minutes." Everybody was rushing off to the bathroom, including me. So we go outside and they said, "Well, we're so glad you're here, and in fact you here, we're going to let you be the lead jumper." They were deferring to my age. I thought, "I don't want to be the lead jumper. I want to go last. If I change my mind, those others won't know that I didn't do it."

And we got in that dern plane, and literally it was an old barnstormin' plane, you know, you don't need the White House plane to do this. As long as it can get off the ground, you've got yourself a good one. It goes flapping down the runway, and I'm talking about rattling and everything, and off we go and then it starts going round and round in circles, climbing at altitudes, probably 5,000 feet every circle. We finally get up to 10,000 feet and that's really tall. You look down and cars look like little bitty ants crawling, and here I am sitting in the jump position. This is all tandem jumping – I wouldn't try it any other way. I don't have the confidence to do that, but these guys are all Screaming Eagles from Clarksville [Tennessee – Fort Campbell], the way they make their living in the off-time is going up and jumping tandem with people. You cannot feel them on your back. You don't know they are there.

He said, "Okay now, Mr. Rice. We're going to have a good time. I want you to giggle and laugh, and when I count three, you roll forward." I started to say, "Well, when you count two, you're going to find me running for the back door." [laughter] But I thought, "I can't back down in front of all of these people, that would be horrible." So, here we go: "One, two, three" – and out of the plane we go.

It was the most fabulous, glorious experience. We started falling at 10,000 feet. When we went over, we did a complete somersault. You just do that when you've got this big guy on your back.

He said, "Alright, you want to fly a little bit? Put your arms out and you can fly exactly like Superman." It's the most euphoric feeling. You tilt your hand to the left, you go to the left. It's just like an airplane. It's the most amazing thing and I can truly say I will never, ever forget that. I'd do it again in a second, and my daughter came right behind me. I was still undoing my stuff when I saw her coming down so I was able to be with her when she landed.

So that's my sky-diving experience that I wouldn't take anything in the world for. It served its purpose and was also a great life experience. I would recommend it to anybody, male or female, regardless of age. Number one, you can't mess up – they won't let you. And when you have the world's greatest jumper on your back – if nothing opens up – he's going to take care of you.

Clore: Did it change how you view the world?

Oh yeah. It made me feel like I had transcended being an ordinary daddy. As you will soon find out, we daddies don't say no, and shouldn't say no. What you're going to end up saying is, "We'll find a way."

Clore: I want to go back to a moment I'll never forget – my first day in class with you at Belmont University. That was a very important moment in my life. Well, the whole upcoming semester, too.

In mine, too.

Clore: Well, thank you, Sir. And I'll never forget you taking off your wristwatch. I was sitting in the front row and you tossed it to me. Do you care to share that story and the idea you were trying to communicate?

Well, it made an unbelievable impression. That was a gold Rolex watch you caught, which I no longer have. That's one way I look at my phases and stages of my life. I'm in the final chapters now, but I wasn't then. There was a time in my life when I sincerely believed that in order to be what I wanted to be, I had to have a gold Rolex watch, and a Cadillac car, and I've had both of them. Today as I'm talking to you, I'm wearing a Timex and I'm driving a 2003 Jeep Wagoneer with almost 200,000 miles on it. I've run through one Cadillac and three Jaguars and you couldn't make me buy a Rolex now.

Clore: Really?

Well, it makes no sense. It makes no sense for something to cost $20,000 and for something else to cost less than $10 and they give me exactly the same service. Help me understand that, will ya?

Clore: I am with you.

The only way I think it makes any sense is if somebody else gives it to you, then takes the write-off as a gift, and they've got to be halfway silly to do something like that. Do you realize that for $25,000 you could endow a scholarship that will help young people just like you were then? It will grow over the years and multiply and endow itself. That's the level I'm thinking on now. I'm at the wonderful stage where, as Jerry Reed used to say, "Give me all of the hamburgers I can eat, and all of the cigarettes I can smoke, and I'm happy as I can be." Ain't that a great line?

Clore: I love it.

There was a time when I thought if I ever made $20,000 a year, back when I was your age, if I ever make $20,000 a year and I get to spend the night, once a month, in a

Holiday Inn, that'll be Valhalla – heaven on earth. I did all of that, but I'm just amazed at perspectives that come to you.

I've also got a friend that says, "Every five years I think we all oughta just turn our lives upside down and start off on a different tangent, to test ourselves, to experience new life." My teaching at Belmont was a new adventure. I loved every second of that.

You know what I'm doing now?

Clore: What's that?

I received a phone call not long ago from a woman with an invitation. She told me she was with the Urban Debate League. In my old age, I've become totally infatuated with debate. I mean totally infatuated. Mainly because right across the street from me is Montgomery Bell Academy [in Nashville]. I go over there all of the time to listen to the debates and watch them. They've even got the "Rice chair" over there where I sit every time, and the professor – Mr. Billy Tate – may be the greatest debate coach in America. They are national champions. If you can make the MBA team, you're automatically bound for a college scholarship at Princeton or Yale or Harvard. It's that strenuous and that difficult. So I've started going over there, this will be about my third year of being caught up in debate.

The Urban Debate League called and said we understand you are infatuated with us, how would you like to become a debate judge? And a debate mentor? Which intrigues me more than being a judge.

Clore: Yeah. I know it does.

But in any event, this coming Saturday I've got another meeting with them. We're going to East Literature High School and there'll be probably 50 young kids out there from that area. These are kids that a lot of them don't have daddies, a lot of them don't have anything, and when they get dressed up to give their presentations, and they look out and see me in the audience, I stand out in the crowd I've got to tell ya. When I smile at them and give them a thumbs-up sign, they almost start dancing, they're so thrilled with joy. How could that not be a glorious growing experience? Right?

Clore: Oh yes.

So that's what I'm doing now. That's my latest hobby. And I'm 73 years old. If my health was not going downhill, I'd probably be happier than I've ever been in my life.

Clore: You're talking about feeling differently about life now than how you did nearly 10 years ago at Belmont. That's the heart of what I'm interested in and what this book is all about – the evolution that happens in a life in the music industry, for people like me and you, on the business side, and for performers. As we go along, as you have thoughts, the life changes that happen, the moments in time when you realized "That doesn't matter anymore."

That's right! It's no big deal. There was a time when I bowed at the altar of that gold Rolex watch and the Jaguar automobile, but I'm not sure I'd even have one if you gave it to me now. I'd much rather fill my gas up with a smaller tank and be available for a young boy or girl who needs a ride somewhere in the Urban Debate League.

But you're exactly right – those things do happen to you, and they're just as natural as anything. For the longest time I was the one that fought change. I'd like to think I'm still a conservative, but by the same token, you can be so damn conservative that you build a wall around yourself. I've got some friends today – this is ironic – I have some friends today that I wouldn't have even wanted to be seen with at one point in my life, and that's nothing in the world but a measure of what we're talking about.

Clore: As we sit here today, I'm just shy of 30 years old. To have your influence in my life over these past eight or nine years, I am so grateful for that, because the things you're telling me now, I'm glad to already know as I'm still just getting started.

Oh sure! The bottom line is, when I was 30, I was a handful. I don't think you would have liked me at age 30, and I don't think I would have liked me. All I knew at age 30 was I had a wife who was pregnant, and we had two other children, and I didn't have an option but to bring in some money. And this is a guy who hadn't spent a lot of time, in his lifetime, working. I had been in the service, but I had to figure out how to make money, and ironically, when I went to work in the Country music field, I did it by default. You know that story. 100% true story, and I love it now. I've loved the friends I've made, including you. You're right there at the top.

Clore: Thank you so much.

But when I was 30, all I knew to do was snuff out the opposition, out hussle 'em, snuff 'em out, put 'em down by whatever means necessary, and then prevail. Well, at age 73, I'm not in to snuffing out anybody, anymore. SOLID [Society of Leaders in Development, an organization I am part of] doesn't teach you to snuff anybody out. SOLID teaches you to make friends and be yourself, be your good self, you don't have to be a badass. I wasn't worth a dern. You could've blown me up with a stick of dynamite and thousands would've applauded during that time period. That's one of the great joys about getting older.

I don't know if I told you this, but in addition to hating Country music, I hated the concept of selling, because everything I knew about selling was all wrong. My picture of a salesman was of a tall, skinny man wearing a fedora and a 3-piece suit, holding a screen back with his foot and hitting the bulldog in the head with his briefcase. And I thought, "No, I wouldn't mind having about thirty salesmen working for me, but if you think I'm going to knock on the door and have a dog try and bite my ankle, you're crazy." And more people kept telling me, "You know, whatever you do, you've got to go in to sales." I said, "I hate salesmen, and I hate selling. You can all go straight to hell."

Next thing I know the phone rings one day. That's something I use a lot of times, "The phone rang." I've had two phone calls today that have just blown my mind. If you'll listen for them. Listen for the opportunities, like Marty Robbins. Classic, classic story. 100% true. In fact, I don't tell things that aren't true. You can check 'em out and they'll check out.

Let me tell you something that I sort of evolved in to, and I'm convinced of it now: the importance of good manners. I went from a "rape, burn and pillage" mentality to the mentality of good manners, which is joyful to live with. You can always help other people. It doesn't cost you a penny, and ironically you can advance your case even quicker by doing that. Whereas if you're out there raping and pillaging and burning down the houses and looting and all that, that's all you're doing. You're not glorifying life, and you're such a blessed person to even be able to be here. Every single member of my family is deceased now. I've had three sisters, all of whom died of cancer. Momma and daddy are gone.

Life is good, especially when you sit back and listen.

Clore: I know the story, but I would love, for posterity's sake, to hear the story about how you got into the music industry.

I graduated from military school in Charleston, South Carolina, and then was assigned to a base in Northern Maine. From Charleston, South Carolina to Caribou, Maine is all the way across the world almost. I went up there and I wanted to fly. They said, "Well, one of your biggest problems is you can't see so we're going to give you a ground job." I said, "What's the ground job?"

"We're going to make you the base information officer."

I thought, "Well, what does that mean? I don't even know what a base information officer does."

Well, there was a light bulb going off.

"There's a 16,000 member base here, and we want you to learn how to run the base radio station, run the base TV station, publish the base newspaper and set up an internal and external public relations for strategic air command."

I had no more idea than a baboon what I was getting in to.

[laughter]

But it ended up being a huge blessing in my life, and the word "Country Music" had never even been articulated to me. When I came home, at the end of three years of service up there, I started looking for a job, going from door to door – knocking on the same doors that my classmates were knocking on: the bank, the insurance company. The first place I went, I got a job offer. It was for $500 a month going into training at the bank. The second offer was for $600 going into training at the insurance company. I didn't know squat about either one of them, but I knew I was making pretty good money because when I was in the Air Force I made $250 a month. So I doubled my income, just in one day of interviewing.

I called my wife and said, "I'm coming home." She said, "Before you come home, go by and get some orange juice. Everybody's crying here, we need to have some orange juice."

I ran in to a cousin of mine by the name of Sarah Ophelia Colley Cannon, "Minnie Pearl," and she said, "Well Tandy, how are you doin'? I heard you were going to be coming to Nashville."

"Yes, Ma'am, I'm glad to be here."

She said, "What are you going to do with your life, now that you're back?"

"I'm going into the insurance business."

"Why?"

"For $600 a month, that's why."

And she said, "Now wait a minute. You should never take a job just for the money."

Now that's hard to tell somebody who has a pregnant wife and two children at home. If I'd been shucking oysters, I'd have gone to do that, but being the competitive person that I was I would want to, a.) be the best oyster shucker that ever lived, or b.) set up a thousand shops of oyster shucking all over the country, but she said, "If you take a job just for the money, it's just a matter of time before you become disenchanted, and leave. You can't work somewhere and not be happy," and I said, "I'm going to be happy with $600 a month."

She said, "What do you know about the music industry?"

I said, "What music industry?"

"The Country music industry."

Well, my first thought was get me a barf bag and let me barf in to it.

Clore: Because you didn't like the music...

Not only did I not like it, I didn't like anybody that liked it. I was doubled-up on prejudice, and I was perfectly comfortable being a doubled-up bigot. I didn't know any different.

Then she started telling me how this small block of old beat-up buildings was evolving into Music Row, and she said, "There's a job over there now for somebody who is willing to travel and willing to become a salesman, and somebody who loves Country music." I said, "How much does it pay?"

"$700 a month."

[laughter]

I said, "Tell me a little more about that job."

I went and interviewed for the job. Got the job and I've been in it ever since.

Clore: And that was '63?

Yeah, it sure was. And here again, it wasn't because of preparation, and it wasn't because of a bunch of things, but it was because the opportunity was there and I just grabbed and embraced.

There's nothing I haven't done in Country music. In a way I'm interested to know what I'm going to do with the next five or six years of my life. I hope I can squeeze that much more life into it, but I want it to be fun and exciting and fulfilling. That's real important to me. I've kissed a lot of toads.

Back when Top Billing was going, we had close to forty employees. All of those service houses are houses of cards. They all depend on one sweet potato at the top, and our sweet potato was Porter and Dolly. When Porter and Dolly decided to go in their separate directions, it totally redefined the life of the corporation, because they were the lead-horse. They were the sweet potato. They were the thing that made the phones ring. You'll find that every agency in town has a sweet potato. Wherever Taylor Swift is, she's the sweet potato.

Clore: I'm vehemently passionate about this topic you're talking about, of power in representation, as I see people around me treat others negatively because they don't have that sweet potato, and it really drives me nuts.

Well, it gripes me, too. If I could do nothing but communicate that point to the folks at SOLID, there's a second point that I'd want to communicate to them, and that's this: sweet potatoes are transient, and life is ever-changing. That's hard to believe when your income jumps from $20,000 a year to $100,000 a year. You suddenly believe, "A-ha, I've finally been discovered. I'm superman at last," and the last thing you would listen to is that this will have a short run. You never know what can happen, a car wreck, a thousand different things. In this case we just had a conflict that we didn't even know was brewing, with Porter and Dolly, and there was nothing we could do to stop it except sit back and pick up the pieces and try and reassemble it. Not one thing we could have done.

When I think humaneness and class, I think of Jerry Clower. When I met Jerry, that was one of the seminal meetings of my life. Here again, I'm driving down the highway and all of the sudden I hear something about a coon hunt, about a coon up in a tree, and a guy named Marcel Ledbetter, and it impacted so strongly in me that I pulled the car off of the side of the road, and I never do that. I just died.

It ends up he and I were business partners for about 35 years on a handshake. On a hand shake. I'm as proud of that as I am of anything, and I adored him. I miss him and I think about him quite a bit [Jerry passed away in 1998], but you can't sit around and live on yesterday's laurels. Here again, all of that was before skydiving, that was before – you know, life goes on. The thing that I'm proudest of all of, I think, is getting my Master's degree from Vanderbilt at age 60. That says a lot. I never read as many books, I never wrote as many papers, and I was never prouder of anything.

Then the second thing that I was equally proud of, was getting an honorary Ph.D. from my college. When they called and told me I thought it was one of my friends playing a joke on me. I came within a hair of doing something that I would have regretted. I literally thought it was a joke. It wasn't a joke. This guy said, "Tandy, this is general so-and-so, I'm calling you from South Carolina." I thought, "Yeah, yeah."

But we all love little pats on the back, and those are two highlights.

Clore: Can you talk about being on the road with Dolly. I know there's the fabulous tattoo story, but can you talk about how that trip came to be?

I sure can. First of all, Dolly's as big as any superstar can be. She's one of the most extraordinary human beings I've ever known. I've never known her to be late. I've never known her to be anything less than courteous to an absolute T. I think I was with her for 15 or 16 years as her agent – Dolly and Porter.

Her husband would come by the office sometimes and pick up her check, and he never would speak to anybody. He's legendary for being so shy. He went for years and never saw her perform. What he would do is he'd come to the front part of the office, and like I said, we had about forty employees then. He'd come in the front reception area and say, "How's old pretty boy doing?" That was me. They'd say, "He's right back there, come on back here, Carl, and meet Tandy." "Nah, he don't have time for me." And they'd say, "Here's your envelope," and he'd be done. I never met him. I never laid eyes on him.

On the European trip with Dolly, there used to be a guy named Mervyn Conn. He was one of the big promoters – this was the Bill Graham of Europe – and this particular time, there used to be a big Country music festival over there, called The International Festival of Country Music at Wembley. They'd fill that blooming thing up, afternoon and night, and he would buy the talent a year in advance. Dolly, Jim Ed Brown, they all came over there through our agency, and we all flew over there together. When we got there, as best I recall, there was just a mad feeding frenzy for Dolly. She drove people nuts, and she's never been flirtatious. She's never brought any of it on. She just looks so unusual, you've got to go have your picture taken with her. You want to touch her and make sure she's real.

But not only would we do those two shows, which we did, but there would be little appearances around, some just plain old sight-seeing, some interviews and that sort of thing. That was the way I toured with her. The rest of the tour we were all together. I'd never seen anybody like her. She gets a lot of credit for being a great businesswoman, and she is a great businesswoman, but you know, John, business is not complicated if you can remove egos from business. It just simply boils down to – what's this thing going to cost me and what am I going to sell it for? The difference is called margin or profit or business – it ain't more complicated than that. If egos come to the table, I'm going to argue about who makes the first bid. I'm going to argue about the size of that apple you just held in your hand – I've got two that are bigger than that. Spitting and pissing and moaning, you see.

Dolly comes to the table, and you talk about bringing power to the table – she'll sit with people and say, "Well, I'm here to work out a deal with you all, who am I going to argue with, who am I going to arm wrestle with?" Naturally, everybody says, "Hey, we're here to please you. You tell us what you want, and we'll see that you get it." Does she use her power or not? Nobody's ever been that powerful. Elvis would've been, but the Colonel [Tom Parker] wouldn't let him even be seen. The Colonel played that like a fine tooth comb.

Clore: How about that Marty Robbins story?

Marty was a very aloof and distant man. I wanted so badly to be a part of his career. I thought that I could help him, and I was fascinated by him. But I never could get through to him. Although he had a secretary who was from Franklin [Tennessee, where Tandy is from]. I knew her when she grew up and she couldn't be more cordial to me, but we couldn't get through to him. Then one night I heard him being interviewed by Ralph Emery, and Ralph said to him, basically, "How does anybody ever get to you?" It's almost like he worked at being like Howard Hughes [see movie, *The Aviator*] used to be – he worked at that. Marty said, "Ah, I'm not all that hard to get to." Ralph said, "But you get tons of mail?" "Yeah, if anybody ever writes me twice, I set a special place for them and I ultimately get to know them. I don't ever forget anybody that writes me twice."

That light bulb went off, and I thought, "I'm going to show you, by God. I'm going to write you a hundred times if that's what it takes."

It's a wonderful story, because the very first letter said, "Dear Mr. Robbins, I know you to be a man of great integrity, and you don't say things you don't believe in, and you don't say things that you don't back up with action. You're a man of honesty and integrity. So I heard you say the other day, that if anybody ever wrote you twice, you never forgot their name. Well, first of all, this is letter number one. Second of all, my name is Tandy Rice. Expect letter number two tomorrow."

Letter number two said, "You knew you'd be hearing from me today, because I'm a man of integrity. My name is still Tandy Rice, and I still want to meet you and I look forward to it because you said I could and I would, and I'm looking forward to it."

And by God, he took off on tour and died while he was on tour.

Now what did I do to prepare for that?

Clore: You were listening.

That's right. Isn't that what we started this interview talking about? I don't know anybody you can't learn something from if you'll just listen, and I don't know anybody you can learn something from if you won't listen. See? All you're doing is ego-tripping to hear the sound of your own voice.

Clore: What are your thoughts on the difference between Nashville, and the general music industry, from 1963 to 2011?

In every industry in the world right now – the Internet caused it. This little machine you've got right here [my laptop] changed everything, and there was no stopping it. I don't think I've ever seen anything impact anything the way the Internet did the music industry. Once students found out they could get something for free, that they used to have to pay $15-$16 for, it was all over. So now, the entire industry is having to reconfigure itself, redefine itself to accommodate that phenomenon. Is that to say it can't be done? Heck no.

It'll do it, and music and entertainment will never go away.

Never.

I heard the greatest thing the other day, I heard somebody say, "People who are determined to do something find a way. People who don't want to do something find excuses."

Have you ever heard the expression that every man in his lifetime should do three things?

Raise a son.

Plant a tree.

And write a book.

Is that strong?

Clore: That's strong. That's good.

And you're doing two of them right now. I really applaud this.

<u>Clore's Summary</u>:

- Notice how drastically Tandy's goals and aspirations have changed over the years.

- Be prepared.

- Listen. Listen for the opportunities. And seek the opportunities.

- Treat others well.

- Go skydiving. Literally and figuratively.

- Have good manners.

<u>Quotes not to miss</u>:

- "When I was 30, all I knew to do was snuff out the opposition, out hussle 'em, snuff 'em out, put 'em down by whatever means necessary, and then prevail...I wasn't worth a dern. You could've blown me up with a stick of dynamite and thousands would've applauded during that time period."

- "All service houses are houses of cards. Every agency in town has a sweet potato."

- "Business is not complicated if you can remove egos from business."

- "People who are determined to do something find a way. People who don't want to do something find excuses."

Jack White is a Smart Man

I am not the biggest White Stripes fan. Don't get me wrong, I like them a lot, but I don't bow at their altar. However, the more I learn about Jack White the more I am convinced of his genius. I don't mean "genius" in some sort of tortured soul, preternatural, indefinable way – although there probably is some of that – but in that he is very intelligent and calculated. Yes, he does have more musical talent than me, you and all of our friends combined (no offense), but unlike most he actually uses it well. He has parlayed his successes into a truly respectable repertoire.

It is refreshing to see a celebrity consistently make good decisions. He has a deep appreciation for history, and that is part of his genius. He actually learns from the blunders of others. Anyone that can develop a relationship with, and eventually produce albums for, Loretta Lynn and Wanda Jackson – that is someone to emulate.

If you haven't read the note from The White Stripes' about their break-up, please do – and consider it a model for how a band should wrap. There are a lot of bands out there today that should have ended a *long* time ago, but that is for another day.

When I watched the documentary, *It Might Get Loud*, which delves into the stories of White, Jimmy Page and The Edge, I was surprised to be most impressed and interested in White.

My only personal interaction with White occurred at the Nashville Airport. We exited the shuttle bus at the same time in the middle of the parking lot. We walked relatively close to each other for a bit, then when he needed to turn to his car, he said the only words uttered between us, "Excuse me."

Gabe Simon

I have a music business degree and the only reason it's worth anything is because I got to meet people, because I went out and networked and made relationships and I got the experience, and that's the degree. The experience is the degree, not the classroom.

When I watched the Kopecky Family Band perform "The Disaster" at 3rd and Lindsley in Nashville on August 8, 2010, I knew there was something very special about them. I feel fortunate to have since become friends with Gabe Simon, co-lead singer of the band. Gabe is a 2011 graduate of Belmont University's Music Business program. He is one of those guys that is so talented that it makes you sick, but you are simultaneously so glad you have found him. He isn't just talented musically, he has a strong business sense about him, which is extremely important for artists.

The Kopecky Family Band formed in the Fall of 2007. Since that time, they have played Bonnaroo, CMJ, SXSW, Next Big Nashville, toured relentlessly and released three EPs. They have performed as part of *Paste Magazine*'s showcase at both CMJ and SXSW. When they played CMJ 2010, they won over Bob Boilen, host of NPR's "All Songs Considered."

Clore: As an artist, how do you stay motivated within our industry that is so cruel and mean at times?

One of the biggest things – when we got to New York to play CMJ – we got to see a lot of our initial team come out to see us play, which was exciting to us, because we kind of make them like family to us. Everybody that we work with, we try to keep them real close to us. So in the midst of that, getting there and getting big hugs from my team and having not seen them for a while, was one of those things where they know we're not a big deal. They see that we're going to be a big deal, and they're hugging us and loving us like we were family. That was encouraging to me. It wasn't just like business to them, and me being the talent, or essentially me being a product, I wasn't just an item anymore.

In order to develop something, especially a human being, you have to show a personality. You have to show an affection. It was really cool to see that it wasn't just the formal system: I can touch you, I can hug you, I can say thank you for all of the work you are doing, and we can develop a relationship, and that was encouraging to me. That's how I got motivated. That's how I stayed motivated – knowing that people believed in me, and that want to be part of my career.

My mom liked this writer when I was younger – Eric Liddell – he wrote a book about how he was a runner, an Irish guy, and how when he would run he would feel God's glory, God's presence, and I feel like that's the same exact way I feel with music. When I would look out in the audience and I see people singing along, it's like they're experiencing what I was experiencing. It was like I could give them a taste of some of the things that give me joy in my life, or sadness, or whatever the experience was – and that keeps me motivated, still.

And then my band, you know? At the end of the day, I can do all of the business that I want. I can meet all of the people and network all I want, but if I don't have those roots of those five people to come back to, I wouldn't be motivated, because they're the ones who create the music. They're the ones who even make it possible for me to have product, because if I ran this business all by myself, I don't know where in the hell it would go. It'd be very selfish and very personally oriented. But having six other people reminds you that it's not just about you. It's about that big picture of how we can all make each other better, how we can develop relationships day after day, whether it be with our team, or with the band.

Clore: In terms of CMJ, SXSW and other things that have been a boost to you all – what has that done for you personally, and as a band? Has it altered your steps?

I think the biggest thing it's shown me is that I can do anything. That sounds weird, but we didn't get accepted to any of those festivals. I wormed our way in. Conniving. We got our people who are part of our team and everybody to really vouch for us to get us into these festivals, and then we made an impact. We had to get through the door, and I was doing whatever I could to get my leg in that door. Anything. But I think that was something – it showed us that we could get anything done. If we worked hard enough and were persistent enough, and I think that showed us if more bands were persistent, if more bands worked harder, if more bands were willing to find the relationships that they had and utilize those, that they could probably do more than what they are doing.

To me that's like a dirty secret I want to keep to myself because I don't want to create more competition. But it's true, a lot of bands just don't have the ambition or the drive to do whatever it takes to get there.

We realized we could do so much more. We didn't have to sit there and wait for it to come to us, we sometimes had to go for it. Part of it, too, is the motivation aspect. It was the little successes that built up to big successes that made us feel like, "Okay, we can actually do this. We can make an impact and we got to these festivals," and we played them, and personally, it was like, "Alright, I guess we're not dicking around anymore, I guess this is for real. I guess this is something – it's not just my college hobby that I do on the weekend, or I do a couple of days during the week and occasionally I get to play with a band I like. Okay, I guess I'm playing with lots of really big bands now. I guess I'm not just this college band. I am an actual band."

This is my career – which is a scary revelation to find out that that's actually your career, because, you know, there's no money in it and there's no anything in it, so it's all about you have to be excited and driven by the music and the love for it. I love getting into these festivals. I love saying we worked for it. We had to work really, really hard for it. We didn't just sit there and wait for it to come to us. We had to tour, tour, tour. We had to call everyone we knew to get any of these things done. The personal effect on me, it was humbling in a weird way.

I know for the rest of the band it's been scary. For a few of them it's been the deciding factor about whether or not they were going to do this for the rest of their life. It's been like, "Okay, this is scary, I thought I was going to be a marketing guy, a banker. I thought I was just going to get married and put aside the touring dream." I think some of us are like, "Well, we can do the touring dream, and get married."

Maybe this is an idea where we have to give up some things. In college I wanted to study abroad so badly, but I couldn't go anywhere. I couldn't go anywhere on the weekends. I couldn't leave for two months in the summer and go to Europe or some place like that and get to study abroad. Maybe I could've, but if I had gone that two months, what would we have not done? We probably would have missed something.

Clore: Having seen you all play live a number of times now, it really genuinely seems like you all have a real connection. Could you talk about what it means to be with people you actually care for, like and respect?

We were actually talking about that this past weekend as we were driving back from Fayetteville, Arkansas. It was like, "What's your favorite moment? What's that one moment when you really get so excited?" We have this song called "Howlin' At The Moon." There's a breakdown, then there's this pause, and in that moment when it transitions back, to me, is like, "Whoa!" I look around and I've got a huge grin on my face and everyone else is excited and pumped up because we're feeling the music. It's still not a song, it's like a whole...it's like when you see *Lord of the Rings* and you're watching the epic battle scenes and the green guys are crawling up the elephants and killing everything. We just watched that on the road this weekend, so it's on my mind. It's like that. You're like, "Ahh, that's so epic!"

I think the thing I continue to recognize is that those moments allow us to have the fun that we do. It's never getting bored of those songs. You have to find ways to give them character, whether it's by dancing around and singing and making them personal – it's real easy to sit there and have a boring show. It's easier for me to just sit there, but in a weird way, yeah, it's easier. There are a lot of things that are easier, but it's not fulfilling. To be honest, that's the biggest part of why we have so much fun, because it's personally fulfilling. Whether or not that's selfish, sometimes I feel like we get more out of it than the people in the audience do, because we are up there having so much fun. I've never had so much fun in a band in my entire life.

When I saw bands like Manamana live for the first time, or when Davie went and saw Arcade Fire for the first time, it was like – "Let down the boundaries, I'm going to scream out every word, I don't care if someone's looking at me." I want to be part of that, and as much as it is for the fan, it's for us. That's for us to go, "That's what's going to keep me dancing. That's what's going to keep me screaming. That's when it's going to keep them engaged."

That's a long explanation for why emotionally we have so much passion. I think it's because we're passionate people, and we can't have a simple argument [laughter]. We argue all the time, and they are intense arguments. They are emotional arguments. We've had to learn how to not take it personally. Like everybody else in this industry, we're all trying to be better, but we're all emotional people and I think that's what comes out through our music. That's what comes out through the way that we dance and sing and play and scream and yell and shout and cry and laugh – everything. And we do all of those things live. That's the weirdest thing to me – I cry and I laugh in the same exact 30 minutes, and in the same three minutes I could be angry and could be trying to be sexy, and I can feel all these things. I've never experienced that in my entire life. I don't think anything can do that other than music. We're not divided, and when our fans are in the room they're not divided, they're connected. It's like one big power surge.

Clore: I'd like to switch gears here for a second and talk about the importance of Belmont University: the role that your college played in your formation. It happened to be Belmont – right across the street from where we are right now. Are there aspects of Belmont that are important to the formation of Kopecky?

Well, I'll tell you that as this band has developed, college has become less of an important role, whether that's good or not. Currently, in 2010, we have an intern who works with us, and he was out with us yesterday and he said, "I don't know if I can come out with you guys in two weeks because it's exam week." And I'm like, "Exams?" I wasn't even thinking about exams. I said, "I have a music business degree and the only reason it's worth anything is because I got to meet people, because I went out and networked and made relationships and I got the experience, and that's the degree. The experience is the degree, not the classroom." He was like, "I agree with you, but I've still got to get As."

[laughter]

Clore: You and Kelsey met in a practice room, right?

Kelsey and I met in a practice room, but she and I had become friends through a friend of hers. I guess it was a boyfriend at the time. So we got to know each other and we started writing with each other. Then we invited Steven, who was a good friend of mine, and he was going to Belmont. Marcus came with him because he was a crazy hippie at Belmont – and Ben and David, and our first bass player, Bennett – were all Belmont students. Corey was a Belmont student. Actually, I sent a Facebook message out to Belmont students saying…"Hey, this is going to be our last show with our current bass player, we're looking for a new bass player." A Belmont student said, "Hey, I want to be in the band."

We were one of his two favorite Belmont bands, in school. How do you get away from the identity of being a Belmont band? How do you say you're a band that formed in college that doesn't do jam band stuff? Nashville's different. In most colleges, when you find bands in college, you think they're playing for ATO and all those fraternities and they're probably just doing cover songs. How do you make yourself individual, and be creative? How do you do it in Nashville? When you're 18, 19 years old coming to school, and there are 31-year olds down the street writing with Taylor Swift, and you're like, "How do I make a career out of this?" How do you not be afraid? How do you not be intimidated?

You have to be ambitious, and you have to have drive. When I look back and I think on my freshman year when we started this band, I think about the other bands who were around us that started at the same exact time. I think about where they are now – only one still exists. That band has struggled, and struggled not because they're working the road and it's tough to be in school – they struggled because they're not doing it. They struggle because they play in Nashville. They struggle because they write songs. They struggle because they don't know what to do with it all. They struggle because they don't want to sell their product, because they think that's "too business." They struggle because they don't know how much work has to go into it, and I think that's the same thing. You know college is supposed to be something that teaches you about life, teaches you how to take the reins of your own life? How do you choose your own classes? How do you get As in your own class without someone having to breathe down your neck saying you need to get As? How do you balance going out and meeting people with actually remembering you need to go to sleep and go to class in the morning? How do you balance everything out?

I think you have to be able to take responsibility for yourself.

Clore: What is life on the road like for you? Loves, hates? Do you look forward to it? Do you look forward to getting back? Do you miss things on the road? Do you miss things back home?

We're family. We're connected to each other. It's probably a lot more fun than most bands get to have on the road, and the fact that we're willing to talk about our issues – we're not a band that just sits there and lets it fester, which makes it worse. We're willing to talk about our issues. I think the hardest thing is – I know for some of the people in the band who are in relationships – being able to go home and see those people. We know we have to sacrifice a lot of time right now and do these kinds of things. It's still hard though.

I mean, school's one thing, but we've missed out on a lot of fun things on the weekend. My best friends right now are my five people in my band. They're the only people I hang out with. I think that's something that's changed for a lot of us. When we're at school, we hang out all the time. Before, we were like, we go home, we have our friends at school, we do whatever, and then we go out as a band. But it doesn't really work like that anymore, especially as you get further along in college, because you start moving out and you're not in the dormitory anymore. It's just different. With that, the likelihood of getting sick of each other is probably a lot higher, with everyone being your best friend and you're around them all the time. But we don't really get sick of each other. We just get frustrated. We want our personal space, and how do you have personal space when you're in a 16-passenger van, only two benches available now, and there's six of us with our intern, so there's seven.

I think the hardest part about it is the lack of things you can do. You are restricted the entire time – and then you have a freedom and you just want to let loose and relax, because it feels like you've been in an office all day long when you're driving in a van. I think people have a misconception of what it's like to be in the van. They think it's, "Oh, you're hanging out, playing with bands, having a good time." Yeah, it is that, about 25% of the time. The other 75% of the time is make sure you actually get paid, show up on time. You've got to do the radio interview, a show, then another show and then you've got to drive home after that. It's not one of those things where it's a simple task.

We're not sleeping in until twelve every day. We're out on the road by 7:30 – 8 o'clock in the morning because we've got to drive nine hours. It's not the most ideal situation. Nobody really wants to be driving for nine hours. It's funny to think that seven to eight hours now doesn't even faze me. It's like, "Oh, we've got seven to eight hours tomorrow. Cool." Seven to eight hours is a long time. You get used to it.

But on playing the show – I think the hardest part is staying motivated every day. Staying excited about playing another venue.

Clore: Knowing what you know now about being on the road, in a 16-passenger van, how do you see it being different if/when you're in a tour bus, you have a road

manager, you have someone that's dealing with all of the business?

From the very beginning, I would say we appreciate so much the times we had a trailer, not having to cram everything together. We will appreciate a bus in an incomparable amount of ways. I already told you about how connectivity is really great about being in a van – that's the one thing that I never want to lose. I never want to lose that, or think, "Well, now we travel in a bus, we're a bigger deal. Now we have a tour manager, we're a bigger deal. Now we can't talk to our fans as much, or we can't do all these things. We can't sit in the venue and hang out and get to know people and get to know the sound guys."

It's funny, some of our biggest fans have become sound guys of venues, which is really weird, because the sound guys usually don't like bands because they do so many of them. They know that most bands are jerks. You know, you try to be nice, that's what we do – we try to be as nice as possible, and usually when they hear us online, they think, "These guys are probably going to be jerks. There's like six of them in the band, the music's kind of super-abstract," and they meet us and they're like, "Man, you guys are super nice. Do you guys want to stay at my house? Do you guys ever need a road sound guy? Let me know."

Clore: What has been your Kopecky highlight(s) so far?

For business, I've made so many relationships that I wouldn't have otherwise. I couldn't plan those things. I love connecting people – that's exciting to me.

Being the manager of six people is like being the manager of a small business. I'm still learning how to communicate. You don't realize how important it is to communicate. Making people feel empowered on your team, motivated, excited. My band knows I'm their motivational guy. I can make them feel really good. I can also make them feel really crappy when I get on to them. How do you manage your peers? How do I become a better communicator? I hate letting them down because they trust me.

Being able to make five people believe and trust in me, that you're willing to defend, that you'd take a bullet 10 times over – that's the exciting thing.

Clore: What advice do you have for people wanting to get into the music industry, especially someone wanting to start a band?

First things first, get an attorney, because someone's going to want to do a deal with you, and you're going to want to sign it but it may not be the best deal. A good attorney, and a good publicist.

You need to play shows, show up, work hard, be creative and smart. However you do that, you need to do that. Recognize early on what you're good at. Be on time, be nice to everyone and don't burn bridges.

Clore's Summary:

- You have to work harder.

- Be respectful to your bandmates.

- Tour, tour and tour some more. Touring is both fun and draining. Be prepared to ride in a van. Even when busses and planes are options, artists find something to complain about. Just be prepared, and try and remain thankful no matter the circumstance.

- Be careful when it comes to who you do business with, and protect yourself by having a good attorney on your side.

- Remain connected to the passion you feel through music.

- Be emotional.

- Be nice to people. You never know what they will be doing next.

The preceding interview took place in November of 2010.

Thank you, John Ondrasik

I wrote the following on September 9, 2010, right in the middle of working on this book. I posted it to my old music blog, Clore Chronicles.

I'm taking a sabbatical from writing this blog. Don't get me wrong, I *love* everything about this platform and the subject matter I attempt to convey, but I am taking a rest. There are a number of reasons why:

1. I am tired of hearing myself talk in this venue. I want to listen and read. My stack of books, magazines and blogs to read is getting silly.

2. I am working on a book based on this blog. It is a little tricky to put together an entire book based on the first 200+ posts on this blog whilst keeping new blogs coming. Did I mention I make $0 from any of this?

3. I am a little worn out by everyone in our society having a voice. Instead of continuing to add mine, I am going to remove it for a bit.

4. This takes a lot of work. I do love every minute of it, but see point #2, and I want to see more of my family and friends.

5. I need new ideas.

Today I was listening to Five For Fighting's John Ondrasik talk to David Hall on my favorite radio station, *Lightning 100*, in Nashville. John was explaining his song "Slice," and, summarizing, he said it's a bit of a call for our culture to not forget about togetherness – that we are so niche-minded these days that we rarely enjoy anything together.

There is a line in the song that references the Don McLean classic, "American Pie," which came out at a point in time when things were much different, and everyone was singing the same songs, or at least were very aware of them.

Consider your own life. I am not encouraging anyone to move backwards. Learn, experience, take each and every (new and old) thing in to the fullest extent.

And remember, just because something occurred in the past, that does not make it wrong, uncool or unworthy of being repeated.

Shannon McCombs

I was doing an afternoon show and my boss came in and said, "Steven Tyler's going to stop by today." I was so green. I literally, physically was praying that it would be after I got off the air, because I didn't want to do it.

From the moment I first met Shannon McCombs when I was doing publicity in the Country music part of Nashville in 2003, I knew she would be a lifelong friend. You know how you rarely meet people that you just know genuinely care about you as a human being? Shannon was one of those people, and remains true to that to this day.

Shannon has conducted well over 5,000 interviews in her career as an integral member of Nashville's music industry. She is one of those people with a ridiculous amount of talent, but you would never know it by how she treats every single person around her. She is a class act.

Between the worlds of radio and television, there are few things that Shannon has not done. She has voiced radio specials for ABC, CBS, NBC, TNN; was an on-air personality, producer and writer at XM Radio; has been a part of CMA Music Festival since 1990; worked at WKDF, both as a Rock station and a Country station; was a producer/interviewer for Access Hollywood; has produced, written, and hosted multiple segments and shows on both CMT and GAC; handles syndicated radio interviews for the "Grand Ole Opry"; and has hosted and/or produced numerous red carpet shows from events and awards shows such as the GRAMMY Awards, ACM Awards and CMA Awards.

On a very cold evening in January 2011, Shannon and I got together in West Nashville for a wonderful conversation about her history and some of her central philosophies.

Clore: Thirty years of interviewing. What really stands out to you?

The first one that pops out to me was a Rock and Roll interview, and it was when I was doing an on-air show at KDF, here in Nashville. I was doing an afternoon show and my boss came in and said, "Steven Tyler's going to stop by today." I was so green. I literally, physically was praying that it would be after I got off the air, because I didn't want to do it. I was scared, and you have to think back, too, this was a time when there wasn't Internet. So, you couldn't [search] somebody to see what they were doing recently. It was whatever you read in *Rolling Stone* last month, and that's three months old.

Clore: So any sort of prep was difficult?

Right, and I say that for a reason, because at the time, they were known for trouble. This was when "Love In An Elevator" was the big hit at the time.

He had come in and told me they might stop by. It was early afternoon and I got off the air at three and I was thinking, "Good, maybe it will be after I get off the air," because I was just green. There's no other way to say it, but green. I had done a handful of interviews and was intimidated by anybody that walked in. I was just really, really shy.

So Steven Tyler comes into the room and he walks up to me, the first thing he does is he curtsies, took my hand and kissed me on the hand, and from that point on I was okay. I remember he sat down to do the interview, we talked for a couple of minutes, then I went to play "Love In An Elevator." As soon as I hit the record, he looks at me and he says, "I have something for you." I said, "Okay."

He walks out of the room and I'm standing there with the music blaring, thinking, "What does he have for me?" He walked out of the studio, and the studio at KDF had this huge picture window in this small hallway, and we had the music blaring out in the hallway. He walks out, and during the song he danced up and down the hallway, and it was the same dance that was in the music video that was out at the time. I guess he knew that I was this shy, naïve, backwards kind of kid and it was kind of his gift to me. He came in just as the song was fading and sat down on the stool like nothing ever happened. I was like, "Okay, Steven Tyler just danced for me. I'm ok now."

Clore: Wow! Was it just him?

It was just him. To tell you another reason it was so great – when he first came in, the whole reputation of Aerosmith at the time was, this was basically before the whole band went to rehab, so there was this reputation about how they treated people and that sort of thing, so that's what was in my mind. Well, unbeknownst to me, that's when they had all just gone through rehab and he was very straight. He had great personality, just a super nice guy to be around. It was a nice surprise.

I think back on some of the people I've been able to meet and it just floors me. I can tell you a near-miss, and this is an odd thing. A few years ago I went to New York and hosted a show for a company called Live on the Net. Live on the Net was before their time. They were doing live-casting before anybody had a computer that could do it. The power of the Internet just wasn't there, but people that wanted to do it were trying to make it happen. So, I was hosting this live Internet show for a Buddy Holly Birthday Bash, which is put on every year by Paul McCartney. And the way it was set up, I was hosting the red carpet and there was a camera with me all night, so I was hosting everything that was going on off-stage, and Paul McCartney was hosting everything that was going on on-stage. So we were co-hosts and we were scheduled to meet at a certain point, like 8:20. We were supposed to meet at a certain place where he was coming from one way and I was coming from the other to do the interview – and it never happened.

It's the near-miss. So we worked for 2.5 hours alongside of each other, but I never got within reach to even say hello to him.

Clore: Was there a time when you knew this is what you would do? When you first were like, "I love learning more about people and actually being able to talk about it with them, and record it, transmit it," or whatever – whether it's through writing or radio. Was there a moment when you were like, "This is my personality, this is me"?

There was a moment for radio, absolutely, and I can remember almost the exact moment, because when I first got in to radio it wasn't about doing interviews, it was about – you know – I've kind of moved into that part of my career, of doing interviews. But when I first got into this business it was hosting radio.

I can remember 1976, I was at a John Denver show, sitting way up top near the rafters...

Clore: Where was this?

It was Louisville, Kentucky. Freedom Hall. And I remember thinking, "I'm going to be in music, somehow, some way. This is what I'm going to do."

I'm a huge John Denver fan, but all through the show – I was fourteen – all through the show I kept noticing all of the different aspects. It was the first time my mind opened up to what it took for one person to do all of this: watching all of the roadies, all of the sound people, the lighting people, everybody working around him – and it was just my first eyes open to the music industry, and I thought, "You know what? I want to be around music. I want to make my life around music." I didn't know exactly what it would be, especially when I went into radio. I never had any intention of doing television or anything like that, it was just how to get into music.

Clore: What are some other interview highlights for you? Isn't there a Johnny Cash story in there somewhere?

There is.

The way I met Johnny Cash was through an interview I did with June Carter Cash. I look back on this and I'm still really thankful that it happened. It was when *Press On*, the album, came out. She had invited three different people to her home for an interview, and I got to be one of them. I still don't really know how that worked out, but I'm very thankful for it.

Clore: That has to be one of those moments.

It was one of those moments. Just going was one of those moments, and going into that house. She was the brightest soul. She had a bright light. I don't know another way to describe it – she carried a light – that's what she did.

And later, I found out – do you remember the "Hurt" video?

Clore: Oh yes.

Okay, you know the table he's sitting at? Well, that table's in their dining room, which I didn't know at the time because this was years before that. But we're sitting at that table doing the interview, near the kitchen, and I hear a noise at the refrigerator and I turn around and it's Johnny Cash getting juice out of the refrigerator. While I'm in the middle of an interview with June Carter, that's how I met Johnny Cash.

And she was so wonderful. I remember leaving that day – I can see her standing in the doorway inviting me back. She invited me to come to a party at their house that was just a couple of weeks later, and I went. The one thing I do regret is not going back [after the party]. She had invited me after that to come back, and I just felt, "Oh, surely not. She probably invites everybody." And, you know, I just kind of felt like I may be imposing and I never took her up on it.

But she was open to everybody, just a bright light.

Clore: Did you talk to Johnny that night?

Very little. He let her have her space. I assumed that's what he was doing. He came in and said hello to everyone and moved on to do his thing, because she was there doing media.

Clore: How about Buck Owens?

Another great memory. I think a lot of that, too, not only that it was Buck, but it was a surprise. Kind of like the Steven Tyler thing, I didn't know it was going to happen. I was sitting in the studio at XM, and if you're familiar with that studio – it was in the Country Music Hall of Fame – and someone from the Hall of Fame popped their head in the door and said, "Hey, Buck Owens is in the building and he wants to know if he can come down and say hello?" Which I was like, "What? Buck wants to know if it's okay? Uhh, yes."

So he came down in the studio, popped in. I remember he had an entourage of people with him, which not everybody travels with an entourage, but he was traveling from California, so he was here [Nashville] with a lot of people. He came in the studio and I remember one of the first things he said to me. He grabbed me and hugged me right off the bat, sat down and I said, "How much time do you have?," which is just a standard thing, because you don't want to keep somebody an hour if they only have 10 minutes. He said, "Well, I'll stay until I'm bored."

No pressure.

Ended up I just pulled out a bunch of Buck Owens songs and we just kept throwing stuff on the air. He stayed for about 10 songs and we went through a lot of stories, told a lot of stories from the beginning of his career all the way up to the last music he recorded. He was great to work with. It was the only time I ever met him, and I never saw him after that.

Clore: It's fascinating, because the assumption with someone like you is that you talk to Garth Brooks, Johnny Cash, Buck Owens multiple times throughout your career. It's interesting that that's not always the case.

You know, and I think you'll understand this. With a lot of artists – well for one thing he was in California – not here very often. When my career started in radio it was 1980, and wasn't at a time when he [Buck Owens] was doing a lot of stuff. I moved to Nashville in '85, started in Country in the '90s, so it wasn't at a time when he was doing a lot of publicity. But with the newer artists, like in the last twenty years, I think of the people I've worked with again and again like Craig Morgan. He and I joke about – I was his first interview – and I've probably put a microphone or a camera on him a hundred times. I don't even think that's exaggerating if we really sat down and counted it. But there's some artists that are like that – you kind of grow up together.

Clore: Are there those that stand out to you in the category you're talking about right now?

Craig [Morgan] is one of those people. It's kind of like talking with you. You're sitting talking with a friend. You're just catching up with a friend.

I love talking to Wynonna – any conversation with Wynonna – because you know that she's going to be deep and she's going to talk to you from her soul.

Clore: Wasn't there a time where you interviewed Mötley Crüe, and then a few hours later, Randy Travis?

Yeah, there was. I was doing a daily radio show at [W] KDF and got this gig doing a show for The Nashville Network, which was the *Country Music Video Album Hour*. The way I would do that show was I would either take a day off from work, use a vacation day, or we'd do it after work. They'd schedule the interviews at night and that sort of thing. So at one point I did a Mötley Crüe interview for KDF that day and went and interviewed Randy Travis. He made fun of it on the show – it was part of the show. There's a bit in that show where he's joking about it.

Clore: As you have seen some artists come and go quickly, but you've seen some artists come and do well – how do you handle the personal side of that? And you're always so nice and genuine to everyone. There are so many changes flying by you, so many publicists that are annoying you...

Publicists make my life though. They schedule my work for me.

Clore: That is true, that is true. But with the realities of the business side of this – I'm heartbroken by it. I know you are too.

You mean watching an artist try to make it then fail?

Clore: Yes. Or maybe they were really big at one point then fell off the charts and now they're not really respected, and then suddenly you're interviewing them somewhere. I know it affects them. I've been around some of these kinds of artists. I'm just curious how you personally stay centered, stay focused and continue to always be so genuine with everyone.

Thank you.

That's a really good question because a lot of times their attitude is different. Sometimes when you're talking to somebody you can feel that they don't quite believe in what they're doing. I think you probably know what I'm talking about. But I think on my part, part of my job is making them comfortable. When I'm working with somebody it really doesn't matter to me personally what their level of popularity is, if they have one hit, or 20 – it matters maybe to the company I'm working for, because there are companies that I work for that will say we need this artist and this artist and this artist. To me personally, there are artists that I'd much rather work with. Some of the new guys that maybe haven't had as much success and sometimes you go up the ladder and it might be a little harder to work with somebody.

Clore: Maybe not when you're actually going to face someone, but just in your own life, do you feel over time that little pieces of your heart are kind of broken along the way when you see things not pan out for people that you really hoped it would?

Yeah, I do. I think a lot of times in the music industry – maybe this way in a lot of industries – but its people's souls. Especially when it comes to songwriters or people that are recording music, it means a lot to them. A lot of times they're putting themselves out there. I mean really, really putting themselves out there and when it doesn't work, it really hurts them. Then again, on the up side, you see a lot of people who started out wanting to be an artist and tried and tried and tried, and couldn't, but yet found that their knack was songwriting. They ended up being a world-famous songwriter that can stay at home and not have to tour and still make more money than the artist on the road. So, there's that turn of it, too.

I think a lot of artists and songwriters, when I talk to them, I can tell you immediately whether they're a songwriter/artist, or an artist/songwriter, which one they are first. Not meaning that they're any less, but that's what they are.

Clore: Is it a polish thing? What is it? Can you even describe it?

I think a lot of it, with a songwriter, when you talk to a songwriter, that's what they are first. They may be an artist, but really they're a songwriter and most artists who write songs will tell you. If you ask them, what are you, they'd say I'm a songwriter, I also sing.

Clore: You were talking about artists that have vulnerably put themselves out there through songs they've written or whatever, and maybe they don't make it – that's heartbreaking to see that happen. There's also the before all of that ever happened – they probably lived something that was heartbreaking to have the experience to even write about – that cycle that happens in an artist's life. It's a soul – they have feelings. It's not a piece of plastic, a product that we're sending down the factory line. It's a person that becomes a product, which is our business...

And I think that's important for artists to learn. I think a lot of them that are really successful do, and you look at artists who put themselves out there as a product, and I don't mean that in any negative way – it's the business. I mean, Taylor Swift, one of the smartest young artists I've ever worked with. Especially for her age, she's made herself a product. When you look at the products that are out there with her name on it – that's the business. Garth Brooks is really smart. Kenny Chesney is really smart. There are artists who really understand the business side.

Clore: Jimmy Buffett.

Jimmy Buffett. Yes, exactly. They understand the business. There are also artists who don't, and that's okay that they don't get the business side, but if they can surround themselves with people who do, that's where they win.

Clore: Do you remember the first year you worked Fan Fair / CMA Music Festival, and I'm assuming you've done it ever since?

Yeah, I have. Wow. Probably the first year wasn't as an interviewer, it was when I was at TNN and was there in a booth to sign autographs because I hosted that show – *The TNN Country Music Video Album Hour* – the longest name in history. That would probably be my first time to Fan Fair. Early '90s. Around 1992.

Clore: Do you remember Garth's famous marathon autograph signing session?

I do remember that. Twenty-three hours straight. I remember that he stood while everybody came through the line and signed autographs.

Clore: I saw the picture where you're reenacting one of Martina McBride's music videos with her.

For the video album hour, they had the picture frame that was used in the video for "My Baby Loves Me," and they set us behind it for part of the interview so that it would look like the video. That's where that frame was from. She had just had a baby and I remember it being a long day because we would stop every thirty minutes or so so that she could take care of the baby. I remember thinking then, and still now – what a wonderful mother because she brought the baby to the set, and we'd stop and make sure everything was okay – feed the baby – then come back and finish another part of the interview.

Clore: Over the course of your career, amidst the goofiest of goofs – that is, our people in the music industry – how have you maintained your class and poise in the middle of all of that?

That's such a great compliment. I don't know how to answer it except to say thank you. I'm glad to be viewed that way, and I take it as a huge compliment.

I don't know what else to say...

Clore: Well, I think that answers it.

Well, thank you. You have a really easy way about you to talk to people. You should be doing this for a living.

Clore: Thank you...

Like you, I have a genuine interest in talking to people. And a lot of times in this business, if I'm working for certain companies, I have to ask certain questions. You don't always get to ask the stuff you really want to because if the company hires you to go and talk about the album, you go talk about the album and it's all publicity. But there are times when you get to sit down with people and really talk to them. That's the part I really enjoy about it.

Clore: Do you have advice for young people wanting to do anything remotely related to what you do?

Don't be afraid to work for free. As much as kids don't want to hear it, I give that advice all the time. I get a lot of e-mails and talk to people that are looking to genuinely get into the music industry, specifically broadcasting – TV and radio. I can't tell you the countless times I've hooked somebody up with an internship that's free, that they've passed on. It's such a great way to get into the business if you can just bite the bullet and take it as a learning experience and know that later on you could make money at it and pay your way. If you can afford to go out and spend some hours and absorb the knowledge, it might turn into a full-time job.

I was fortunate enough that it happened for me, and I've seen it happen for a lot of people.

Clore: What's the most intense situation you've ever been in? I'm thinking red carpet, backstage at an award show?

Award shows are intense, but they're a great challenge. What a lot of people don't realize when you're watching on television is that when you're doing an interview you've got somebody talking in your ear saying, "Wrap that up because we've got another interview coming down the line." It becomes a juggling thing between who's the most popular, because if you're interviewing somebody that is a B artist and the A artist comes along, you don't want to push the B artist out of the way, but if you've got a network telling you to do it, you've got to do it in a very kind manner.

I'll never forget working the red carpet one year and we were doing live television interviews and Loretta Lynn comes walking down. Everyone's trying to grab her and I remember her publicist at the time was in a hurry to get her into the building. And like a publicist has to sometimes, you take the artist by the arm and you walk them up and say, "Come on, we're going." And as I'm doing a live break, all of a sudden, Loretta walks right up to me and goes, "How're you doing, honey?" And that's just Loretta. That was a gift that fell from the sky. Which would be a publicist's nightmare, but sometimes you can schedule all that you want, and sometimes things like that will just fall in your lap. That's what I love about red carpet, you just never know. It's a challenge.

Clore: Loretta is an artist I'm fascinated by. Have you talked to her many times?

I have. Working at the Opry, I work with her a couple of times per year. The thing with Loretta and everybody knows, is she just says what's on her mind. Every time I interview her there's another story that tops the other one. I walked into her dressing room and you know how she wears those wonderful, big Loretta dresses, as I like to call them – and when she sits down it flares out. So I walked over to her with my microphone, and the first thing out of her mouth was, "Squat right down here, honey, and talk to me." So I did. I "squatted" right down with my microphone and talked to her. That's Loretta.

Clore: She is so classic. Were you at the GRAMMY Salute to Loretta? It was in October 2010 at The Ryman.

I didn't go to that.

Clore: It was one of those moments for me. Garth was there, Kid Rock, Gretchen Wilson, Martina McBride, Reba McEntire, Jack White, Lee Ann Womack – quite a line-up. It was a GRAMMY Salute to Loretta Lynn. Most of those artists came out and did Loretta songs, and then at the end they brought her up on stage to present her this award, and it seemed she really had no idea why they were there. It was a total surprise to her, and she started crying. Jack didn't perform, but he talked about her for a while before they brought her up on-stage. It was such a glowing presentation, hearing Jack White talk about her. To me that's what's so cool about

music. **People may not like Country Music, but maybe they like The White Stripes, and maybe they learn Jack has worked with Loretta Lynn. I love that kind of stuff.**

He's archiving history. He's working with Wanda Jackson right now.

There's the people you run into, the people I work with at the Opry. I walk in those doors and go, "Oh my God, I work at the Grand Ole Opry." I think of that every time I walk through the backdoors. I think of being a kid. I make it a point to think back to what it was like when I was a kid. We joke at the Opry that we work with Little Jimmy Dickens, which is a treat in itself.

Clore: There's one artist I would love to ask you about, because of how much he has impacted me, and that is Ray Price. As I was sharing with you, I lean Rock and Roll, but when I was able to work with Ray Price he truly changed my life. Working with him is what helped me realize my love for music history. I was Ray Price's publicist for nine months of my life and I am so proud of that, and always will be. I was able to have some conversations with him that are some of the most prized moments of my music industry career, talking about Hank Williams, and...

Weren't they roommates?

Clore: Yes, they were. I'm assuming you've talked to him a few times?

Talk about class and poise. That's Ray Price. I love working with Ray Price and I've learned a lot from him, too. I've actually learned a lot about interviewing from Ray Price. The way I have learned is that when you speak with him, and he tells a story, a lot of times on radio you're trying to make things go – "snap, snap, snap" – and he very slowly, very deliberately tells stories. His speech pattern, which is very important to pay attention to when you're doing interviews – his delivery is very slow. The first time I interviewed him I kept cutting him off because I thought he was through talking. He would say a couple of sentences and he would pause, and you working with him know this, his pauses sometimes were three, four, five, six, seven seconds and I would jump in and then he would start talking, then it would be on top of each other. But from working with Ray Price, I learned how to interview. It was another aspect of learning interviews.

I'm still learning. I can't say that there are secrets, just things that I've learned that I try to apply, and still mess up. I still think that the single most important thing going into an interview is somebody being comfortable. You could have all the questions in the world and know their whole background, but it won't help you unless that person is comfortable. I've learned over the years to try to read, to get a temperature on someone, when they come in. I mean, if you pay attention to somebody's demeanor, not only in an interview, but just when you see a friend of yours, you can look at their face and see if they're upset, whether they're in a bad mood, whether they're in a hurry, which can make a big difference. All of those things, you know sometimes going into an interview I only have 60 seconds to get a read on that, but if you can zoom in on it, make somebody comfortable, it will pay for itself.

He used to come into the studio a lot when I was at XM, because he is a [Country Music] Hall of Fame member. When he would be in the Hall of Fame, he would stop by the studio, which was a great advantage to that studio. I remember one day he came in, of course XM had tons of music, and we'd sit and just play song after song, anything they'd want to hear when the artist came in. There was an album of his that we didn't have. I can't recall the title, but we talked about it in the interview. The interview ended and I said goodbye to him and he left and I looked out a couple of minutes later and I saw him standing in line at the gift shop. Standing in line! I was like, "What is he doing?"

He bought the CD. He bought it. Gave the Hall of Fame cash for it. I don't think he got a discount either.

He walked over and brought it back into the studio for me to have. He said, "Here, I thought you should have this."

Conclusion

U se your brain. Learn from those that have made asinine decisions in the past.

Do your best to make better decisions: for your own sake, your family, and all of those around you. Live life, have fun – do fun things that will provide countless memories to relive with those near you – just consider the bigger picture.

We are all dealt a different hand, some far better than others. All you can do is strive to handle yourself in the best possible manner, no matter your upbringing or current realities.

The music industry doesn't have to kill you. That is what I want to communicate now, and for the rest of my life. I am committed to and passionate about this crazy industry of music and entertainment. I want to do my part to encourage those around me to see the positive, the good – and work to push away the dark side, the negativity, that so quickly destroys – and learn from those that have come before.

Now, let's rock it.

Additional Information

For further information about the remarkable people in this book, please visit the following:

Gene Bowen – www.roadrecovery.org

Charlie Brusco – www.redlightmanagement.com

Fred Buc – www.lightning100.com

Thomas Cain – www.candycanemusic.com

Peter Cooper – www.petercoopermusic.com

John Ettinger – www.ettingertalent.com

John Feldmann – http://en.wikipedia.org/wiki/John_Feldmann

Pinky Gonzales – www.pinkygonzales.com

Mark Hollingsworth – www.markahollingsworth.com

Sage Keffer – www.sagekeffer.com

Brenda Lee – www.brendalee.com

Ebie McFarland – www.ebmediapr.com

Alan Parsons – www.alanparsonsmusic.com

Dolph Ramseur – www.ramseurrecords.net

Gabe Simon – www.kopeckyfamilyband.com

Shannon McCombs – www.shannoncountry.com

Acknowledgements

M ichael Lasley, Mallory Redel, Matt Ingle – I cannot begin to explain how fortunate I am to have you all in my life. Each of you have been an absolutely amazing source of encouragement for me, especially in the toughest of times during this process. Your support, wisdom and attention to detail has meant more than you will know. Thank you for the hours you will never get back. Thank you. Thank you.

Dr. Harrington, you gave me an interview, but more than that, thank you for believing in me. Your guidance, wisdom and encouragement are invaluable to this book, my life and my future.

Dr. Rice, I know you will always be one of my biggest fans, and you will always tell everyone that I was your best student. There is simply no way to express to you how much that means to my soul. You are as classic as they come. Thank you from the bottom of my heart for loving and supporting my every move.

Jim Foglesong, years ago you told me I could buy your lunch someday when I'm the head of a company. I'm not the head of a company, but your time and overall encouragement that day played a significant role in pushing my professional development forward. You are a legend. Thank you for everything.

Chris Hauser, I know of no one in the world who so similarly shares both my worldview and my passion for the history of Rock and Roll. Our conversations mean the world to me. Thank you for all you do.

John Feldmann, you are a hilarious and extremely talented individual. Thank you for unknowingly being my brother's hero.

Mark Hollingsworth, thank you for always being a great example for me to follow. You truly helped me get my start in the music industry by giving me my first internship with you at Compassion. Thank you for the endless support ever since.

Brenda Lee, you are an amazing woman. Thank you so much for being a part of this. It is a tremendous honor.

Gene Bowen, I appreciate what you do. You are constantly changing lives of our young people. Thank you for standing strong during the thankless hours.

Thomas Cain, you are a great man. Thank you for your strong example in humility, perseverance and loving others.

Liberty DeVitto, your contribution to music is indelible. Thank you for your undying spirit and ridiculously good drumming.

Michelle Tigard Kammerer, I can think of few people in my life that display the constant energy and excitement that you do. Thank you for always supporting me.

Sage Keffer, keep up the good work, my friend. You are an inspiration to many.

John Ozier, thank you for being a part of this. Speaking in Muscle Shoals with you will always be a highlight for me.

Ebie McFarland, I am so glad we were office neighbors in 2005 and got to know each other. You will always be one of my favorite publicists, and people, in general.

Dolph Ramseur, if everyone in the music industry was like you, I would have no reason to write this book.

Fred Buc, thank you for *Retro Lightning* and your leadership and vision for WRLT/Nashville.

Alan Parsons, thank you for your great attitude, and your important role in the history of recorded music. We would live in a much different industry without some of the legendary music you have helped create.

Shannon McCombs, you have always treated me with the utmost respect. Thank you for that. Thank you for being such a sweet and strong woman. I am very honored to include you in this book.

Gabe Simon, I like your style and your tunes. Keep up the good work. I am glad to know you.

Charlie Brusco, I am in awe of your experience, and experiences. Thank you for being part of this.

Peter Cooper, your talent and energy, combined with how kind you are, easily makes you one of my favorite people anywhere.

John Ettinger, you are a good man. Thank you for telling us all that family and friends are always more important than work.

Pinky Gonzales, you are a class act. I am very thankful to call you friend.

Jackie Monaghan, you have guided so much of my music industry career. Thank you from the bottom of my heart for being one of the most wonderful women the good Lord has ever created, and thank you for connecting me with the wonderful Brenda Lee.

Tyler Clark, your friendship and guidance through this has been essential. Thank you for everything you have done.

Andrew Osenga, you are one of my favorites artists, and you are one heck of a dude. Thank you for letting me plug some of your amazing lyrics in to this book.

Chuck Klosterman, your writing style and approach has significantly influenced me. Thank you for what you do.

C.C. Chapman, you literally gave me the idea and encouragement to want to write this book. Thank you, Sir.

To my wonderful friends and colleagues that have supported me in countless ways: Bob Bartel, Justin Levenson, Chip Petree, Nicole Pope Gaia, Angela-Marie Lampton, Lisa Parsons, Marcia Raubach, Heather Lewandoski, Jim Colella, Jackie Marushka, Steve Strout, Melanie Wetherbee, Andrea Kleid, Rod Riley, Sarah Lai, Tim Marshall, Ben Brown, Jimmy Wheeler, Brandon Frankel, David Smallbone, Phil Hawkins, Sarah McGrady, John Hood, Jeff Savage, Betsy Walker, Tony Grotticelli, Derrick Seiner, Rachel Pinkerton, Meredith Herberg-Waldron, Rachel Mowl.

To my family and closest friends – you all genuinely keep me on-track in life, in many, many ways. I love each and every one of you, and thank you from the bottom of my heart. You all play major, continuous and essential roles in my existence. Thank you so much: My sister, Emily Clore, and niece, Genevieve, Kent Morris, Lee Plunkett, Todd Ramey, Nate and Betsy Oldham, Jason Deadmond, Dave Hopper, Christian Lobb.

Mom and Dad (Tom and Chloe Ann Clore), you are the best parents a guy could ask for. I have genuinely always been thankful for you both, but now that I'm a dad, I truly see just how much you have sacrificed and loved for all of my years. Thank you for providing a foundation of love, understanding, stability and respect – and then challenging me to be my own man at the right time. I love you both.

Andrew Clore, my little brothers in arms. I can't imagine my life without you and I am glad I don't have to. I will never understand how we both developed such an undying love for the entertainment industry, but I am so glad we did. Thank you for everything, my dear friend and brother.

Harvey Clore, you are my little music buddy. Among the music we have intently listened to together as of the initial printing of this book: Billy Joel, Hank Williams, Chuck Berry, Jimmie Rodgers, Metallica, Rich Mullins, The Hold Steady, The Beatles, The Rolling Stones, Elton John, Pearl Jam, Ben Folds, and so many more. We are just getting started – get ready. You will never understand your precious and profound impact on my life.

Charlie Clore, you were born during the creation of this book, and I cannot express how much that means to me. As I am writing this line, you were born just four days ago. My, how life has changed in that time. You are my little music buddy, too. Thank you for continuing to change my life for the better.

To my beautiful bride, Sarah, your unending support, patience, encouragement, advice, wisdom and love is truly key for any of this to be remotely possible. You forever changed my life and brought me to a loving place of peace, where I could sit long enough to collect my thoughts, and dream. You are grace revealed to me. You are the most amazing human being I will ever know and love. Thank you more than you will ever understand.

Made in the USA
Charleston, SC
25 May 2012